RSPB

BIRDFEEDER GUIDE

BIRDFEEDER GUIDE

Robert Burton

DORLING KINDERSLEY

LONDON, NEW YORK, MELBOURNE,
MUNICH, AND DELHI

Senior Editor Angeles Gavira
Senior Art Editor Ina Stradins
DTP Designer Rajen Shah
Production Controller Bethan Blase
Managing Editor Liz Wheeler
Managing Art Editor Phil Ormerod
Category Publisher Jonathan Metcalf
Art Director Bryn Walls

Produced for Dorling Kindersley by cobalt id,
The Stables, Wood Farm, Deopham Road,
Attleborough, Norfolk NR17 1AJ
www.cobaltid.co.uk

For cobalt id
Editors Marek Walisiewicz, Kati Dye
Art Editors Paul Reid, Darren Bland,
Pia Hietarinta, Lloyd Tilbury

Published by Dorling Kindersley Ltd
in association with the RSPB

First published in Great Britain in 2003
by Dorling Kindersley Limited
80 Strand, London WC2R 0RL

A CIP catalogue record for this book is
available from the British Library.

ISBN 1-4053-0072-8

Reproduced by Colourscan, Singapore
Printed and bound by
Star Standard Industries (Pte.) Ltd, Singapore

See our complete catalogue at
www.dk.com

Contents

Foreword

Feeding birds matters. Let's not pretend otherwise. In our suburban areas, we have created an artificial ecology where a super-abundance of good quality and regular food means that certain species can not only survive, but may also prosper. Prosper at a time when their country cousins are really struggling due to a lack of food in our too efficient, too intensive farmland. Species such as Blue Tits, Great Tits, and especially Great Spotted Woodpeckers have shown significant increases in their populations, which may well be in part due to back garden feeding. The RSPB have been feeding birds too, species that need that little bit of help to get started or hang on. Thus supplementary feeding of the re-introduced Red Kites has fuelled their establishment and spread, the Cirl Buntings in Devon have enjoyed some winter feed treats and responded accordingly, and several Tree Sparrow colonies are now doing much better thanks to what the RSPB gives them. So whether it is on your patio or the wilds of the shire, feeding our feathered friends makes a difference, and not just for the birds.

As I write, tea and biscuits to hand in the comfort of our kitchen, I am watching some speckly young Greenfinches vie with some glamorous Goldfinches on our feeder. Every now and then a Nuthatch buzzes in to upset everyone. It has "mudded up" a nestbox in the garden and I'm really excited about that. You see in return for some sunflower seeds and peanuts, I have a smile on my face and a great show taking place on my balcony. The quality of my life has been enriched by the birds in my community. There's a kind of harmony there, a sort of co-existence between me and the birds and I think I like that most of all. You should try it too. We can all be conservationists, and the only cost is peanuts!

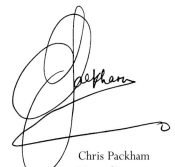

Chris Packham
Naturalist, writer, and broadcaster

Introduction

THERE ARE ABOUT 25 BIRDS that appear in gardens so regularly that they can be called "garden birds". But almost every species can be seen in a garden at some time or another – in passage or when blown off course by extreme weather. Observing, studying, and caring for these birds is a fascinating pastime and a significant industry, with more than 20,000 tonnes of bird seed sold annually in the UK alone. Gardens have become vital sanctuaries that help maintain the populations of birds under threat.

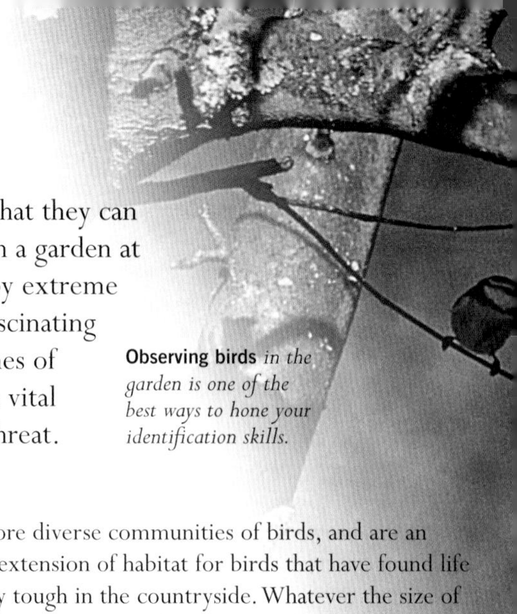

Observing birds *in the garden is one of the best ways to hone your identification skills.*

Birds for all

Garden birdwatching is a pastime that everyone can enjoy. The setting may not be exotic, but the encounters with garden wildlife are always close and personal. Birds bring to the garden a fascinating diversity of colour, form, movement, and song, and watching their behaviour is the most immediate introduction to natural history for anyone – whatever their age.

Even pocket-sized city gardens are visited by a few species, and nearby parks provide many opportunities for both birds and birdwatchers. Suburban and country gardens support more diverse communities of birds, and are an important extension of habitat for birds that have found life increasingly tough in the countryside. Whatever the size of your garden, providing food, water, and shelter will always tempt more species to visit, increasing your enjoyment of birds and enhancing their chances of survival.

Some bird species thrive near human habitation, feeding and nesting in gardens. Others, which may be common in the countryside, rarely come near houses, or only enter the largest gardens with mature trees and shrubs. Others still may just pass through gardens, perhaps swept off-course when on migration or driven by hunger to search for food outside their normal habitat. The predictability of old friends, the seasonal shifts of migrant populations, and the prospect of unexpected visitors makes the garden the best of all bird observatories. And by adding feeders, nest-boxes, and bird-baths, and planting bird-friendly plants, it can be transformed into a bird sanctuary that will provide wildlife interest all year round.

Birds visiting gardens *include rare birds of prey, such as the Red Kite (right), and old friends like the Blackbird (below). Watching, studying, and understanding the behaviour of common species throughout the year is every bit as rewarding as the occasional glimpse of a rarity.*

Garden successes

Many more birds now come into gardens than they did 20 years ago, and the variety of species seen has increased dramatically – a survey by the British Trust for Ornithology recorded a staggering 162 species of birds feeding in British gardens. Some of these species, notably the Siskin, Goldfinch, and Long-tailed Tit, have only recently become regular visitors. Siskins, for example, were once rather rare birds in the south of England, but in 1963 they started to come into gardens to feed on peanuts in plastic mesh bags, and now they are common winter visitors in many gardens around the country. New research is revealing new kinds of food that will lure even more species into gardens.

PAST PRACTICES

Historical documents show that people have been feeding and caring for wild birds for centuries. The poet Geoffrey Chaucer wrote of the "tame ruddock" (the ancient name for the Robin), which suggests that it was already a garden favourite in the 14th century. Burgeoning interest in wildlife and bird conservation in the late 19th century gave bird feeding an environmental perspective, and today its importance to the survival of wild bird populations is acknowledged.

By the 19th century, *putting out crumbs for Robins and other birds was an accepted pastime.*

The diversity *of birdfeeders available today has quadrupled the number of species that regularly visit European gardens over the past two decades.*

Disappearing birds

Throughout Europe, wild birds are in trouble. The last 30 years have seen dramatic declines in numerous once-familiar garden species – especially those which spend part of their lives in the open countryside. Rural House Sparrow and Song Thrush populations, for example, have plummetted by more than 60 per cent since the 1970s across much of Europe. Yellowhammers, Linnets, Bullfinches, and Tree Sparrows, as well as ground-nesting birds, such as the Skylark, Lapwing, and Curlew have all also followed downward trends.

Changes in European *agricultural practices have profoundly affected bird numbers. Traditional grazing meadows (above) are now a rare sight, while today's intensively farmed fields (left) produce barren monocultures.*

Threats in the wild

Explaining the decline of one species is never easy, because a combination of factors is usually involved. Some blame increasing numbers of predators and nest robbers, such as Sparrowhawks and Magpies, for falling songbird populations, but there is little evidence that these predators ever have more than a local effect. It is more likely that declines are linked to the degradation and disappearance of habitat. New buildings and roads have caused hundreds of square kilometres of countryside to be consumed by developers, while changes in agricultural practices have seriously affected the feeding and breeding opportunities for many bird species.

The move to gardens

The intensification of agriculture has replaced a varied farmed landscape of fields, hedges, and rough corners with dense monocultures of crops, depriving birds of habitats. Fruitful hedgerow shrubs, such as hawthorn, wild rose, and sloe, have been grubbed out, and effective pesticides and herbicides have removed the invertebrates and weeds on which many birds depend for food. Sixty years ago, a square metre of ordinary ground contained an average of 2,000 seeds, many of them vital weed seeds, but now an average square has just 200 seeds.

More efficient harvesting of cereal grain and better storage have depleted the amount of grain left on the ground for birds during the tough winter months. New varieties of cereal crops can be grown at such high densities that birds are unable to move between the plants to feed and nest. A particularly significant change to farming practices has been the move from spring-sown to autumn-sown cereal crops, resulting in the disappearance of stubble, which was once an important source of winter food.

With all these changes in the countryside, and the growth of birdfeeding as a hobby, it is no surprise that domestic gardens are becoming increasingly important as a source of food and a safe refuge for birds, particularly in the winter months.

The garden provides *many nesting opportunities for enterprising birds, such as this Spotted Flycatcher.*

Plants – even those grown *for their ornamental value – may be a useful food source for birds. Greenfinches (far left) visit sunflower seedheads, while House Sparrows (left) sometimes take nectar from red hot pokers.*

Helping garden birds

Studies by ornithologists show that gardens are rather poor habitats for birds when compared to woodland and traditional farmland. With time and planning, however, it is possible to transform almost any garden into a haven for birds. This involves planting and landscaping the area in such a way that it provides natural sources of food for different birds throughout the year, and so that it contains suitable cover for roosting and nesting (see pages 44–49). A mixture of trees, shrubs, lawn, and herbaceous beds, for example, recreates a woodland glade habitat and provides opportunities for food and shelter for a range of species, from Wrens to Sparrowhawks.

Feeding

Creating a wildlife garden is an immensely rewarding project, but there are more immediate ways to attract birds into your garden. The simplest is to put out home-made or proprietary food in your garden, using purpose-built bird-tables and feeders.

In the 1970s, kitchen scraps, half-coconuts, and strings of monkey nuts were the most popular foods left out for birds. In the 1980s, red plastic nets filled with shelled peanuts appeared in millions of gardens as a quick and convenient way of feeding. However, the nets also proved very convenient for squirrels, which could rip them open and steal their contents. These were replaced by purpose-built, tubular, metal-mesh and clear plastic feeders, which could be filled with peanuts, sunflower seeds, and food mixes specially formulated for birds. Today's feeders are highly sophisticated, can be sited in almost any garden location (see page 23), and are designed to attract or exclude particular bird species.

When to feed

Birds benefit most from supplementary feeding at two times of year – towards the end of winter and during the nesting season. In winter, insects are scarce, and birds take seeds as the main part of their diet. When the previous autumn's seed crop is used up, birds flood into gardens in search of food, and in years when hard frosts and snow lock up food supplies, some birds may starve. Wrens are particularly susceptible, and populations can be halved in bad winters. Lack of food makes others less alert, and so more likely to fall prey to predators.

Gardens are also often short of natural foods when birds are rearing their young. Summer feeding encourages tits and finches into the garden, and these may stay faithful through the autumn. Greenfinches nest earlier in gardens if fed on sunflower seeds, and Blue Tit survival is improved if the birds can take a quick snack of peanuts while searching for insect food for their nestlings.

NEW HABITATS

As the farmed countryside provides ever fewer opportunities for birds, the role of gardens as wildlife sanctuaries has increased. Britain alone has 270,000 hectares of private gardens and a further 150,000 hectares of parks. There are also large areas of roadside verges, "brownfield" sites, playing fields, cemeteries, and other open spaces which support birds.

Wrens starve *because they cannot find food when the ground is covered with snow and ice. Clearing the ground in sheltered places and putting out grated cheese can be a critical aid.*

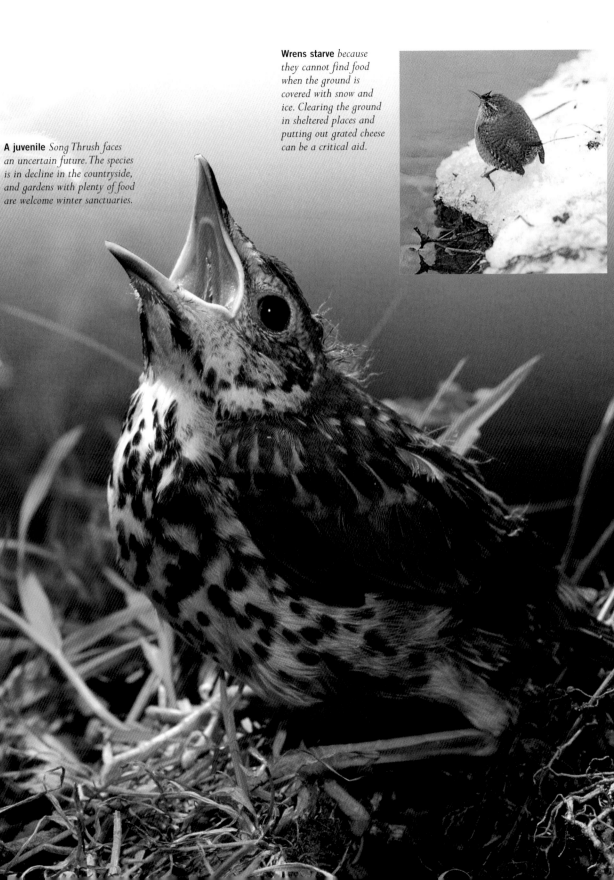

A juvenile *Song Thrush faces an uncertain future. The species is in decline in the countryside, and gardens with plenty of food are welcome winter sanctuaries.*

What birds need

Success in attracting birds depends on how well you can provide for their basic needs. Even if your garden does not contain a natural wealth of food, or large, mature trees, you can copy these features in the garden by providing food, birdfeeders, and nest-boxes.

The basics

MOST WILD ANIMALS ARE DEPENDENT on four major factors in their habitat – food, cover, water, and space. Even in the smallest rooftop garden, it is possible to provide birds with food and water, while the average suburban garden can passably recreate the woodland favoured by most common bird species. Knowing what birds need from their habitat can help us boost the number of species that visit, and help birds to survive adversity.

Water as well as food *is an important resource that you can provide in your garden.*

New habitats

Until about 7,000 years ago, much of Europe was covered in primeval woodland. Our Neolithic ancestors converted much of the forest to farmland, but even in the early Iron Age, about 2,500 years ago, about half of the continent was covered in forest. Since that time, a total transformation has taken place. Habitats have changed beyond recognition, and a new one – suburbia – has been created. Suburbia is where most of us live, and our suburban gardens are where we have our closest contact with nature.

DAILY FOOD INTAKE

Daily food intake differs from species to species. The higher the calorific value of the food, the less the birds need to find. A Yellowhammer feeds on seeds that have a higher nutritional content than the slugs and snails favoured by Song Thrushes.

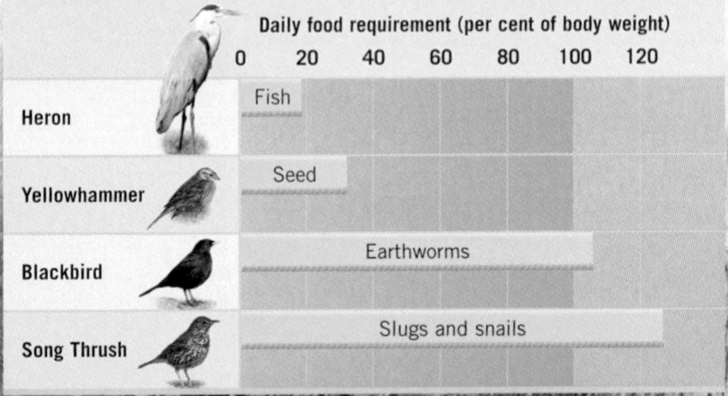

Even with our help, *life is tough for garden birds. Of this brood of Blue Tits, on average only two will survive until the next spring.*

The mixed forested landscape of our ancestors has become a blend of different habitats, most of which appear in microcosm – a clump of trees here, a grassy clearing there, and perhaps a few isolated shrubs. Some of the old forest residents have learned to thrive in this new habitat, while others need human assistance.

Food and drink

The easiest way to attract birds into the garden is to provide them with nutritious, energy-rich foods in the winter months. Food gives birds the energy to stay alive, and the colder the weather, the more they need. Small species lose heat quicker than larger ones and so have to feed more frequently. A Blue Tit, for example, spends 85 per cent of a winter's day searching for food. A Blackbird will take over 300 berries a day from a pyracantha bush and a Waxwing can eat more than 600 cotoneaster berries in a single day – twice its own body weight.

Feeding in the summer is also important. While there is more daylight and more food, a growing brood makes great demands on its parents. A pair of adult Blue Tits, for example, will gather as many as 1,000 caterpillars each day to feed to their young. Water, too, is essential for birds, both for drinking and bathing. Seed-eaters in particular need to drink plenty of water, because this is lacking in their diet. Your garden may already contain a pond or stream, or even natural hollows at the bases of tree limbs that trap rain water. Adding water holes or bird-baths to the garden will attract all sorts of interesting wildlife, not least birds.

Specially made *birdfeeders can be used throughout the year. Some designs (left) allow birds to take only the correct size food, so there is no danger to the adults or young. Others are enclosed in cages (above) to protect the food from bandits, such as rats and squirrels.*

NIGHT AND DAY

The amount of time a bird can spend feeding is limited by daylight, which varies greatly with the seasons, especially at northern latitudes. In winter, a bird may have just eight hours or less to feed; it converts its food to fat, and burns the fat reserves to survive the following hours of darkness. Small birds cannot store enough fat to last through more than one night.

Safe places

All birds need cover from predators and protection from the elements, especially in the breeding season. Cover can be provided naturally by trees, shrubs, banks, hedgerows, or artificially, by nest-boxes. Thorny bushes, thoughtfully planted, make excellent protective thickets, and an old teapot upended in a tree or bush makes a good nest site for a Robin. Leave a window open in your garden shed, or make a special entrance under the roof; birds are great opportunists, and a Blackbird or Song Thrush may well take this chance to raise its young out of the reach of cats.

This chapter contains a wealth of ideas to help you to transform your garden into a rich bird habitat that will bring you pleasure year-round.

Hanging birdfeeders

THE FOOD THAT MANY BIRDS NEED, especially in winter, often grows at the ends of slender branches and twigs: thousands of seeds make up birch catkins, for example, and alder seeds are hidden in small cones. Many small, agile species are well adapted to feed from this hanging harvest, and it is easy to tempt these attractive birds into the garden by putting up hanging birdfeeders. Different designs favour different species, so variety is the key to bird diversity in the garden.

HANGING BIRDFEEDER BIRDS

Birds you are most likely to see on a hanging birdfeeder include:

- Blue Tit
- Great Tit
- Coal Tit
- Long-tailed Tit
- House Sparrow
- Great Spotted Woodpecker
- Starling
- Greenfinch
- Siskin

The specialists

The birds most likely to come to hanging birdfeeders are those adapted to living high in trees or shrubs where they naturally cling to swinging twigs or hang upside down to grab food from under leaves. Blue and Great Tits are the most familiar visitors, but Coal Tits, Greenfinches, and Siskins are also regulars. Surprisingly, Long-tailed Tits, which are well adapted to a hanging style of feeding, have only begun to take food from feeders in recent years. Among other birds, Nuthatches, which are often seen clambering jerkily up and down tree trunks, have learned to visit garden feeders, as have Great Spotted Woodpeckers.

Siskins feed *by hanging from branches of birch or alder to take seeds, and so can easily adapt to feeding on the hanging feeders you provide in your garden.*

Feeders fitted with perches enable less agile species – such as the Chaffinch and Goldfinch – to feed alongside the accomplished acrobats. Hanging feeders are typically filled with peanuts, but using other foods, including sunflower or nyjer seed (see page 28), helps to increase the variety of visiting species.

Learning the ropes

Hanging feeders will also attract species that do not normally eat suspended food. House Sparrows and Starlings have, for many years, copied the tits and finches and learned to cling – usually rather clumsily – on to the feeders.

TYPES OF HANGING BIRDFEEDER

A large wire mesh feeder *holds enough peanuts to last several days before refilling. It attracts species like the Nuthatch.*

Mesh feeders *are coated with zinc to prevent corrosion, and offer excellent protection against squirrel damage.*

Log-style feeders *blend into the garden landscape – ideal for gardeners who favour the natural look.*

A simple wire basket *filled with peanuts is sufficient to attract unusual birds, such as the Siskin, into the garden.*

Peanut feeders *are designed to ensure that parent birds cannot take whole nuts, which could choke their young.*

Robins have also learned by observation: they will often hover, hummingbird-like, at a feeder, as they take dainty pecks at the hanging food.

In a garden setting, hanging birdfeeders can be a target for larger birds that have observed the flurry of feeding activity and learned to exploit this ready-made food source. Jackdaws, Rooks, and other crows, for example, will sometimes raid feeders, while a local Sparrowhawk may make occasional dashing raids into the garden to prey on unsuspecting small birds that are using a hanging birdfeeder.

Exciting species, *such as this Great Spotted Woodpecker, can be seen at feeders throughout the year, but are most likely to visit in the winter. They favour gardens where there are mature trees and shrubs nearby.*

Warm fat *studded with seeds, set in a ceramic "bell", is particularly good for birds that feed upside down.*

This seed feeder *has an opening at the base that allows seeds to fill a shallow tray. A roof keeps the seed dry.*

Clear plastic tubes *can be filled with a mixture of seeds. Specially designed feeding ports allow access for birds.*

A seed tray *fitted to the base of a tube feeder catches spilt seed. Drainage holes ensure the seed remains dry.*

The multiple feeding *ports on this giant feeder have perches and are offset to maximize feeding access.*

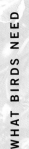

Specialist birdfeeders

MOST BIRDFEEDERS are designed to attract the widest possible range of common species, though they tend to be visited predominantly by tits and finches. As gardening for birds has become more popular, feeders have been developed that attract specific birds, particularly more unusual ones, or which deter certain birds or mammalian predators. A good bird garden – one that draws in an interesting mix of visitors – is likely to contain a variety of feeders.

Careful selection *of food and feeders can attract species like the Linnet into the garden.*

Unwanted visitors

Hanging feeders are an excellent means of delivering food to garden birds because they keep seeds or nuts beyond the reach of mice and rats. Grey Squirrels, however, are harder to exclude because they can climb the thinnest branches, jump gaps of 2m (6ft) or more, and chew their way into all but the most robust feeders. In many cases, they not only eat the food, but render the feeders unusable after chewing off the top or bottom.

There are a number of squirrel deterrents available for garden feeders. These include plastic domed baffles with steep sides to prevent squirrel access, and wire cages around the container. The cages allow small birds to enter, while denying entry to squirrels, as well as excluding larger birds, such as pigeons and crows, which quickly consume the seed. Cages also give protection against Sparrowhawks –

Sparrowhawks *soon discover the feeding places of their prey, and make bold attacks at garden birdfeeders.*

BIRDFEEDERS AND ACCESSORIES

Window feeders *attached with plastic suction caps give close-up views of birds, ideal for people who live in flats.*

Wall-mounted *peanut feeders are perfect for smaller gardens with no trees. They attract smaller species, such as Blue Tits.*

Rings *made from mixed seeds and melted fat can be hung from low branches to make an excellent high-calorie snack.*

The "squirrel baffle" *over this feeding station has a pivot, and tips to the side when a squirrel attempts to get a foothold.*

Corrosion-proof poles *can elevate a feeder if there are no trees in the garden, or help make the best use of limited space.*

Grey squirrels are *highly resourceful and will exploit any food source in the garden. They have chisel-like front teeth and well-developed jaws which can cut through the wire of a hanging feeder.*

swift, agile predators that frequent the feeding haunts of small birds. Protective cages must be large and robust enough to stop a squirrel reaching the food with its paws (Sparrowhawks too have a remarkably long reach). Care must be taken when attaching the heavy assembly to a branch – squirrels have been known to gnaw through the supporting rope or wire and carry off the entire feeder.

Feeding for diversity

Increasing the range of foods available in the garden will almost always attract a greater variety of birds. Specialized birdfeeders are designed to hold particular types of food: millet and nyjer seed, for example, are finer than most other bird foods and fall out of conventional feeders; they need to be held in custom feeders with small port holes.

Robust, heavy *gauge steel bars protect a tubular polycarbonate feeder with metal feeding ports.*

Nyjer seed *is held in a feeder with small feeding ports. It is a favourite of Goldfinches, but also attracts Siskins.*

A guard *with a mesh size of about 5 x 5cm (2 x 2 in) allows small birds to feed, but excludes larger species and squirrels.*

Holders *for fat-based bird foods, such as this peanut cake, allow the cake to be hung from a branch or pole.*

Peanut cake *studded with seeds can be placed into a rustic, natural feeder, made from bent reeds tied with twine.*

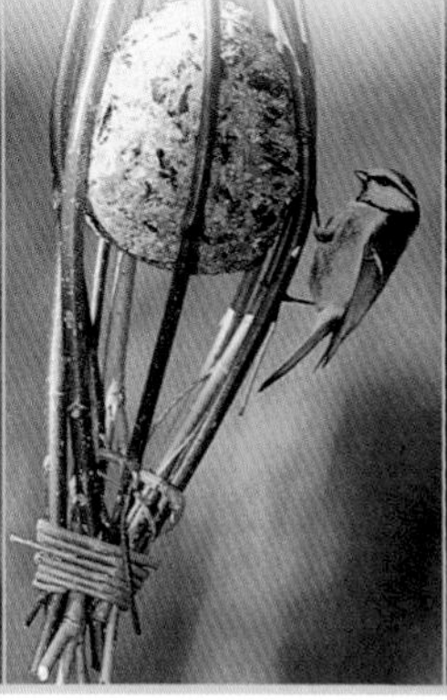

A woodpecker *feeds at a peanut cake. Starlings can be discouraged by placing a CD over the top of the cake.*

Ground feeders

SUCCESS IN ATTRACTING a wide variety of birds to the garden depends on how well the natural feeding habits of different species are catered for. While many common garden birds readily adapt to hanging birdfeeders and bird-tables, others are much happier feeding at ground level. A well-planned bird garden needs to consider these and all the species that may visit and ensure there are the appropriate feeders to meet their needs.

GROUND FEEDER BIRDS

Birds you are most likely to see on a ground feeder include:

- Collared Dove
- Pied Wagtail
- Dunnock
- Mistle Thrush
- Song Thrush
- Starling
- Chaffinch
- Greenfinch

Feeding on the ground

Some birds, such as tits and finches, are adept at finding food in the slender branches of trees and shrubs and they readily adapt to feeding on hanging feeders and on bird-tables. Others, such as Robins, House Sparrows, and Starlings, have watched and imitated this behaviour. A number of species, however, including Dunnocks and Song Thrushes, visit gardens but mainly forage for food on the ground, only rarely venturing on to bird-tables, especially those without roofs.

Food can, of course, simply be spread on the ground to make it available to all species, and ground-feeding birds, such as Chaffinches, are a common sight feeding on spilled food under bird-tables and hanging feeders. Food lying on the ground can quickly be spoiled by wet or snowy weather, however, potentially causing hygiene problems, so it is best to provide food on low bird-tables (see page 26) or in ground feeders, such as hoppers.

Feeder variety

Many of the larger species that feed mainly on the ground tend to arrive in flocks, quickly snapping up any available food. Supplying the food in hoppers (see below) allows a controlled release of food, ensuring that there is some remaining after the flock has left, and also prevents seed from being blown away by strong winds. Caged hoppers, which restrict species by size, help to ensure that the smaller, shyer species get their fair share, and also give protection from predators, such as cats and squirrels.

The Song Thrush *is more at home feeding on the lawn than visiting a bird-table, and it never visits hanging feeders.*

TYPES OF GROUND FEEDER

This plastic hopper *releases food from a lower tray as the birds eat. Prevent damage to the lawn by moving it every few days.*

Plywood hoppers *are simple and inexpensive. This hopper is easily dismantled so that it can be cleaned inside and out.*

Caged hoppers *allow small birds like Dunnocks to feed undisturbed, while larger species such as Woodpigeons are excluded.*

Metal hoppers *are sturdy and weather-resistant. The cage prevents large birds and squirrels from feeding.*

SITING FEEDERS

To attract the maximum number of birds to the garden, it is best to have a variety of feeders in different locations. As a general rule, place hanging feeders near the house for less shy species and away from the house for those that are timid. Put ground feeders and low bird-tables on the lawn for those species that cannot normally be encouraged on to a bird-table or feeder. There is considerable overlap between species and the feeders they use, so the secret is to experiment with different feeders in different positions until all are being fully used. When choosing where to put feeders and tables, however, make sure that they are safely out of reach of predators, such as cats.

Positioning *a bird-table close to the house will give you a good view. Blackbirds are frequent visitors.*

The boldest birds, *such as the Blue Tit, visit window feeders, giving wonderful viewing opportunities.*

A caged hopper *is good for an open position. Small birds, like the Chaffinch, can see predators coming and are afforded some protection.*

A hanging peanut *feeder, sited close to cover, will attract regular visitors, like the Siskin.*

Starlings *visit birdfeeders and tables to feed. Hanging feeders from the edge of a bird-table is a simple way of providing both options.*

Birds that *do not usually feed on bird-tables, like the Collared Dove, may venture on to a hanging table just above the ground.*

Pole-mounted feeders *can be moved around the garden to find the most popular spot. They attract birds like House Sparrows that feed on seeds and peanuts.*

Tubular feeders *attract acrobatic visitors, such as Coal Tits. When siting a feeder in a tree, be sure there are no overhanging branches that allow easy access to cats and squirrels.*

Greenfinches *often visit birdfeeders in small flocks, and so make good use of larger tubular feeders attached to trees.*

A well-stocked *low bird-table close to shrubs and bushes will attract ground-feeding birds, such as the Song Thrush.*

Making feeders

AS THE POPULARITY of feeding birds in the garden grows, so more feeding equipment becomes commercially available. It is, however, relatively easy to make some basic feeders at home using commonplace materials. The results may be just as successful at attracting a variety of species at considerably less expense, and the rustic look of home-made feeders blends well with the garden environment.

To a visiting bird *like this Brambling, it is not the look of a table that matters, but the food that it offers and its location.*

Simple feeders

There are many simple methods of feeding garden birds that do not involve expensive feeding equipment or complicated construction. A coconut sawn in half and suspended on string, for example, is very attractive to Blue and Great Tits, while hanging whole peanuts in their shells threaded on a wire will also attract the same species. Bones from cooked meat suspended on string from trees and bushes will usually be pecked clean by a variety of birds within a few days.

Fatty food is very valuable to birds as a winter supply of protein. A log can be smeared with cooked fat, or have large holes drilled in it into which suet or other fat can be pressed (see below). This is enjoyed not only by tits, but also Nuthatches and woodpeckers. Another way of serving up fat is to pour it into yoghurt pots or half-coconut shells while warm. It can be mixed with bird food and kitchen scraps to make a nutritious "cake" (see page 31). If attached to a wire, this can then be suspended from a branch or bird-table.

Home projects

Commercially made bird-tables come in all shapes and sizes, and some are very elaborate. Home-made bird-tables need not be complex, and can be a satisfying project to attempt (see opposite). A simple tray on a post or suspended from the branches of a tree is all that is required to hold the food and keep it off the ground. Adding a roof helps to keep the food dry and the table cleaner, but is not essential. If even this level of construction is daunting, however, try simply attaching a small tray to a windowsill. Although it may take birds some time to discover this source of food, many species will eventually become bold and approach the window, giving you unsurpassed views from within.

Seed hoppers keep food dry and stop it from blowing away in the wind. A simple hopper can be made using household materials (see opposite). Small versions can be fixed to trees or posts, while larger hoppers can be placed on the lawn for ground-feeding birds. The hopper can be filled with mixed seeds or small fruits, but remember to cover the jar with a piece of card while fitting it in place so that the contents do not spill out.

Hanging half a coconut *makes a simple feeder, but allow it to face downwards so water does not collect in the shell.*

Drill holes *along the length of a log and smear and push fat into them. The log can then be hung from a tree or bush and attracts tits as well as other small species.*

MAKING A BIRD-TABLE

First construct the tray: fix the side pieces to the base with 30mm (1¼in) rustproof nails. The side pieces do not butt together – leave gaps at each corner to allow rain to drain away. To make the roof, fit a piece of triangular dowel between the long edges of each roof panel so that they butt together neatly. Fix together with wood adhesive. Cut the uprights from 20 x 20mm (¾ x ¾in) wood, and angle the top of each one by cutting off a 6mm (¼in) wedge. Nail the uprights into the corners of the tray. Attach triangular gables to the uprights, and then, finally, nail the roof to the structure.

Materials

① 12mm (½in) plywood
② 20mm (¾in) wood
③ 20 x 20mm (¾ x ¾in) wood
④ 9mm (⅜in) plywood
⑤ 9mm (⅜in) triangular dowel

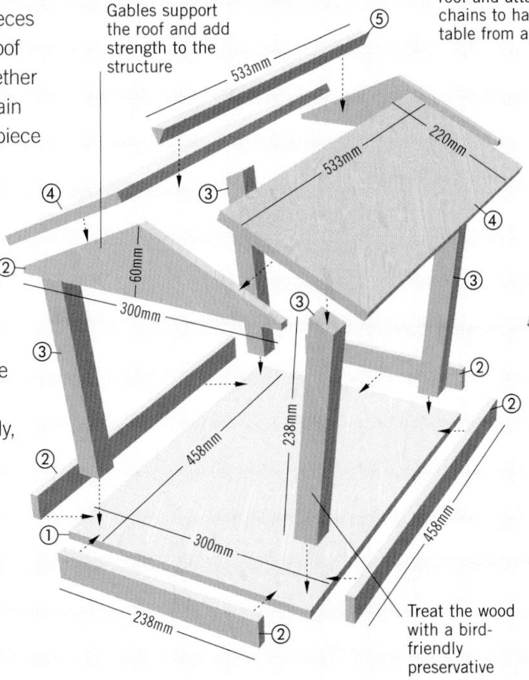

Gables support the roof and add strength to the structure
Fix hooks to the roof and attach chains to hang the table from a tree
533mm
533mm
220mm
60mm
300mm
458mm
238mm
300mm
458mm
238mm
Treat the wood with a bird-friendly preservative

Completed bird-table

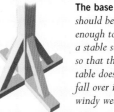

The table *can be mounted on a pole. This can be driven into the ground or a free-standing base can be constructed.*

The base *should be wide enough to form a stable support so that the table does not fall over in windy weather.*

MAKING A SEED HOPPER

This homemade hopper uses a 450g (1lb) jam jar, but the sizes of the back panel, base, and sides can be adjusted to fit other jars. Fix the back panel at a right angle to the base with long, rustproof screws. Attach the sides with nails to form a tray, leaving gaps at each corner for water drainage. Drill two holes in the base to fit the dowels, which steady the jar, and tack the webbing to the back panel to secure the jar. Screw three short screws into the base; the inverted jar rests upon them.

Materials

① 25mm (1in) wood
② 20mm (¾in) wood
③ 12mm (½in) plywood
④ Rustproof screws
⑤ Strip of webbing
⑥ Glass jar
⑦ 80mm (3in) dowel pegs

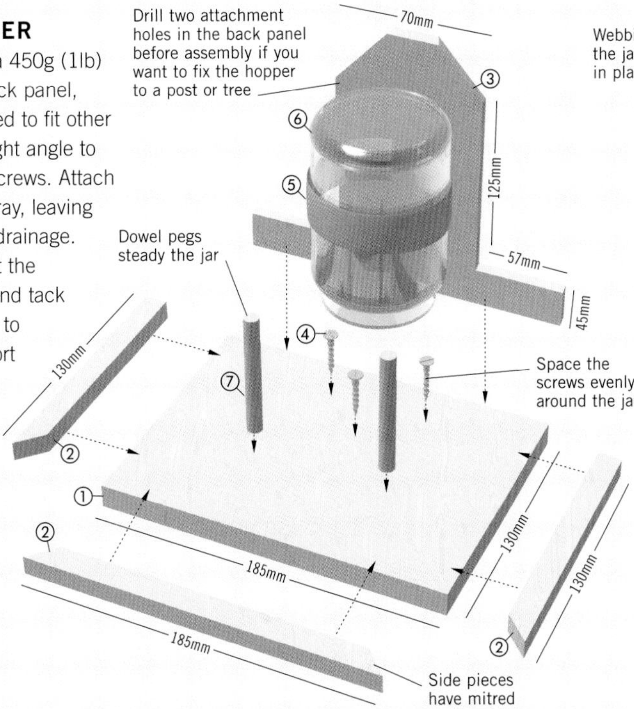

Drill two attachment holes in the back panel before assembly if you want to fix the hopper to a post or tree
70mm
125mm
57mm
45mm
Dowel pegs steady the jar
130mm
Space the screws evenly around the jar
130mm
130mm
185mm
185mm
Side pieces have mitred ends to form a neat corner

Webbing holds the jar firmly in place

Completed seed hopper

Adjust the gap *between the jar rim and the tray by turning the three support screws. This controls the flow of food from the jar.*

Bird-tables

NO BIRD GARDEN would be complete without a bird-table. This traditional feature remains the most efficient feeder for the greatest number of common species, attracting birds as varied as Blackcaps, Coal Tits, and Collared Doves. Bird-tables do a simple job – keeping food off the ground and providing a safe place for birds to feed, but there are many variations on the basic design.

A well-stocked bird-table *will occasionally reward its keeper with the visit of a less common species, such as this Bullfinch.*

BIRD-TABLE BIRDS

Birds you are most likely to see on a bird-table include:

- Woodpigeon
- Collared Dove
- Robin
- Blackbird
- Blackcap
- Blue Tit
- Great Tit
- Nuthatch
- Jackdaw
- Starling
- House Sparrow
- Chaffinch
- Greenfinch
- Feral Pigeon
- Wren
- Goldfinch
- Song Thrush
- Mistle Thrush

Table features

A well designed bird-table has a number of features that maximize the safety and comfort of visiting birds while preventing the loss and spoilage of food. It should be easy to clean and have good drainage (usually a base of stainless steel mesh) to prevent waterlogging of the food. It should have raised edges to prevent food blowing away in strong winds, and be open in aspect rather than confined, so that feeding birds can spot approaching predators, such as cats and Sparrowhawks, and make their escape in good time.

A raised table will bring together small birds, such as Blue Tits and Great Tits, larger Starlings, and really big species like the Rook and Woodpigeon. Even Pheasants have been known to visit. Aggregations of birds that do not normally feed together may result in behaviour called "dominance", where some birds drive off others – even those larger than themselves. Blackcaps visiting bird-tables in the winter, for example, are notorious for driving other birds away from the feeding site.

BIRD-TABLE DESIGNS

Low bird-tables *attract birds like Pied Wagtails and Song Thrushes, which prefer to feed on the ground.*

A traditional *table attracts the most birds and the greatest diversity of species, including Blue Tits and Nuthatches.*

Metal bird-tables *may be more costly than wooden models, but they resist the elements more effectively.*

A tray hanging *from the branch of a tree can be very effective in attracting more timid species, such as Goldfinches.*

Mixed species *often feed together on bird-tables – a good opportunity to observe how different birds interact.*

STYLES TO AVOID

Certain designs of bird-tables are not suitable for wild birds and should be avoided. Tables with integral nest-boxes (right), for example, may seem a good idea, fulfilling two tasks in one, but in practice birds are very unlikely to nest where so many others feed in their territory. Tables that are enclosed or walled should be avoided too, because birds feel far less secure if they do not have clear sight of their surroundings. Tables should be easy to clean, without cracks and crevices in which food and excrement can collect.

Ideal locations

The classic bird-table is mounted on a pole set into the ground, but tables that hang from trees or wall brackets are just as attractive and effective. All types should be set up on lawns away from trees or shrubs that provide cover for cats, and far enough from overhanging branches to deter squirrels from raiding the food. At first, the table should be placed away from the house to minimize disturbance, but once the birds get used to feeding, it may be moved closer to a window for better observation.

This popular type *of table has a heavy base for stability, yet can be moved easily round the garden if required.*

A roof protects *feeding birds from the worst of the winter weather, and an inverted metal collar below the table deters squirrels.*

A multi-tiered table *can hold several different types of food, so increasing the number and variety of visiting birds.*

This wall-mounted table *is made from sustainably-produced timber that has been treated with bird-safe preservative.*

Choosing bird food

OUR MOST FAMILIAR BIRDS naturally eat a wide variety of food. Song Thrushes feast on snails in summer, while Robins search for insects. Siskins take seeds from alder cones and Blue Tits from silver birch catkins. By carefully choosing the food that we put out for birds, we can attract a range of visitors to the garden and help them survive through the year, particularly in the difficult winter months. Today, it is possible to choose from a vast range of proprietary bird foods or to make your own from seeds or kitchen scraps.

A hanging peanut feeder *is a magnet to tits. The sturdy wire mesh prevents the nuts from being taken whole.*

Energy to live

The amount that a bird needs to eat depends on the energy content of its food. Insects and other invertebrates are the most nutritious foods for birds, followed by seeds, and finally berries. A Blackbird feeding on cotoneaster in autumn, for example, must consume more than 300 individual berries in a day just to stay alive.

Proprietary bird foods usually consist of seeds or nuts. Mixtures are popular because they offer balanced nutrition similar to the birds' natural diet. In recent years, the range of foods has expanded enormously: free-flowing seed mixtures have been formulated for use in tubular feeders, there are special mixes for ground feeders, and even "no mess" mixes from which seed husks have been removed. "Table seed" contains seeds that appeal to birds that prefer to eat off the bird table, such as sparrows, Robins, and Chaffinches. There are mixes that contain oystershell grit – a good source of calcium which birds need to make egg shells – and mixtures specially developed for different types of birds, such as ducks, geese, and swans.

Young birds *in particular benefit from the high-quality protein in live foods, such as mealworms.*

Peanuts – perhaps the best-known bird food – should be used in purpose-built feeders that prevent birds such as tits and Nuthatches from taking entire nuts, which can choke nestlings. It is wise to buy peanuts from a reputable bird food supplier; they may otherwise contain aflatoxin – a poison produced by a fungus, which can kill birds.

PROPRIETARY BIRD FOOD

Safe, high-calorie, nutritious bird foods can be bought from specialist dealers. Seed mixes are the most popular, and attract the widest range of species, but pure single foods favour selected garden species. Dealers produce variety "starter packs", which allow you to experiment with different bird foods.

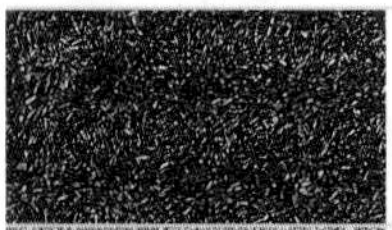

Nyjer seed *is very attractive to Goldfinches, but due to its small size, it must be put in a special feeder or mixed with other foods.*

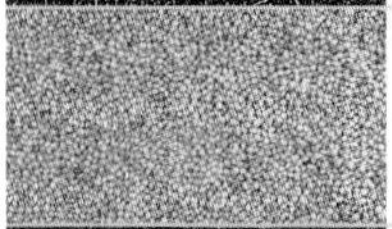

Millet seed *has a high fat content. Placed in ground feeders or on bird-tables, it appeals to smaller species, such as finches.*

Black sunflower seeds *are popular with many species including Greenfinches. Their husks can be added to the compost bin.*

Feeder seed mix *is a free-flowing mixture of sunflower seeds, chopped peanuts, millet, and oatmeal, suitable for hanging feeders.*

Table seed mix *for use on bird-tables contains wheat, sunflower seeds, kibbled maize, oatmeal, and chopped peanuts.*

Peanuts *are rich in oil and protein. They mainly attract tits, but are also popular with species such as Greenfinches and sparrows.*

Raisins and sultanas *are best when placed on a bird-table and mixed with other foods. A favourite of Blackbirds and thrushes.*

Mealworms, *waxworms, and earthworms placed in smooth, steep-sided bowls add a new dimension to bird feeding.*

ANNUAL FEEDING REQUIREMENTS

Birds benefit from additional feeding year round, not just in the winter months. The amount of energy that a bird needs varies considerably through the year (see below); extra food is taken in when the calorific value of the food is low, when additional fat reserves are needed (for example before migration), and when feeding the young.

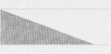

High food intake
Low food intake

SPECIES	Jan	Feb	Mar	Apr	May	Jun	Jul	Aug	Sep	Oct	Nov	Dec	PREFERRED FOOD
Collared Dove													*Mixed corn, seed mixes, table seed, grain.*
Dunnock													*Nyjer seed, pinhead oats.*
Robin													*Mealworms, waxworms, peanut granules, sunflower hearts.*
Song Thrush													*Fruit, earthworms, mealworms, peanut granules.*
Blackbird													*Fruit, peanut granules, mealworms, earthworms.*
Great Tit													*Peanuts, peanut cake, seed mixes, sunflower hearts.*
Blue Tit													*Peanuts, peanut cake, black sunflower seeds, seed mixes.*
Starling													*Scraps, seed mixes, peanut cake, live foods.*
House Sparrow													*Mealworms (when breeding), sunflower hearts, seed mixes.*
Chaffinch													*Peanut granules, sunflower hearts, seed mixes.*
Goldfinch													*Sunflower hearts, nyjer seed, black sunflower seeds, peanuts.*
Greenfinch													*Black sunflower seeds, sunflower hearts, seed mixes.*
Siskin													*Sunflower hearts, peanuts, black sunflower seeds, nyjer seed.*

Making bird food

FEEDING GARDEN BIRDS need not be costly. Domestic kitchen scraps are often rich in the very fats and carbohydrates that birds need to maintain vital reserves of body fat in the winter months. And even if proprietary seed mixes are used, they can be safely augmented with recycled food from our kitchens, or with windfall fruit. More dedicated bird gardeners may be inclined to make special bird cakes.

Once you start *to provide food for birds, continue throughout the cold season, because the birds will begin to count on your offerings. It helps to keep the same food type at a particular feeder throughout the winter.*

Food for free

Kitchen scraps placed on a bird-table will be eaten by a variety of species, from Robins to Song Thrushes. Bread, cake, and biscuit crumbs are all popular, as are cooked potato, cheese, and chopped bacon rind. Even the timid Dunnock may be tempted to a bird-table for some of the smaller scraps. Bones from cooked meats suspended from a bird-table will be pecked clean by Starlings as well as by smaller species, such as Robins.

In autumn, windfall fruits can simply be left on the ground for the birds, or collected for use as a bird food later in the year. Fruit is popular with members of the thrush family, especially Blackbirds; any left over in late autumn may become food for migrant thrushes, such as Redwings and Fieldfares.

Smearing warm fat on a tree trunk, or pushing suet into a crack in a log makes a quick treat for tits and Nuthatches, while melted fat poured into a yoghurt pot and then pressed out on to the bird-table (or suspended on a string) provides energy-rich food for House Sparrows, Starlings, and tits. More complex home-made bird cakes (see opposite) will attract tits and finches.

Seeds *from plants like flax, sunflower, beech, and teazel can be collected from the garden for use as bird food.*

KITCHEN SCRAPS

Food for birds should be free from moulds, some of which can cause respiratory disease. Always remove any food that goes stale on the bird-table – it will cause salmonella, which is fatal to birds like Greenfinches and House Sparrows.

Cake and bread *should be soaked in water. They are good "filler" foods but lack the protein and fat that birds need in their diet, so should be used sparingly.*

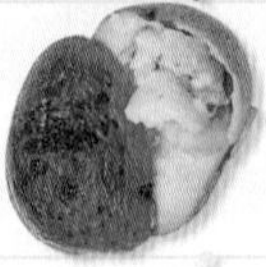

Cooked potatoes *are high in protein. These left-overs are popular with many species, especially Starlings, which will peck out the soft centre, leaving the outer skin.*

Cooked rice *quickly vanishes from the bird-table, and is favoured by House Sparrows and Starlings. Avoid putting out rice that has been highly flavoured.*

Fruits, *such as apples, pears, and grapes are all popular foods. Thrushes, especially Blackbirds, Starlings, and tits all like to feed on fallen apples in late autumn.*

Dry cheese *is a protein-rich food that can be a life-saver for small birds in hard weather. Sprinkled under bushes it will sometimes be eaten by Wrens.*

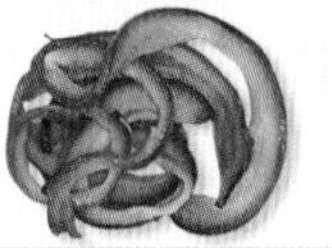

Bacon rind *is popular with nearly all birds, and can attract larger species, such as Magpies and gulls. It should be cut into small pieces before serving.*

TABLE MANNERS

In nature, it is rare for birds to congregate frequently to feed at one spot. Busy bird-tables can become breeding grounds for diseases, some of which can be passed on to humans. Old food and droppings should regularly be scraped off, and the table washed with a mild detergent to prevent problems. Food scraps on the ground should also be cleared regularly to deter rodents.

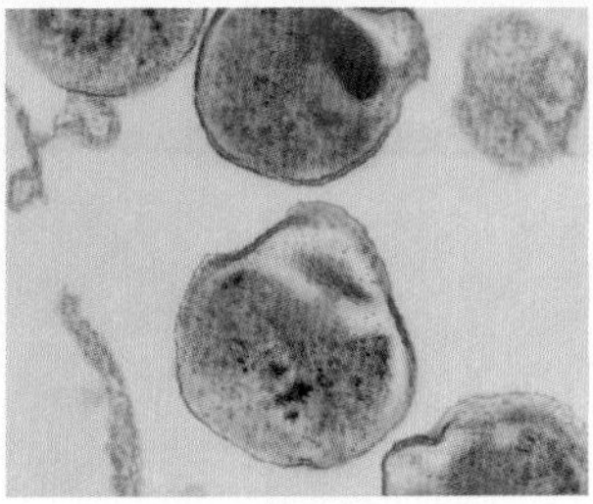

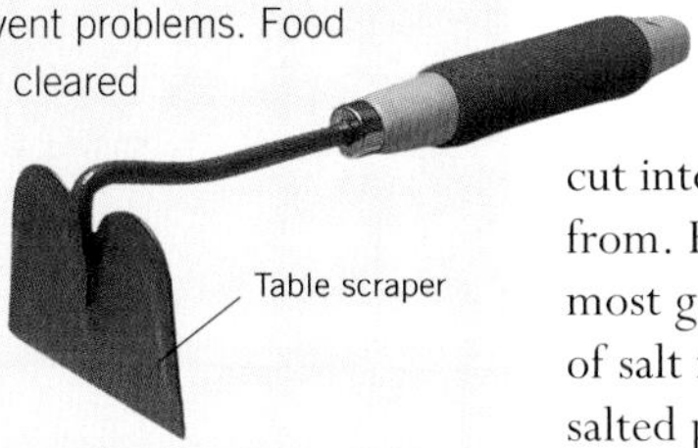

Table scraper

Psittacosis *is a bacterial disease that can be transmitted from birds to humans, in whom it causes pneumonia-like symptoms.*

Foods to avoid

Many food scraps are safe for birds, but some should be avoided. Uncooked rice and desiccated coconut, for example, will swell up inside a bird's gut, often with fatal results. For similar reasons, it is better to soak dry bread in water before placing it on the bird table. Bacon rind is nutritious, especially uncooked, but large pieces can choke small birds. The rind should be cut into cubes, or tied firmly and suspended for tits to feed from. Birds should not be given spoiled or spicy food, and most garden species are unable to cope with large amounts of salt in their diet, so salty fats, cured foods, crisps, and salted peanuts should be avoided.

While birds adore saturated fats, such as raw suet and lard, unsaturated fats may be harmful. These fats, which include margarine and vegetable oils, can become smeared on to the bird's body, where they destroy the waterproofing and insulating qualities of its feathers.

Making your own *bird cake is easy. Melt shredded suet or dripping in a saucepan and add kitchen scraps, bird seeds, or unsalted peanuts. Pour into a container and allow to set. The resulting cake can be cut and put on to the bird-table.*

Drinking and bathing

WATER IS AN ESSENTIAL ingredient in any bird garden. It will attract a wide range of species throughout the year, including birds that feed elsewhere but need fresh water for drinking and bathing. The simplest way to provide water is in a bird-bath, but garden ponds with shallow edges provide the same facilities, with the added benefit of giving a home to aquatic animals, including frogs and toads.

A Goldcrest *soaks itself while bathing, which helps to keep feathers in good order and keeps it cool in hot weather.*

The importance of water

Small birds, particularly those that feed on dry seeds, need to drink regularly (at least twice a day) to replace the fluids lost through respiration and in their droppings. Water is also essential for bathing, which plays an important role in feather maintenance; dampening the feathers loosens the dirt and makes the feathers easier to preen.

Some woodland birds may drink water from droplets on leaves, but the easiest way to provide water in the garden is in a bird-bath or a pond. A good bird-bath is simple and sturdy, but light enough to clean and refill. It must have sloping sides with a shallow approach to the water. Depth should range between 2.5 and 10cm (1–4in) to allow every species to bathe at its ideal depth. The surface of the bath should be rough so birds can grip it with their claws, and it should be large enough to hold sufficient water to withstand a vigorous bathing session by a flock of Starlings.

WINTER WATER

In cold conditions, check your bird-bath daily. Break through the ice so that birds can bathe and drink. Avoid additives that prevent freezing, because these can poison birds or damage the waterproofing of their plumage. If possible, add a water feature such as a fountain; running water lets birds drink even when standing water is frozen. House Sparrows are particularly quick to take advantage of running water supplies.

A garden pond *not only provides a place for birds to bathe and water for them to drink, but certain birds, like the Grey Heron, may even hunt for fish or frogs.*

TYPES OF BIRD-BATH

A stone bath *on a pedestal has a traditional appearance, but is heavy, so difficult to move around the garden.*

Ceramic baths *may benefit from a thin layer of gravel on the bottom to give the birds a surer footing.*

This stone-effect *fibre-glass bath is light and easy to move. It has deep and shallow areas, so is suitable for birds of all sizes.*

Shallow metal containers *are fine, but water freezes quickly in cold weather. A floating tennis ball delays ice build-up.*

The simplest bird-bath is a large plant saucer with a stone in the middle to serve as a perch, or an inverted dustbin lid sunk into the ground; custom-made bird-baths are available from garden centres or specialist bird care suppliers. All types should be cleaned weekly to remove algae and droppings. Use dilute non-toxic disinfectant and rinse thoroughly.

This shallow pond *edge attracts many Blackbirds in spring. The birds visit to drink, bathe, forage for food, and gather mud, which they use to build their nests.*

Safety first

Birds are distracted while bathing, making them vulnerable to predator attack. Siting the bath near bushes or trees, where birds can retreat, perch, and preen, will attract more visitors, and planting thorny shrubs such as roses or pyracantha will keep cats away from the birds' cover.

During periods of drought, birds may try to use water barrels or troughs for drinking, and sadly many drown. If these containers cannot be covered, they can be made safer by floating a plank of wood or a branch on the water surface, so that birds can land and drink.

When bathing, *most garden birds crouch in the water, ruffle their feathers, and flick their wings, which helps spread the water over the body. After bathing they shake off the water and preen the feathers into position.*

Nest-boxes

EVEN IF A GARDEN IS WELL STOCKED with food, birds will leave in the breeding season unless they can find suitable nest sites. The way to keep birds in the garden year round is to put up nest-boxes that replicate the birds' natural nesting preferences. More than 60 species are known to use nest-boxes – from tits, House and Tree Sparrows, and Spotted Flycatchers, to Kestrels and Tawny Owls. Much depends on where the box is sited and on its surroundings.

Nest-boxes that are in use *should not be inspected. It is best to watch and enjoy from a distance or to buy a tiny nest-box camera. This can be linked up to your television for a front-row view from inside the box.*

Enclosed and open boxes

Many garden birds prefer to nest in crevices in trees. Great Spotted Woodpeckers usually excavate their own holes, but other species either use old woodpecker nests or exploit natural cavities in old trees. In towns, where old trees are in short supply, the bird gardener can help by providing artificial holes in the form of "enclosed" nest-boxes.

A typical box is rectangular, upright, with a small hole at the front. Its exact dimensions depend on the nesting species: small boxes attract tits, while the largest may be used by birds up to the size of Jackdaws. Social species, such as House Sparrows, may be tempted to a collection of several adjacent boxes, but most birds defend larger territories and prefer boxes spaced out around the garden.

"Open-fronted" nest-boxes are used by species that naturally nest on ledges and partly enclosed spaces – birds like Spotted Flycatchers, Robins, and Pied Wagtails – and

OPEN AND ENCLOSED NEST-BOXES

A half-open nest-box *is simple in design and easy to clean. They are particularly attractive to Robins, Spotted Flycatchers, and Wrens if positioned low down within dense cover.*

An open nest-box *gives species such as Blackbirds a platform on which they can build their nest. It is easy to maintain and offers excellent viewing opportunities.*

Tits prefer enclosed boxes *like this traditional style nest-box. Choose boxes with a hinged or removable roof or front panel to allow access for cleaning.*

CHOOSING A NEST-BOX

Nest-boxes are designed with various hole sizes suited to particular species. This table lists birds that prefer open and enclosed boxes, and the hole dimensions they require.

ENCLOSED NEST-BOXES

Bird species	Diameter of hole
Blue Tit	25mm (1in)
Great Tit	28mm (1in)
Tree Sparrow	28mm (1in)
Nuthatch	32mm (1¼in)
House Sparrow	32mm (1¼in)
Starling	45mm (1¾in)
Great Spotted Woodpecker	50mm (2in)
Little Owl	70mm (2¾in)
Mallard	150mm (6in)
Stock Dove	150mm (6in)
Tawny Owl	150mm (6in)
Jackdaw	150mm (6in)

OPEN NEST-BOXES

Bird species
Wren
Pied Wagtail
Robin
Blackbird
Spotted Flycatcher
Feral Pigeon
Kestrel

occasional Blackbirds and Wrens will also use this type of box.

When choosing a wooden nest-box, check that the exterior has been treated with preservative. Woodcrete boxes – made from a mixture of sawdust and concrete – are sturdy and rot-proof. They may offer improved nestling survival, because they are better at maintaining internal temperature, and exclude most predators.

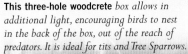

A House Sparrow *feeds its young at a nest-box. These birds rarely nest far away from buildings.*

This tough resin nest-box *provides added safety for the nesting birds, because predators cannot enlarge the entrance hole to gain access to the eggs and chicks inside.*

This birch log nest-box *blends in perfectly with its rustic garden surroundings. The lid can be unscrewed for routine maintenance at the end of each nesting season.*

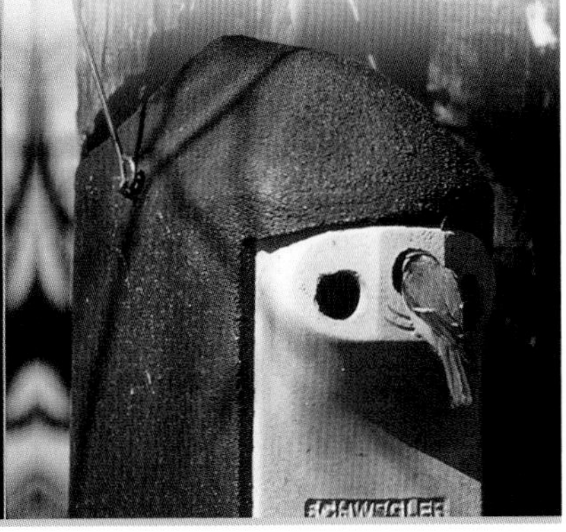

This three-hole woodcrete *box allows in additional light, encouraging birds to nest in the back of the box, out of the reach of predators. It is ideal for tits and Tree Sparrows.*

NEST-BOXES AND SPECIES RECOVERY

Some of our most familiar garden birds are in decline. House Sparrow populations, for example, have halved in some parts of Europe over the last 20 years. The use of suitable nest-boxes can locally boost numbers of these once-common birds. House Sparrows use Blue Tit-sized boxes, with entrance holes of 32mm (1¼in) diameter. Siting several nest-boxes close together in a garden may produce a visible increase in the sparrow population within a single year.

The Great Spotted Woodpecker *is a natural hole nester. It uses its tail as a prop when balancing on a tree trunk to excavate its hole or feed its young.*

Boxes should be put up in early January through to the end of February, when pairs of birds are already exploring potential nest sites. If a box is occupied, great care should be taken to minimize disturbance until the young take flight. After nesting, the nest material should be removed and the box disinfected to prevent a build-up of parasites (see opposite). The box should immediately be put back up again because it may be used in winter as a roost.

Do not despair if your nest-box is not used in the first year – chances are that it will be occupied in years to come.

SPECIALIST NEST-BOXES

Kestrels naturally nest *on ledges on cliffs or buildings, or in large tree holes. They will sometimes occupy large, open nest-boxes sited high on mature trees.*

Starlings may appear *to be common, but European populations are in decline. Large nest-boxes with 45mm (1¾in) holes provide suitable nest sites.*

Tawny Owls *can be tempted to nest in long wooden boxes situated high in trees. Boxes must be well away from public places, because nesting owls sometimes swoop on passers by.*

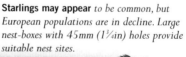

Putting up several boxes increases the chance of at least one being used, and by introducing a variety of styles there is a good chance that unusual species will arrive and nest.

Rarer nesters

Some birds will almost never nest in artificial nest-boxes, and others have strict nesting requirements. Swifts, for example, long ago moved from their traditional sites in caves and crevices to nest almost entirely in niches in the roofs of buildings, often in towns. Modern houses are built with few crevices for Swifts, yet putting up nest-boxes for the birds does not attract nesters. Studies showed that the Swifts often did not recognize the boxes as potential nest sites, but if they were played recordings of Swift calls, apparently originating from the boxes, this increased the chances of them investigating and then adopting a box.

Nest-boxes not only encourage garden birds to stay and breed near our homes, but also help species that are declining in their natural habitats (see opposite). Many specialist boxes are used on nature reserves, but they can also be put up in suitable gardens (see below).

Wrens are opportunists *when it comes to nesting. This one has found a good site in an old woolly jumper hanging in a shed.*

HYGIENE AND NEST SITES

Most birds' nests harbour fleas and other parasites, which remain to infest young birds that hatch the following year, so old nests should be removed in late autumn. Boiling water can be used to clean the nest-box and kill any remaining parasites. Insecticides and flea powders must not be used. Placing a handful of clean hay or wood shavings (not straw) in the box once it is thoroughly dry increases the chances that it will be used in winter by small mammals or birds.

Opening a nest-box *in the breeding season could cause birds to abandon their eggs or young.*

Swallows naturally *build bowl-shaped nests of mud lined with white feathers. Artificial nests made from a mix of wood and concrete (woodcrete) can be put inside a shed or barn.*

Treecreepers usually *nest in narrow gaps and clefts in mature trees. Purpose-designed Treecreeper boxes are wedge shaped, and have unique triangular entrance holes.*

Dovecotes originally *held doves, which provided fresh meat throughout the winter, but today they are a highly decorative addition to the garden.*

Making nest-boxes

MAKING A NEST-BOX DOES NOT require great carpentry skills and can be fun. Design your box to suit the birds visiting your garden in winter, and you may persuade some to remain there to nest. There is no guarantee that a nest-box will attract birds, but careful siting increases the likelihood of it being adopted. Be patient: some boxes are not adopted for several years after installation.

Position boxes *facing away from the prevailing wind and rain, and out of the midday sun.*

DIY nest-boxes

There are two basic designs of nest-box that can be made relatively simply: enclosed boxes with a small hole for tits, or open nest-boxes, favoured by Robins and Pied Wagtails. One of the advantages of building your own nest-box is that you can tailor it to the species you want to attract; the size of an enclosed box and the diameter of its entrance hole, for example, will determine which species use it (see page 35).

Boxes should be made from strong timber and can be treated with a harmless wood preservative on the outside to prolong their life. Be sure that the cavity in the box is large enough for a nest and several young; boxes that are too small can lead to overcrowding, poor circulation, and over-heating in warm weather, while too large a space will simply be filled with more nesting material. At the end of each season, old nests need to be removed and the nest-box cleaned (see page 37). To allow access to the interior of enclosed nest-boxes, fit them with a tight-fitting, hinged lid.

HOW TO BUILD A NEST-BOX

To make a standard enclosed nest-box, cut surplus floorboards or plywood into the sizes shown here. Saw the side of the lid that butts on to the back panel at an angle, so that it fits tightly to the back of the box. Secure a metal plate on the inside of the front panel to reinforce the hole. With 38mm (1½in) nails, fix the sides of the box to the edges of the base, then attach the front and back panels. Use a strip of waterproof material or a metal hinge to attach the lid to the back panel, and secure it with a hook and eye on each side panel.

Materials

① 15mm (⅝in) thick floorboard or plywood

② Metal plate or tin lid to reinforce the entrance hole

③ Metal hinge or strip of waterproof material

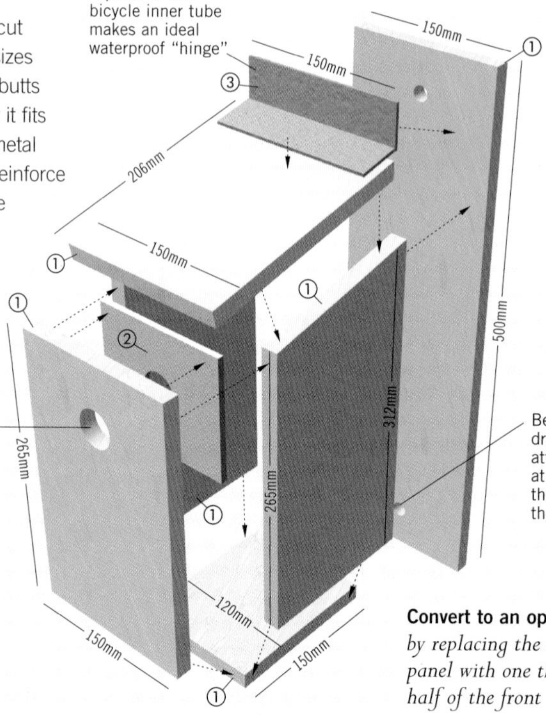
A piece of old bicycle inner tube makes an ideal waterproof "hinge"
150mm
150mm
206mm
150mm
500mm
312mm
265mm
265mm
120mm
150mm
150mm
①
②
③
Tailor the size of entrance hole to the bird species you want to attract
Before assembly, drill a small attachment hole at the top and the bottom of the back panel

Completed enclosed nest-box

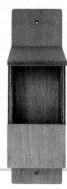

Convert to an open *nest-box by replacing the entrance-hole panel with one that covers half of the front of the box.*

SITING NEST-BOXES

There are few hard and fast rules when it comes to choosing where to position nest-boxes around the garden. Birds like privacy when nesting, so nest-boxes should be put where there will be minimal disturbance and where predators, such as cats, find it difficult to attack. Installing several boxes increases the chance that one will be used, but as most species require a territory, they should be spaced out around the garden. It is a mistake to position nest-boxes too close to a bird-table or feeder, because it makes it more difficult for the resident birds to defend a territory around their home.

House Sparrows *prefer to nest close together, and use special "House Sparrow terraces" that allow several birds to nest in the same box.*

Starlings *use large enclosed nest-boxes with entrance holes 52mm (2in) in diameter. Position on a wall or tree.*

Treecreepers *naturally nest in gaps and crevices in trees, and use special wedge-shaped nest-boxes positioned on the trunk of a tree.*

Kestrels *nest in large open nest-boxes positioned near the top of a mature tree, or at least 5m (16ft) above the ground.*

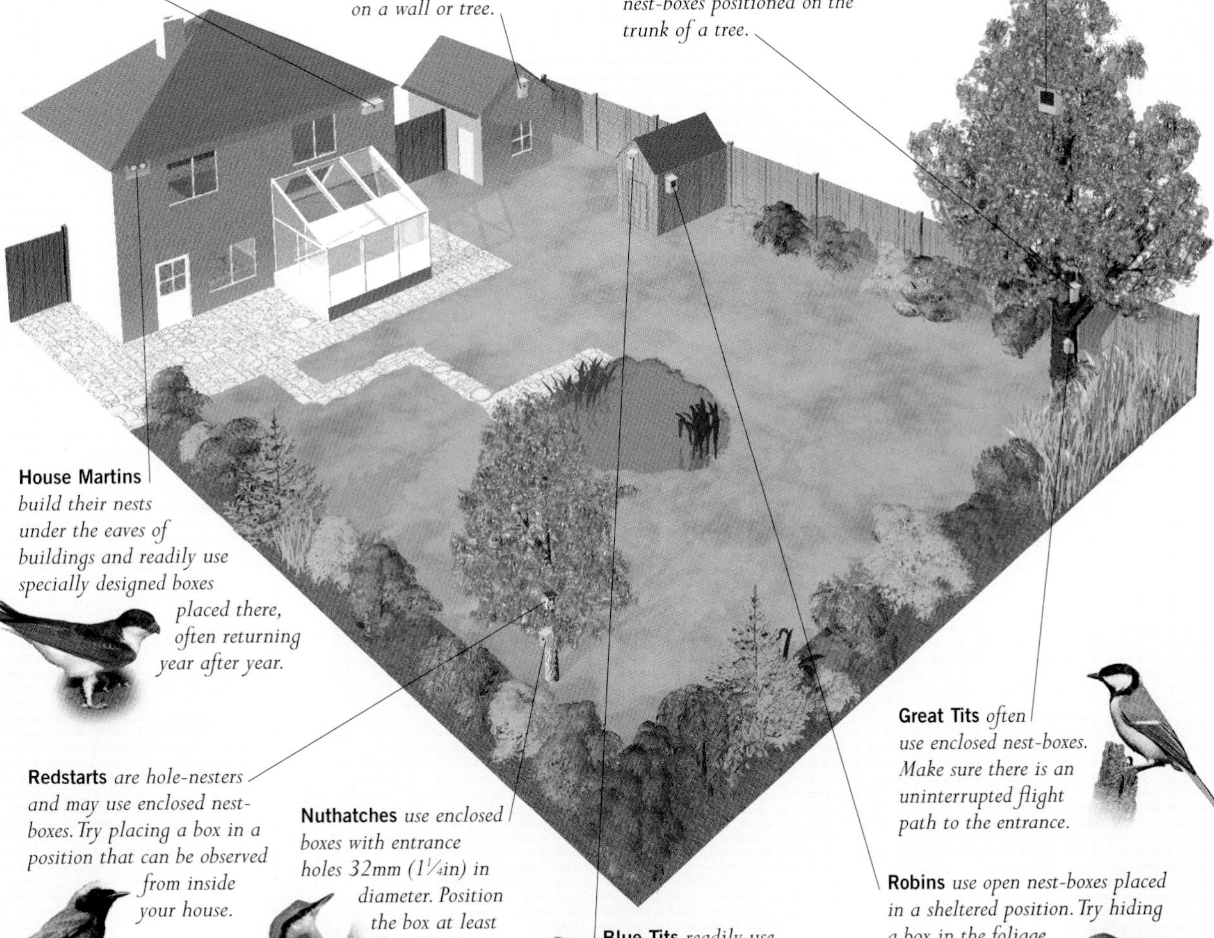

House Martins *build their nests under the eaves of buildings and readily use specially designed boxes placed there, often returning year after year.*

Great Tits *often use enclosed nest-boxes. Make sure there is an uninterrupted flight path to the entrance.*

Redstarts *are hole-nesters and may use enclosed nest-boxes. Try placing a box in a position that can be observed from inside your house.*

Nuthatches *use enclosed boxes with entrance holes 32mm (1¼in) in diameter. Position the box at least 2m (7ft) from the ground.*

Blue Tits *readily use enclosed nest-boxes. Angle the boxes downwards to prevent rain from entering.*

Robins *use open nest-boxes placed in a sheltered position. Try hiding a box in the foliage of a climbing plant, such as ivy.*

Garden threats

ATTRACTING BIRDS INTO THE GARDEN is not always consistent with other activities around the home. For example, garden birds may be disturbed or attacked by domestic pets, endangered by chemicals used in the home or the garden, or injured in strikes with windows. Birds are also threatened by other wild species that may steal their eggs or take their young. A few simple measures can help you avoid many of these problems, and maximize the benefits that your garden offers to wildlife.

Undesirable visitors

Many wild animals are tempted into gardens to take advantage of birds or bird foods: grey squirrels take not only bird seed and nuts, but also nestlings; rats, stoats, and Magpies raid nests for eggs; and Sparrowhawks prey upon feeding songbirds. In most cases, cages or baffles around feeders and bird-tables are enough to humanely deter the raiders.

The most dangerous garden visitors, however, are not wild animals, but domestic cats. Cats are opportunistic hunters, and birds account for just 20 per cent of the animals they catch, but with an estimated 8 million cats in the UK alone, conservationists believe that they have a significant effect on wild bird populations.

Nest-boxes and feeders should always be positioned out of a cat's reach (see box, right). Cat repellents – either strong-smelling chemicals or ultrasonic devices – can be used to repel the more determined hunters, although success is not guaranteed.

NEST PROTECTION

Predators are quick to make a meal out of a clutch of eggs or a brood of young. Siting nest-boxes high in trees, or surrounded by thorny shrubs (below) or tangles of chicken wire will make their approach more difficult. Nest-boxes can be fittted with plastic or metal "protectors" which lengthen the entrance hole, so preventing access by squirrels and cats. Metal plates around the entrance will prevent predators enlarging the holes to steal eggs.

Large glazed doors *are a danger; birds see the reflected sky and trees, and attempt to fly through. Stickers, especially raptor silhouettes, help to warn them off.*

Pesticides *used in the garden rarely harm birds directly, but they kill the insects on which many birds depend. Natural, "biological" pest control is better for birds.*

Mesh bags *should be avoided because they can trap birds' feet and cause broken legs. They also attract squirrels, which tear open the bags and steal the nuts.*

Grey squirrels *will exploit the easiest supply of food, even if this is eggs in a nest-box. Providing squirrels with their own dedicated cache of nuts in a suitable feeder may persuade them to leave birds and bird foods alone.*

Cat owners can *take measures to prevent their pets from catching birds. Cats should be kept indoors when birds are most vulnerable, especially around sunset and sunrise. A simple bell, or a more sophisticated sonic device, attached to the collar, warns birds of the cat's approach.*

The bird-friendly garden

Changes in the countryside and in agricultural practices have made gardens a vitally important bird habitat. Maximizing your garden's appeal to birds is about making the most of what you already have, and planting with wildlife in mind.

Woodland gardens

ONE OF THE RICHEST NATURAL HABITATS for wildlife is the woodland edge, which offers a mix of vegetation, light and shade, and shelter. Birds have evolved to live in different sections of this habitat: Blue Tits in the tree canopy, Greenfinches and Robins among the lower branches and bushes, and Dunnocks and Blackbirds on the ground. There is space to create a woodland area even in a small courtyard garden.

Hazels are small, *fast-growing trees that provide good cover for nesting birds. Insects thrive in their foliage and hazelnuts are taken by some bird species.*

The garden compromise

Creating a garden for birds is almost always a compromise. It may not even be worth trying to encourage birds if your garden is already a playground for small children or cats. Similarly, if you have serious horticultural objectives, it may be hard to reconcile your standards of neatness and planting with the more overgrown, unkempt look of a wildlife garden. But for most gardeners, a compromise is possible. Plants can be chosen that are attractive to both birds and humans, and pruning, cutting, and trimming can be reduced to allow insects to flourish and seeds and fruits to ripen. Maintaining a bird garden has become more acceptable in recent years as a natural outdoors look has become more fashionable. For example, the dead stems of perennials, which were traditionally cut after flowering, are now often left on the plants, because seedheads (with their rich load of bird food) and stems are considered to be decorative. And patches of lawn are often left unmown allowing clover to emerge, so providing food for Woodpigeons and Bullfinches.

Many garden birds *are natural woodland edge species (below), preferring a mixture of dense, tall foliage, tall herbs, and open space. The shrubs and herbaceous beds of an effective bird garden (below right) create the same effect.*

Natural engineering

To make a garden attractive for birds, try to recreate their natural habitat. For most of our common garden birds that means woodland – specifically, the boundary between woods and open ground, or the similar hedgerow habitat.

Lavender *is a popular garden plant, grown for its fragrance and colour, but it also attracts Goldfinches that eat its seeds.*

INSECT ATTRACTIONS

Hebes are decorative, evergreen shrubs that grow in sunny, well-drained places. They are planted in borders and rock gardens for their foliage and flowers. They are also a good food source for birds because they are attractive to insects, such as hoverflies and small bees. Insects of this size are the preferred prey for Spotted Flycatchers.

Spotted Flycatcher

To provide "natural" food successfully in the garden, think about the year-round requirements of different birds. Choose annuals and herbaceous perennials, and some fast-growing lavender, cotoneaster, pyracantha, ivy, and bird cherry, which will quickly provide food and shelter. Plant fast-growing bird-friendly trees, such as birch, and replace walls or sections of fences with hedges, which add wildlife value (see box below).

Dense bushes and climbers and taller trees will attract birds to nest, especially Blackbirds, Robins, and Dunnocks, but many more species will be attracted to carefully selected nest-boxes (see pages 34–37).

Creating a "woodland-edge" garden calls for long-term planning, because the plants brought into the garden need time to establish and grow. Finding out what plants and features are successful for birds in your garden is partly a case of trial and error, and partly dependent on your surrounding environment. Mistle Thrushes, for example, have recently expanded into suburban gardens. The reason for this has little to do with gardening practices, however, and more to do with the fact that amenity tree-planting is providing them with the high perches they need when singing.

Little Owls *are exciting visitors to gardens, settling on perches where they can be seen even in broad daylight. Logpiles and compost heaps provide them with small mammals, insects, and worms.*

HEDGE HABITATS

A well-established, *thick hedge provides ideal nesting and roosting sites, and is often the only hiding place in the garden. Hedges also provide better shelter from winds than solid walls and fences, preventing eddies that disturb nesting birds and that kill delicate plants.*

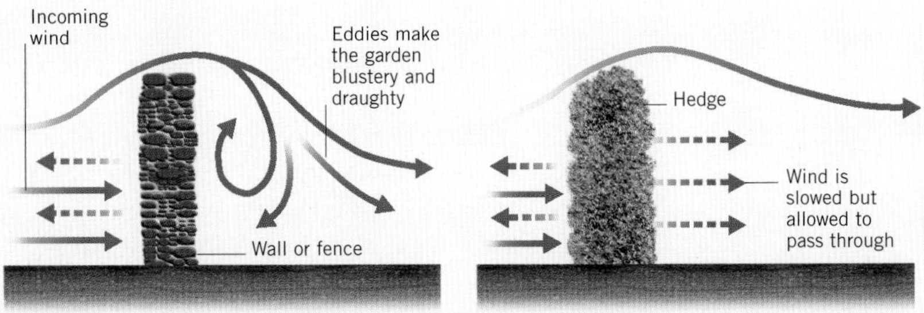
Incoming wind
Eddies make the garden blustery and draughty
Wall or fence
Hedge
Wind is slowed but allowed to pass through

Any shrub *that stands being clipped can be trained to form a hedge. A mixture of fast-growing evergreens and broadleaf species is ideal.*

Water gardens

Moorhens may nest *on garden ponds secluded by high vegetation. The pond should be at least 20m (66ft) square.*

WATER FEATURES CAN BE integrated into virtually any garden, whatever its size. Pools are used for drinking and bathing, and larger ponds may attract water birds, from Mallards to Kingfishers. Muddy pond margins draw in species like wagtails, which come to forage for worms and insects, while Blackbirds, thrushes, and House Martins use pond mud for nesting material.

Attracted to water

Wildlife is drawn to ponds. The boundary between land and water, usually sheltered by dense foliage, presents an ideal habitat for varied invertebrates, amphibians, and birds. Gardeners, too, adore water, because it allows the planting of exquisite water plants and exciting and attractive species that thrive in wet margins.

Pond construction

There are many ways to build a pond. The simplest is to lower a moulded rigid fibreglass container into the ground, although these preformed ponds are limited in shape and size. Another alternative is to line a hole with tonnes of impermeable clay, although this daunting undertaking is most suited to the largest of ponds. Perhaps the best way to create a wildlife pond is to use thick neoprene sheeting to line a hole; today's long-lasting, inconspicuous, flexible pond liners make this a fairly straightforward process. Using flexible liner allows gradations of shape and depth, which maximize the appeal of the pond to wildlife.

A pond should have gently sloping sides; birds will drink and bathe in the shallows and the low gradient permits animals such as hedgehogs to clamber out. As a rule, the more varied the slopes and the longer the shoreline, the better the pond will be for wildlife. However, it should also have areas in which the depth exceeds 60cm (23in) deep, so that the water does not freeze solid in hard winters.

PLANNING AND PLANTING

When making a bird pond, leave shallow edges on at least part of the circumference, and plant them with marsh species, including flag irises, sedges, and marsh marigolds. The edges of the pond should shelve away gently so that a bird can wade in up to its middle. If this is not possible (for example, if using a preformed pond), build a platform from bricks or stones that is submerged just deep enough for birds to stand in.

Birds bathe *in ponds year-round (above), but especially in winter when good feather maintenance is essential to keep warm. In the nesting season, some species collect mud as cement for their nests (left).*

Moving water features, *such as waterfalls and fountains, prevent water from freezing in winter.*

Position and stocking

Avoid siting the pond under trees – it will fill with autumn leaves and growing roots could puncture the pond lining. Instead, plant a low bush near the pond to provide cover for bathing birds. Do not automatically place your pond in a wet or damp hollow, because such areas may already be important for wildlife; having more than one wet area in a garden can increase the variety of wildlife.

The pond is incomplete without plants, which provide food and nesting material. The best time for planting is late spring when the water is beginning to warm up. Submerge the plants in plastic baskets or flowerpots and, if necessary, weight the pots with stones until the trapped air has dispersed. The weights may need to be retained for tall plants that will be blown over by the wind. Place the containers on large stones or bricks so that the leaves are at surface level. The plants can gradually be lowered as the leaves spread. Only one or two plants are needed for a small pond.

Pondweed, which has submerged or floating leaves, adds interest to the surface of the water, while marginal plants as such as sedges, purple loosestrife, and kingcups provide colour and variety around the edge of a pond. Tall waterside plants may help attract shyer birds and deter herons, which like a clear view of their surroundings.

Amphibians are good *colonizers, and appear once your pond is established enough to support them. Newts favour ponds next to wild areas with plants like water forget-me-not, water speedwell, and water starwort.*

Bulrushes provide birds *with food and nesting material. Their seedheads attract feeding birds in autumn.*

A brand-new, freshly-filled pond is barren at first, but life soon appears in the form of water beetles, dragonflies, and other insects that fly in and settle. Frogs, toads, and newts may also discover the pond for themselves and establish breeding populations. Snails, and other animals that are aquatic rather than amphibious, have to be introduced from another pond. Populations of creatures such as water fleas, which are food for larger animals, can be started by adding a bucket of water and mud from an established pond. Fish, such as sticklebacks, are an interesting addition, but check that the species you choose do not eat tadpoles.

A natural pond *(below) takes years to develop into a focus for wildlife. If designed carefully, a garden pond (below right) can reproduce the conditions that exist in the wild.*

Easy gardens

Fat hen *is an annual weed, not loved by most gardeners, but its seeds are an important food for many birds.*

PEOPLE WITH GARDENS are not necessarily keen gardeners. Some prefer to maintain their garden rather like their home, tidying regularly but refurbishing rarely. This approach is highly compatible with wildlife gardening because birds are most likely to be attracted to less "managed" areas where there are weed seeds and insects on unkempt foliage. However, this does not mean that a wildlife garden is a neglected garden.

Soil and aspect

The key to maintaining a successful wildlife garden with minimum effort is to adapt to local conditions. Use bird-friendly plants that are sympathetic with the soil type and aspect of your garden. For example, if your soil is poor and dry, don't try to enrich it with fertilizer; instead, give it a Mediterranean look with lavender and aromatic herbs. If your garden is shady, typical woodland floor plants come into their own – bluebell, Solomon's seal, dog's mercury, bugle, and herb robert, for example.

Practise sensible, low-intensity cultivation. Do not trim all your herbaceous plants in the autumn, because they provide shelter for insects later in the season. Similarly, do not clear away all fallen leaf litter. It can be home to ground beetles and centipedes, and ladybirds will nest in bunches of sticks. Regularly mulch any areas of bare soil with bark chippings to control weeds and encourage earthworms.

If you have a large lawn, give parts of it no more than two or three cuts a year. This will allow broad-leaved plants to flower and set seed amongst the grass – excellent food for birds. In summer, your flower-rich lawn will swarm with insects that help feed hungry broods, but remember that the grass should be cut before it turns into hay and becomes untidy. Grass can also be allowed to grow and seed

Working with the garden *means paying attention to light and soil conditions. Shade-tolerant plants work in a walled or woodland garden (below), while plants like gorse thrive on acid soils (right).*

around trees and in tight corners; the long growth gives shelter to animals, from insects and snails to mice and voles. This will encourage Kestrels or owls to hunt in your garden.

Native or exotic?

Most successful wildlife gardens are well stocked with native plants. These species have evolved hand-in-hand with native animals – mainly birds and invertebrates – so provide the habitat that resident wildlife needs. For example, teazel and thistles provide birds with seeds, flowers such as foxgloves

A damp, grassy patch *can be transformed into a flower-rich meadow, attractive for birds, bees, and butterflies. It can be planted with specialist meadow flowers such as the fritillary (right).*

and lavender yield nectar to attract bees, and native trees, such as rowan and elder, produce berries. Grass species, such as fescues and bents, provide seeds for sparrows and continue to feed birds through the winter. Plants with "flat" flowers, such as sedums and *Limnanthes douglasii* (also known as "poached eggs"), attract hoverflies and lacewings.

Native species are the obvious choice, but exotics can also be valuable in the wildlife garden. Verbena (*Verbena bonariensis*), for example, is a native of South America. Its seeds are eaten by finches and tits, and it produces plenty of nectar, which is a great draw for butterflies and hoverflies, and these, in turn, draw in hunting birds. Choosing exotic plants allows you to extend the growing season in your garden, making it attractive to birds for longer periods of the year. Different species of cotoneaster, for example, flower at different times throughout the summer. When choosing exotics, take care to avoid invasive species, such as the common rhododendron, *Rhododendron ponticum*.

CHOOSING PLANTS

Selecting plants for your garden calls for research. You must take into account soil type, aspect, and maintenance, as well as a plant's size, appearance, and value to wildlife. The following pages list a handful of species of known value to birds. In general, you should choose old-fashioned, single varieties, because modern, double petal varieties produce little or no nectar. Also, remember that varieties which are susceptible to attack by caterpillars and other insects may be the best choices for planting in bird gardens.

Primroses are *native plants that spread naturally in gardens. They bring colour in spring in a variety of soil and shade conditions.*

Buddleia is an exotic *plant that is easy to grow. It produces copious nectar and is a favourite of butterflies and other insects.*

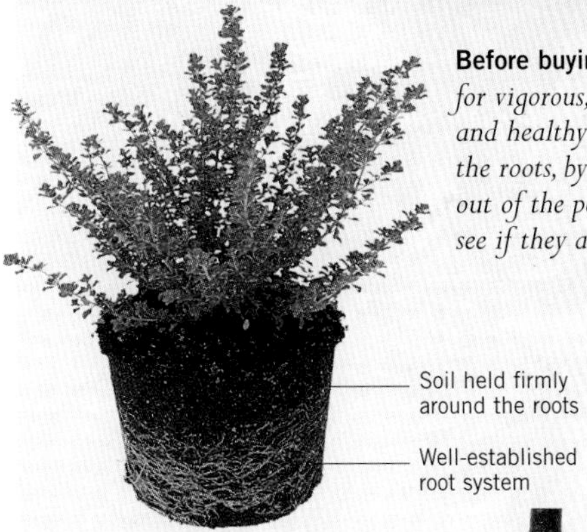

Before buying, *check plants for vigorous, balanced growth and healthy leaves. Look at the roots, by easing the plant out of the pot if possible, to see if they are overcrowded.*

Choose a bare-root *tree or shrub with roots spread evenly around the stem. It should have plenty of small "feeder" roots.*

Plant guide: trees

Trees create habitats for birds in the garden by providing nesting places, song-posts, and an important variety of foods. Growing a tree is a long-term investment, but choosing fast-growing or smaller species will give a quicker return. Larger species can be coppiced or pollarded to make them more suitable for garden use. Choose species carefully: years can be wasted if the tree does not flourish in the conditions in your garden.

Silver birch

Betula pendula

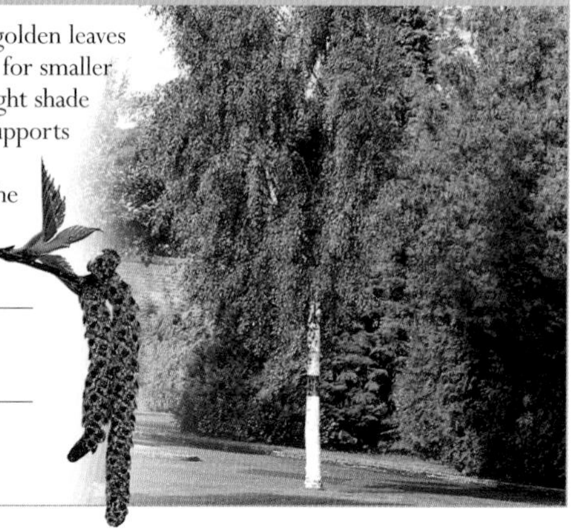

Grown for its attractive silvery bark and golden leaves in autumn, this decorative tree is suitable for smaller gardens because it will coppice. It casts light shade and is tolerant of poor and acid soils. It supports over 200 types of insect, and birds from crows to warblers eat its winged seeds. The trunk is good for woodpecker nest holes.

HEIGHT 20m (66ft) **SPREAD** 10m (33ft)

CULTIVATION Grows in dry soil in a sunny position. Do not grow near buildings or other trees, because its roots grow near the surface.

RELATED SPECIES Monarch birch (*B. maximowicziana*) is a quick-growing species; *B. var jacquemontii* has very white bark.

Alder

Alnus glutinosa

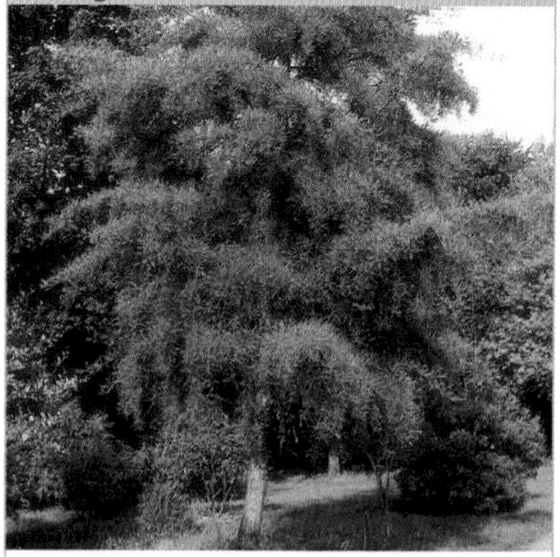

This medium-sized, deciduous tree is not suitable for small gardens. Birds, such as Siskins, eat the seeds when the woody cone-shaped fruits open in dry weather.

HEIGHT 25m (83ft) **SPREAD** 10m (33ft)

CULTIVATION Grows in moderately fertile, moist soil. It can be coppiced.

RELATED SPECIES Italian alder (*A. cordata*) grows on dry soil; grey alder (*A. incana*) thrives in cold, poor soils; *A. i.* 'Aurea' has yellow foliage and red catkins.

Bird cherry

Prunus padus

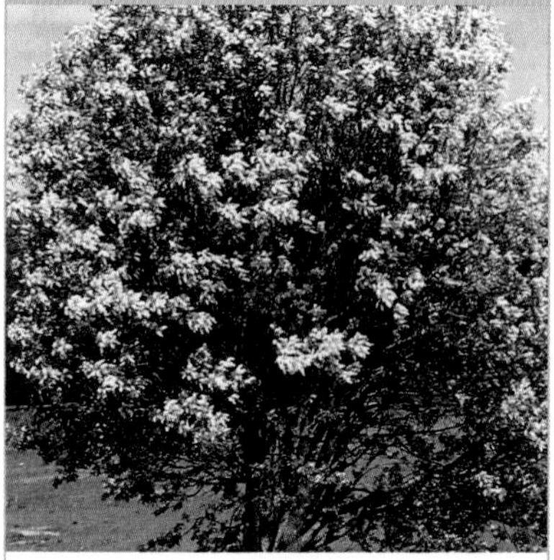

A small deciduous tree or bush with small, fragrant white flowers. These develop into bitter, black cherries that are enjoyed by many birds, including Hawfinches.

HEIGHT 15m (50ft) **SPREAD** 10m (33ft)

CULTIVATION Prefers full sun and grows in moist but well-drained soil. Its shallow roots hinder underplanting, and it throws up suckers.

RELATED SPECIES Some *Prunus* varieties do not produce fruit. Wild cherry (*P. avium*), the ancestor of cultivated cherries, is a common garden tree.

Crab apple

Malus sylvestris

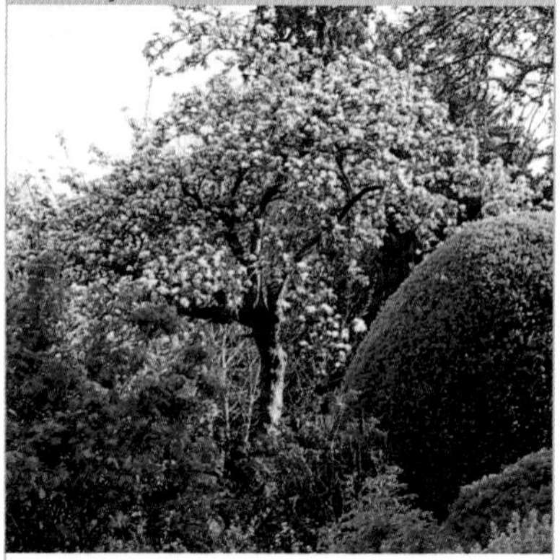

This small tree of woods and hedges is suitable for smaller gardens. The fruit and seeds are eaten by birds, such as Blackbirds, and the leaves support caterpillars.

HEIGHT 10m (33ft) **SPREAD** 10m (33ft)

CULTIVATION Prefers full sun but will grow in part-shade, in any soil. Prune in winter.

RELATED SPECIES *M. sylvestris* is the ancestor of cultivated apple species (*M. domestica*). *M.* 'John Downie' and the Siberian crab apple (*M. baccata*) retain fruit on the tree into late winter.

Rowan

Sorbus aucuparia

The red-orange berries of this small, deciduous tree are eaten by many birds; if there is a good crop, the autumn migrations of Fieldfare and Waxwing may be delayed.

HEIGHT 15m (50ft) **SPREAD** 8m (26ft)

CULTIVATION Prefers sun or light-dappled shade and needs moist, light soil. It will tolerate extreme acidity.

RELATED SPECIES Wild service tree (*S. torminalis*) and whitebeam (*S. aria*; good in chalky soils) will grow in gardens; service tree (*S. domestica*).

Holly

Ilex aquifolium

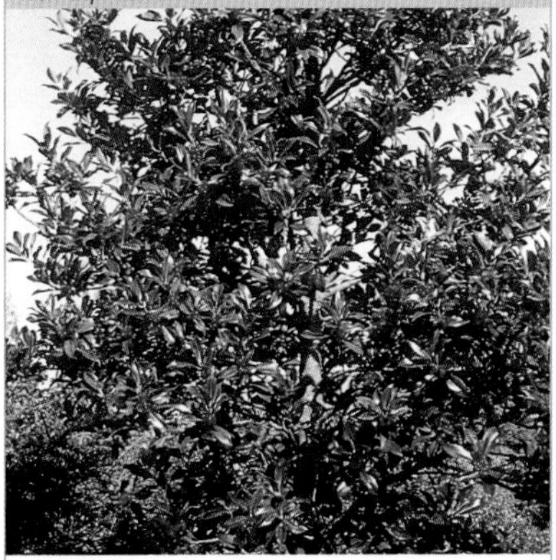

A small, evergreen tree that grows in hedges and woods. The small flowers open in May and June and the red or yellow berries are eaten by many birds.

HEIGHT 3–15m (10–50ft)
SPREAD 5m (17ft)

CULTIVATION Grows in sun or shade, and withstands pollution and salt spray.

RELATED SPECIES *I. a.* 'Argentea Longifolia' is good for berries.

Goat willow

Salix caprea

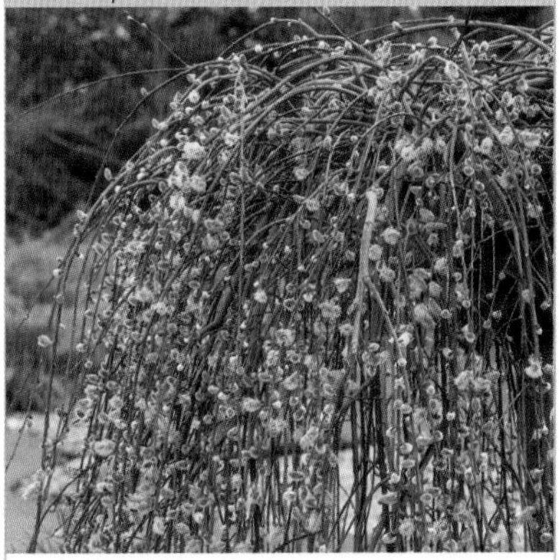

This small, deciduous, fast-growing tree bears catkins in late winter, attracting early insects. Blue Tit and Blackcap will drink the nectar, and finches eat its seeds.

HEIGHT 10m (33ft) **SPREAD** 8m (26ft)

CULTIVATION Prefers full sun, and can grow in dry, but not chalk, soil. It coppices freely, and cuttings will readily take root. Site away from drains which can be invaded by roots.

RELATED SPECIES Grey willow (*S. cinerea*) is similar but smaller and more bushy.

European larch

Larix decidua

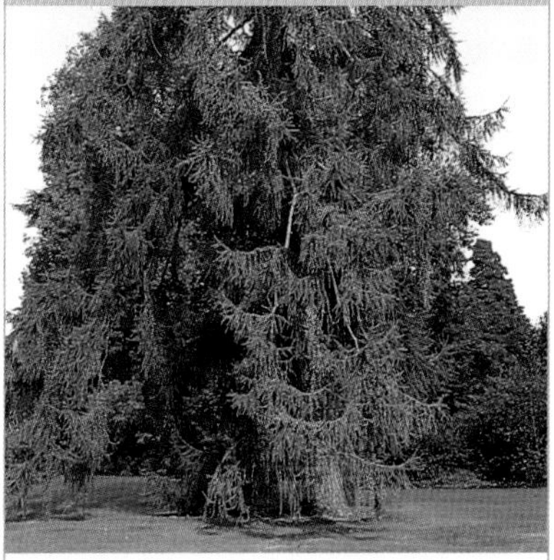

Unlike most conifers, the larch is deciduous. It bears cones which ripen in autumn, shedding seeds that attract many birds, including Great Spotted Woodpeckers.

HEIGHT 50m (165ft) **SPREAD** 5–15m (17–50ft)

CULTIVATION This fast-growing tree prefers full sun and deep, well-drained soils. Avoid wet soils and dry, shallow chalk.

RELATED SPECIES Fast-growing and disease-free Japanese larch (*L. kaemferi*) and hybrid larch (*L. x. eurolepis*) are commonly grown.

Common lime

Tilia x europaea

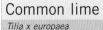

A tall deciduous tree that is a natural, fertile hybrid. Insect-eating birds are attracted to aphids that feed on its leaves, while other birds enjoy the seeds.

HEIGHT 35m (116ft) **SPREAD** 15m (50ft)

CULTIVATION Grows in sun or part-shade in moist but drained soils. It is suitable for lopping and coppicing.

RELATED SPECIES Silver lime (*T. tomentosa*) and pendant silver lime (*T.* 'Petiolaris') have leaves with silver undersides.

Common oak

Quercus robur

Suitable only for large gardens, this large, slow-growing, deciduous tree is an important resource for insect-eating birds. It supports more insect species than any other European tree, including caterpillars, which are vital for nesting birds. The acorns are eaten by a variety of birds, including Jays.

HEIGHT 30–40m (99–132ft)
SPREAD 25m (83ft)

CULTIVATION Grows in deep soil in a well-drained position. It retains dead leaves through winter until it reaches 2.5m (8ft) in height.

RELATED SPECIES Fast-growing red oak *Q. r. rubra* survives air pollution.

Jay

Plant guide: shrubs

Shrubs are used by gardeners to give structure and colour to the garden, and for hedging. A shrub is essentially a small tree, but the term is used more for a woody plant that produces a mass of branches from the base rather than a single trunk. Certain trees can be grown as shrubs, especially in hedges, by pruning. Like trees, shrubs are valuable for birds, their dense growth providing shelter for nesting and roosting.

Blackthorn (sloe)

Prunus spinosa

Common in hedgerows and woods, this small, deciduous shrub or tree bears masses of small white flowers which open in April, before the leaves. The round, shiny black fruit – the sloe – remains on the tree through the winter and is enjoyed by a variety of birds. The dense foliage provides good nesting places.

HEIGHT 4m (13ft) **SPREAD** 3m (10ft)

CULTIVATION Prefers full sun, and soil that is neither waterlogged nor too acid. Trim in winter, once the nesting season is over.

RELATED SPECIES Bullace (*Prunus domestica*) is a hybrid that grows in the British Isles.

Cotoneaster

Cotoneaster microphyllus

An evergreen shrub with rigid, often drooping, branches. The small, dark-green leaves make dense cover, and it bears red fruits which are popular with many birds.

HEIGHT 1m (3½ft) **SPREAD** 2m (7ft)

CULTIVATION Prefers dry sites in sun or part-shade. Good for seaside sites.

RELATED SPECIES Prostrate *C. horizontalis* is good for walls, banks, and ground cover, especially in small gardens; *C. dammeri* is ideal for banks and ground cover beneath other shrubs.

Hawthorn (may)

Crataegus monogyna

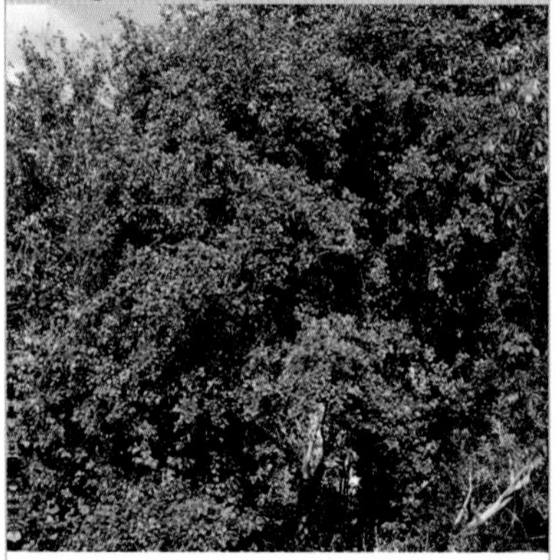

This small, deciduous tree with spiny twigs is often used for hedging. The crimson berries, or haws, are eaten by many birds, the leaves by Woodpigeons.

HEIGHT 10m (33ft)
SPREAD 8m (26ft)

CULTIVATION Prefers sun but will grow in shade, and will grow in polluted or exposed sites.

RELATED SPECIES *C. laevigata* is useful for garden hedging.

Firethorn

Pyracantha coccinea

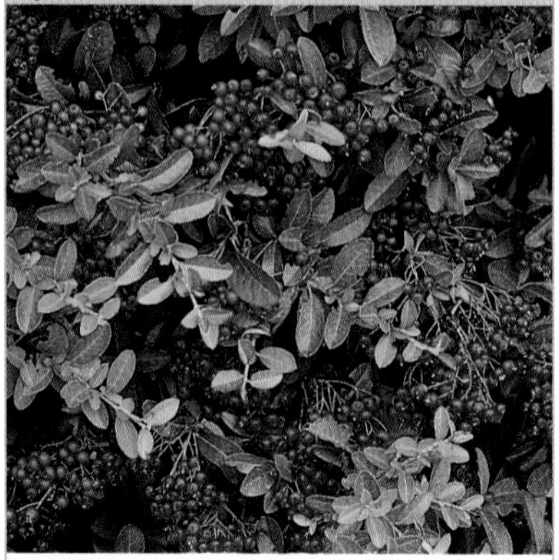

A dense, spiny, evergreen shrub, which can be grown in a hedge or against a wall. The scarlet berries are eaten by some birds, but its main value is as a secure site for nests.

HEIGHT 2m (7ft) **SPREAD** 2m (7ft)

CULTIVATION Prefers sun or part-shade and grows in any well-drained soil. Train against a wall with trellis or wires for support.

RELATED SPECIES *P.* 'Golden Dome' forms a dense mound with yellow berries; *P. angustifolia* grows on north-facing walls.

Juneberry (serviceberry)

Amelanchier lamarckii

The foliage of this deciduous shrub or small tree turns from dark green or bronze to red and orange in autumn. The clusters of berries are popular with birds.

HEIGHT 6m (20ft) **SPREAD** 3m (10ft)

CULTIVATION Requires full sun or part-shade, and prefers moist or well-drained, fairly acid soil. Prune during winter to keep plant shape.

RELATED SPECIES *A. arborea*, *A. laevis*, and *A. canadensis* are similar species that are often confused with *A. lamarckii*.

Elder

Sambucus nigra

This deciduous shrub or small tree bears purple-black berries that are extremely popular with birds, including thrushes. It can become rampant if left unchecked.

HEIGHT 4m (13ft) **SPREAD** 4m (13ft)

CULTIVATION Needs a sunny position and moist, fertile soil. Prune old shoots in winter and dig out unwanted seedlings.

RELATED SPECIES *S. n.* 'Aurea' is smaller and less rampant than the native species; it has attractive gold foliage and is very hardy.

Yew

Taxus baccata

Often used for hedging, this evergreen tree has dense foliage of dark green, flattened leaves. It bears bright red, fleshy, cup-shaped fruits, or arils, each containing a single green seed. These ripen from late August, and are enjoyed by many birds, including finches and Waxwings. All parts of yew, however, are poisonous to humans.

HEIGHT 15m (50ft) **SPREAD** 10m (33ft)

CULTIVATION Grows almost anywhere in sun or shade and is tolerant of drought, exposure, and polluted air.

RELATED SPECIES *T. b.* 'Dovastonii Aurea' has golden foliage and grows to 5m (17ft); *T. cuspidata* is dwarf and very hardy.

Greenfinch

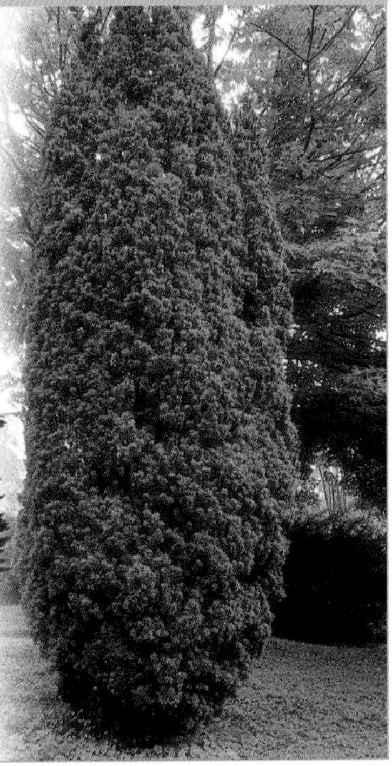

Mezereon

Daphne mezereum

This small, deciduous shrub bears fragrant pink flowers. Round, yellow fruits ripen in May and June and are eaten by many birds, and Blackcaps drink its nectar.

HEIGHT 1m (3½ft) **SPREAD** 1m (3½ft)

CULTIVATION Grows in moderately fertile, well-drained soil in full sun. Mulch regularly to keep the roots cool, but keep pruning to a minimum as it is prone to die-back.

RELATED SPECIES *D. m.* 'Alba' has white flowers and translucent amber fruits.

Hazel

Corylus avellana

A deciduous shrub that bears long, yellow male catkins in January. The nuts (known as cobnuts or hazelnuts) are eaten by several birds, including Nuthatches.

HEIGHT 6m (20ft)
SPREAD 6m (20ft)

CULTIVATION Prefers sun or part-shade and well-drained soil but grows wild on damp soils. Nuts are borne after seven years.

RELATED SPECIES Corkscrew hazel (*C. a.* 'Contorta') has strangely twisted twigs.

Privet

Ligustrum vulgare

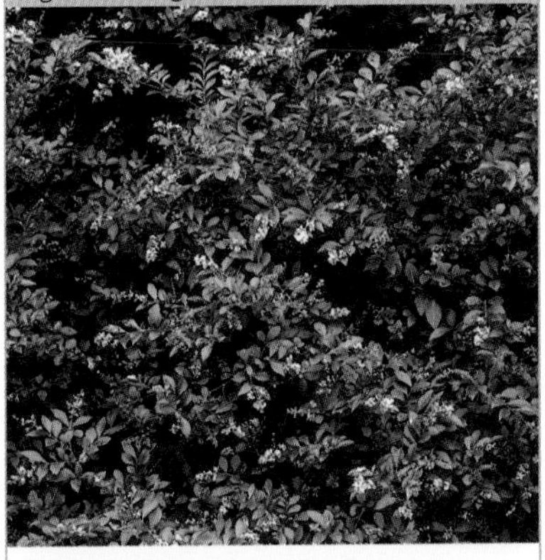

Ideal for hedging, this fast-growing, deciduous shrub bears small, white, scented flowers that attract insects, and black berries eaten by many birds.

HEIGHT 5m (17ft) **SPREAD** 3m (10ft)

CULTIVATION Prefers well-drained, limestone soil and full sun. Hard cutting improves its value as cover for nests but leave untrimmed for fruit.

RELATED SPECIES Japanese privet (*L. japonicum*) and golden privet (*L. ovalifolium* 'Aureum') are suitable for ornamental hedges.

Guelder rose

Viburnum opulus

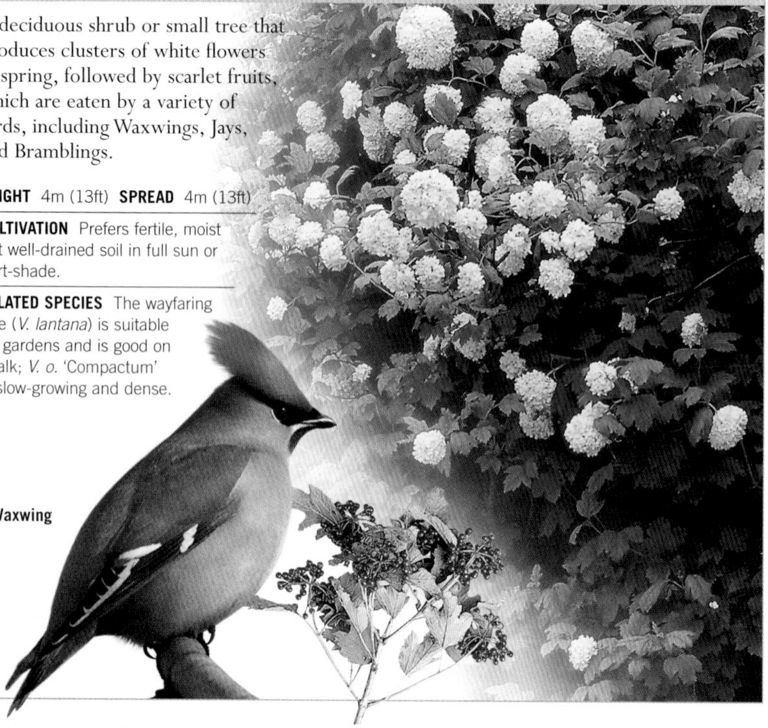

A deciduous shrub or small tree that produces clusters of white flowers in spring, followed by scarlet fruits, which are eaten by a variety of birds, including Waxwings, Jays, and Bramblings.

HEIGHT 4m (13ft) **SPREAD** 4m (13ft)

CULTIVATION Prefers fertile, moist but well-drained soil in full sun or part-shade.

RELATED SPECIES The wayfaring tree (*V. lantana*) is suitable for gardens and is good on chalk; *V. o.* 'Compactum' is slow-growing and dense.

Waxwing

Blackcurrant

Ribes nigrum

A deciduous shrub cultivated for its soft fruit. The small black berries ripen in June and July and are popular with many birds, including Blackbirds.

HEIGHT 2m (7ft) **SPREAD** 2m (7ft)

CULTIVATION Grows in moderately fertile soil in full sun. It can be trained against a wall. After fruiting, cut out old stems.

RELATED SPECIES Redcurrant (*R. rubrum*) and gooseberry (*R. uva-crispa*) are close relatives also cultivated for their fruits.

Dogwood

Cornus sanguinea

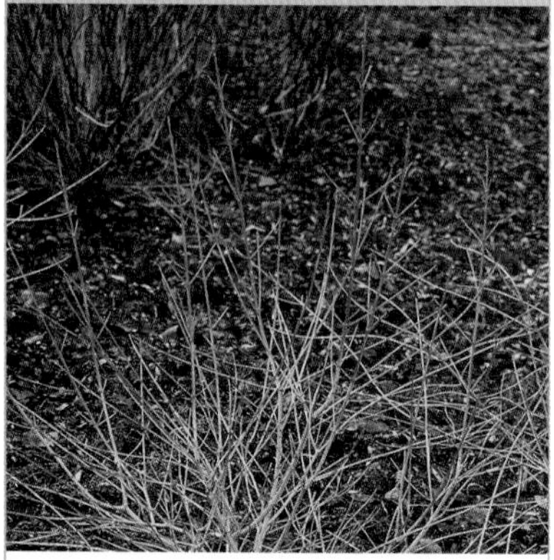

With its bold red twigs, this deciduous bush or small tree gives colour to the garden in winter. The small black berries are popular with several bird species.

HEIGHT 4m (13ft) **SPREAD** 3m (10ft)

CULTIVATION Grows in fertile, chalky soil, and needs a sunny position to produce red stems. It grows from suckers so will colonize an area without assistance.

RELATED SPECIES *C. canadensis* grows in acid soil and is suitable for ground cover.

Oregon grape

Mahonia aquifolium

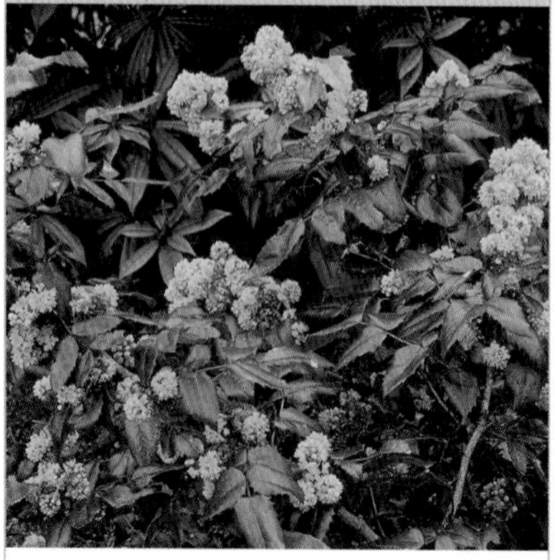

This evergreen shrub bears yellow, fragrant flowers, which are visited by birds for their nectar and pollen. The blue-black berries are eaten by Blackbirds and thrushes.

HEIGHT 1m (3½ft) **SPREAD** 1.5m (5ft)

CULTIVATION Prefers some shade. Cut down old stems in April.

RELATED SPECIES Varieties range from the 3m (10ft) *M. japonica* to the 30cm (12in) *M. repens*, which spreads by underground stems.

Barberry

Berberis vulgaris

An evergreen shrub with finely branching twigs and sharp spines, suitable for hedging. It bears brilliant orange-red berries that are eaten by many birds.

HEIGHT 4m (13ft) **SPREAD** 4m (13ft)

CULTIVATION Grows in sun or part-shade and in almost any well-drained soil. Full sun produces the best autumn colours. Good for seaside sites.

RELATED SPECIES The evergreen *B. darwinii* is good for hedging and is attractive to birds; *B. coryi* is suitable for small gardens.

Beech

Fagus sylvatica

Often grown as a hedge, this deciduous tree provides places for birds to nest and roost. The seeds, known as beech mast, are important for several bird species.

HEIGHT 30m (99ft) **SPREAD** 25m (83ft)

CULTIVATION Grows in well-drained, chalky soil, and prefers a sunny position or part-shade. When grown as a hedge, trim in summer. Trees under 2.5m (8ft) in height keep their leaves in winter.

RELATED SPECIES Copper beech (*F. s.* var. *purpurea*) has purple-brown leaves.

Spindle

Euonymus europaeus

A small, deciduous shrub grown for its autumn leaf colour and brightly coloured seed pods. The seeds are eaten by many bird species, including finches.

HEIGHT 6m (20ft) **SPREAD** 2m (7ft)

CULTIVATION Grows in full sun or part-shade, and prefers calcareous soils.

RELATED SPECIES *E. fortunei* var. *radicans* is a creeper that provides good ground cover; Japanese spindle (*E. japonicus*) is evergreen and tolerates air pollution and salt spray.

Bay laurel

Laurus nobilis

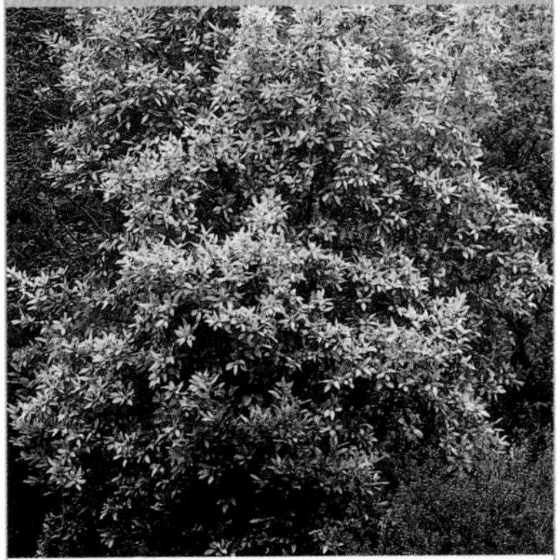

This evergreen shrub, often grown in containers, has shiny, green leaves and bears small black berries. The dense foliage provides useful nesting places for birds.

HEIGHT 12m (40ft) **SPREAD** 10m (33ft)

CULTIVATION Grows in full sun or part-shade in fertile, well-drained soil. It should be sheltered from strong winds and watered in dry weather.

RELATED SPECIES Cherry laurel (*Prunus laurocerasus*) and Portugal laurel (*P. lusitanica*) are cherries that look similar to bay laurel.

Lavender

Lavandula angustifolia

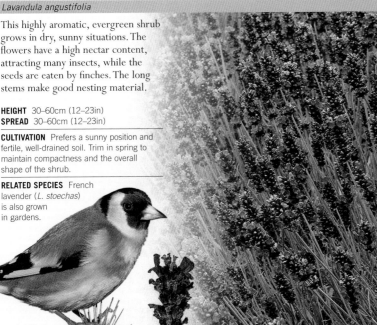

This highly aromatic, evergreen shrub grows in dry, sunny situations. The flowers have a high nectar content, attracting many insects, while the seeds are eaten by finches. The long stems make good nesting material.

HEIGHT 30–60cm (12–23in)
SPREAD 30–60cm (12–23in)

CULTIVATION Prefers a sunny position and fertile, well-drained soil. Trim in spring to maintain compactness and the overall shape of the shrub.

RELATED SPECIES French lavender (*L. stoechas*) is also grown in gardens.

Goldfinch

Garrya

Garrya elliptica

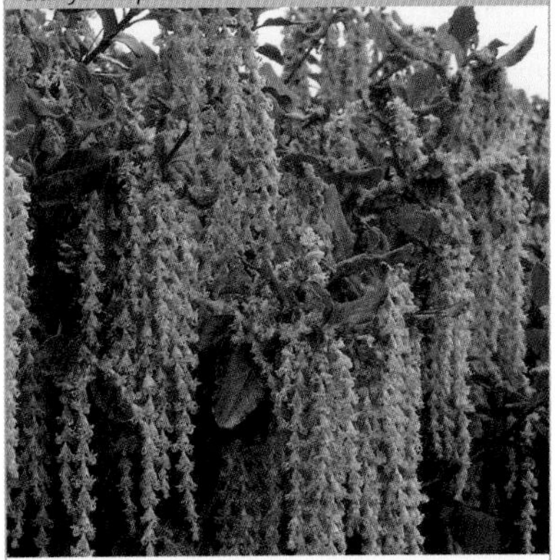

A dense, evergreen shrub grown for its dramatic, long grey catkins in late winter. It is valuable for birds because it provides good cover for early nests.

HEIGHT 4m (13ft) **SPREAD** 4m (13ft)

CULTIVATION Can be grown in part-shade against a wall even in poor soil, but it prefers a well-drained soil. It can tolerate salt spray, but requires protection from frosts and strong winds. It should be pruned only to maintain shape.

RELATED SPECIES None.

Plant guide: climbers

Climbers provide a quick and simple way of adding to the vertical dimension of the garden, especially where there is too little space to grow trees. They are indispensable for covering unsightly buildings or even sprawling over bare ground, and add flowers, fruit, and foliage to bare walls, pergolas, and pillars. While some yield fruit that attracts birds, their main value is in providing cover for roosting and nesting.

Golden hop

Humulus lupulus

This herbaceous, twining climber has male and female flowers on separate plants. The female flowers develop into clusters of hops, which are used in brewing. Golden hop is often used for covering sheds and trees, and provides valuable cover for nests and roosts.

HEIGHT 5m (17ft)

CULTIVATION Grows in sun or part-shade in humus-rich soil. Water well in dry weather. Support the stems and cut back in spring.

RELATED SPECIES None.

Ivy

Hedera helix

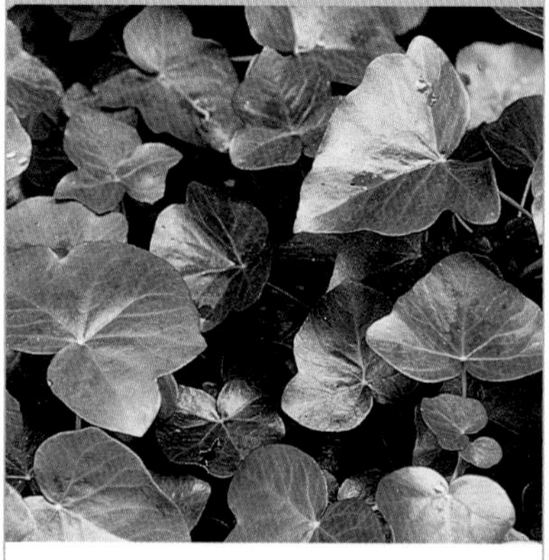

This evergreen climber clings to trees or walls and provides good cover for nesting and roosting. Its berries are a valuable winter food for many birds, such as Jays.

HEIGHT 10m (33ft)

CULTIVATION Tolerates shade but only flowers in the sun and prefers well-drained soils.

RELATED SPECIES *H. h.* 'Cavendishii' is good for growing against walls.

Honeysuckle

Lonicera periclymenum

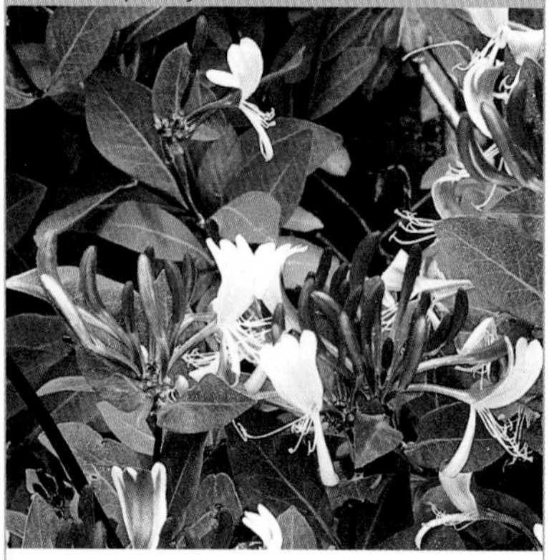

Grown for its scented flowers, this twining, deciduous climber attracts large insects and Blackcaps, which drink the nectar. The red berries are popular with many bird species.

HEIGHT 7m (23ft)

CULTIVATION Grow in sun or shade on fertile soil. Immediately after flowering, thin and cut back old flowering shoots to 1cm (½in) of old wood.

RELATED SPECIES *L. pileata* is good in shade; *L. nitida* is a dense, quick-growing, evergreen shrub; *L. fragrantissima* is a winter-flowering shrub.

Virginia creeper

Parthenocissus quinquefolia

This quick-growing, deciduous climber clings to supports with tendrils tipped with suckers. It provides good cover for nests, and the berries are eaten by some birds.

HEIGHT 20m (66ft)

CULTIVATION Will grow in shade or part-shade. Support young growth until it clings to supports. Trim in early spring to restrain and direct the growth of this vigorous climber.

RELATED SPECIES Chinese Virginia creeper (*P. henryana*) is good for ground cover.

Grape vine

Vitis vinifera

A cultivated fruit crop in many parts of the world, this woody, deciduous climber bears clusters of green, red, or purple fleshy fruits, enjoyed by many birds.

HEIGHT 30m (99ft)

CULTIVATION Requires full sun and rich soil, and can be trained on trellises, pergolas, or against walls. Protect against late frost.

RELATED SPECIES The ornamental vine *V. v.* 'Purpurea' has inedible fruit.

Blackberry (bramble)

Rubus fruticosus

A perennial, deciduous climber whose prickles are used as hooks to anchor the stems as they scramble over each other or up trees and shrubs. It bears white flowers in summer, followed by plump black fruits in early autumn, enjoyed by many bird species, including Blackcaps.

HEIGHT 3m (10ft) **SPREAD** 3m (10ft)

CULTIVATION Grows in fertile, well-drained soil and prefers sun, but evergreen varieties tolerate shade. Blackberries grown for their fruit are trained against a wall or wires and stems are cut to the ground after flowering. To provide nesting places for birds, blackberry stems should be left to form a thicket, if space allows.

RELATED SPECIES Dewberry (*R. caesius*), cloudberry (*R. chamaemorus*), and raspberry (*R. idaeus*) bear edible fruits.

Blackcap

Dog rose

Rosa canina

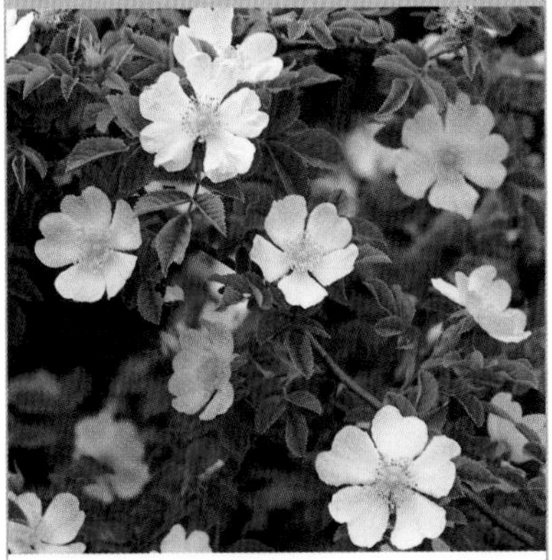

A deciduous, scrambling shrub that bears red, fleshy fruits (hips), attracting finches, tits, and other birds. Bushy growth makes good nest sites for Blackbirds and thrushes.

HEIGHT 3m (10ft)

CULTIVATION Prefers sun and fertile soil. Occasionally trim to shape or thin in winter. Prune in February to allow fruiting.

RELATED SPECIES *R. rugosa* bears large hips, which are popular with many bird species.

Climbing hydrangea

Hydrangea petiolaris ssp *petiolaris*

A deciduous, woody climber that clings to walls by aerial roots on the stems. It is grown for its showy flowers, but the tangle of stems can give valuable shelter to birds.

HEIGHT 7m (23ft) **SPREAD** 7m (23ft)

CULTIVATION Grows in sun or part-shade, and will thrive against a north-facing wall. In dry soil, it requires a more shady position. It is self-clinging, and can be pruned after flowering.

RELATED SPECIES *H. aspera* and *H. macrophylla* are bushy species.

Wisteria

Wisteria chinensis

Grown for its dramatic, drooping purple flowers, this elegant, deciduous climber has thick, woody stems, which make good supports for birds' nests.

HEIGHT 30m (99ft)

CULTIVATION Grows best in full sun (with its roots shaded) in a well-drained soil. It can be trained to wire attached to a wall, and will cover a pergola. Prune after flowering.

RELATED SPECIES Japanese wisteria (*W. floribunda*) produces very long, purple blooms.

Clematis

Clematis montana

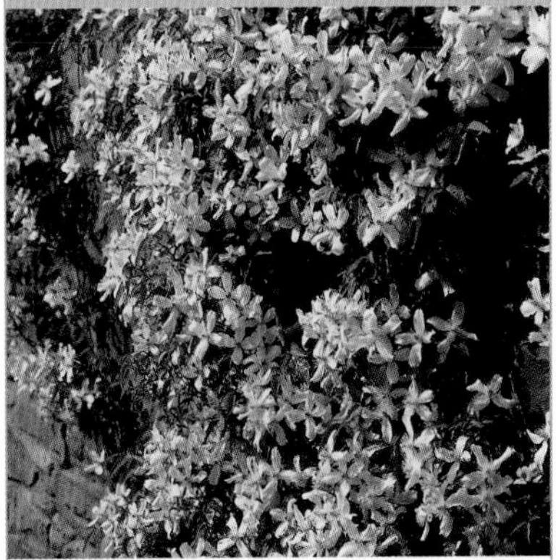

This evergreen, twining climber produces a mass of small white flowers in spring. It provides good cover for nesting, and the seeds and buds are eaten by some birds.

HEIGHT 12m (40ft) **SPREAD** 3m (10ft)

CULTIVATION A vigorous, hardy climber that will grow in sun or shade, but will flower best in a sunny postion. Plant in well-drained soil, and prune in May or June, after flowering.

RELATED SPECIES *C. alpina* is suitable for north-facing or very exposed sites.

Plant guide: herbaceous plants

Herbaceous plants are an important part of any garden designed to attract wildlife. In summer, they harbour rich insect life, and the wide variety of invertebrates attracted to their flowers and foliage is appreciated by many insect-eating bird species, while the seeds they produce are an important food source for birds. Allow seedheads to ripen and stand until the seeds are shed, and they will provide food for birds into the winter months.

Red clover

Trifolium pratense

Considered a weed when growing in a lawn, this low-growing perennial herb is a colourful addition to a stretch of garden meadow. The round heads of pink-purple flowers appear between May and September, and the seeds ripen in tiny pods. Several bird species feed on the seeds, and Woodpigeons also eat the leaves.

HEIGHT 20cm (8in) **SPREAD** 20cm (8in)

CULTIVATION Naturally invades the garden but can be grown from seed. It grows best in well-drained soil in full sun, and self-seeds very readily.

RELATED SPECIES *T. incarnatum* has red-yellow flowers.

Angelica

Angelica sylvestris

This tall perennial herb grows in damp places. The heads of white or pink flowers attract large numbers of insects, while the seeds are eaten by tits and finches.

HEIGHT 2m (7ft) **SPREAD** 1m (3½ft)

CULTIVATION Grows in sun or shade, in damp soil. Sow in autumn or spring and, after flowering, allow seeds to form. Best grown as a biennial, it will self-seed freely.

RELATED SPECIES Archangel (*A. archangelica*) is native to northern Europe.

Amaranth

Amaranthus caudatus

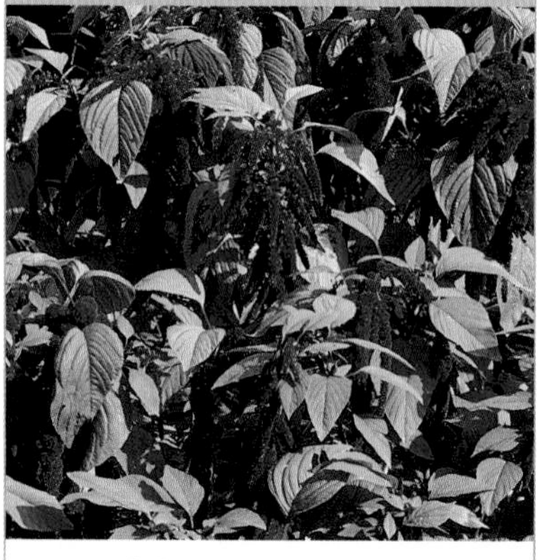

Commonly known as love-lies-bleeding, amaranth is an annual grown for its tassels of tiny flowers and colourful foliage. The seeds are eaten by a variety of birds.

HEIGHT 1.2m (4ft) **SPREAD** 45cm (18in)

CULTIVATION Sow seeds under glass in March or in a sunny, sheltered site in April.

RELATED SPECIES Joseph's coat (*A. tricolor*) is grown for its multi-coloured foliage.

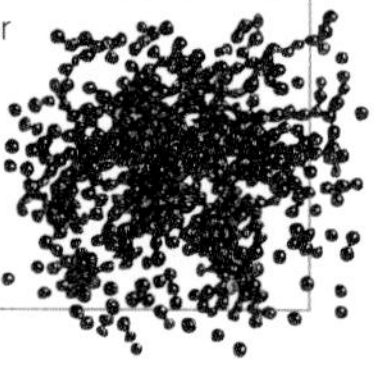

Field forget-me-not

Myosotis arvensis

This small annual or biennial, usually treated as a weed, bears small, bright blue flowers from April to September. The tiny seeds are popular with finches.

HEIGHT 15cm (6in) **SPREAD** 10cm (4in)

CULTIVATION Prefers sun and well-drained soil. Cultivated forms are sown as seed in autumn, or bought as bedding plants.

RELATED SPECIES Water forget-me-not (*M. scorpoides*) is suitable for bog gardens; *M. sylvatica* is a cultivated species.

Argentinian vervain

Verbena bonariensis

A favourite for attracting butterflies and other insects, this perennial bears clusters of small purple flowers. Greenfinches, Goldfinches, and Blue Tits enjoy its seeds.

HEIGHT 1.5m (5ft) **SPREAD** 50cm (20in)

CULTIVATION Prefers sun and well-drained soil. Sow seeds in autumn and spring. Divide clumps in spring, when necessary.

RELATED SPECIES *V. alpina* is a low spreading perennial; *V. x hybrida* is slow-growing and is cultivated as an annual.

Teazel
Dipsacus fullonum

This short-lived perennial herb bears heads of tiny purple flowers. In winter, Goldfinches and Crossbills extract seeds from the dead seedheads.

HEIGHT 2m (7ft) **SPREAD** 60cm (23in)

CULTIVATION Grows in moderately fertile soil, including clay, in sun or part-shade.

RELATED SPECIES Fuller's teazel (*D.f.* subsp. *sativus*) is grown for its stiff, spiny seedheads which are used for raising the nap of cloth.

Common nettle
Urtica dioica

With its stinging leaves and rapid growth, the nettle is considered an unpleasant weed, but it is of great value to wildlife, attracting caterpillars and the birds that feed on them.

HEIGHT 1.5m (5ft) **SPREAD** 15cm (6in)

CULTIVATION Grows best in rich, well-manured soil, but should only be planted in a confined area. Cut mature stems to promote fresh growth for caterpillars.

RELATED SPECIES Annual nettle (*U. urens*) is a smaller, less invasive species.

Evening primrose
Oenothera biennis

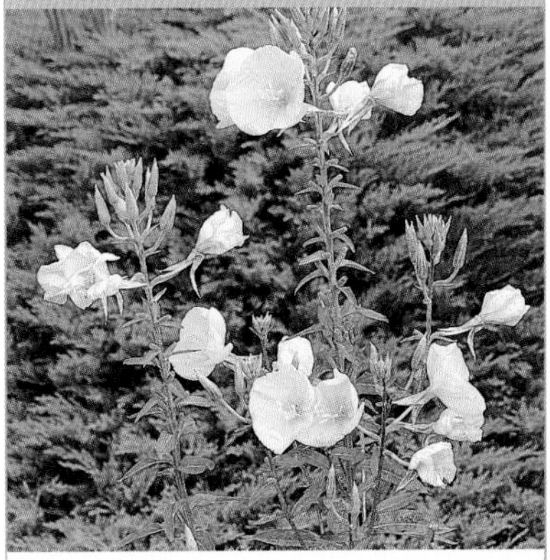

A biennial herb grown in gardens for the succession of short-lived yellow flowers that open in the evening. The flowers attract insects and the seeds are eaten by finches.

HEIGHT 1m (3½ft) **SPREAD** 40cm (16in)

CULTIVATION Needs full sun and well-drained soil. Self-seeds and can be divided in spring.

RELATED SPECIES *O. acaulis* and Ozark sundrops (*O. macrocarpa*) are 15cm (6in) high and suit small gardens.

Greater plantain
Plantago major

In gardens, this perennial herb is a weed that grows on lawns and in gravel paths. If left uncut, its seeds may be eaten by Woodpigeons, buntings, and finches.

HEIGHT 30cm (12in) **SPREAD** 60cm (23in)

CULTIVATION A common weed that spreads easily and can be invasive. It does best in full sun and well-drained soil.

RELATED SPECIES Ribwort plantain (*P. lanceolata*) is another garden weed; *P. nivalis* is a compact species that suits rock gardens.

Aubretia
Aubrieta deltoidea

This evergreen perennial forms mounds or carpets which trail over rocks, banks, and walls. The display of purple to lilac flowers lasts from March to June, and Starlings and House Sparrows take early flowers for nesting.

HEIGHT 8–10cm (3–4in)
SPREAD 40–60cm (16–23in)

CULTIVATION Grows in well-drained soil in full sun. Cut back after flowering to maintain the compact mound.

RELATED SPECIES *A. x cultorum* 'J. S. Baker' bears purple, white-eyed flowers.

Starling

Fat hen

Chenopodium album

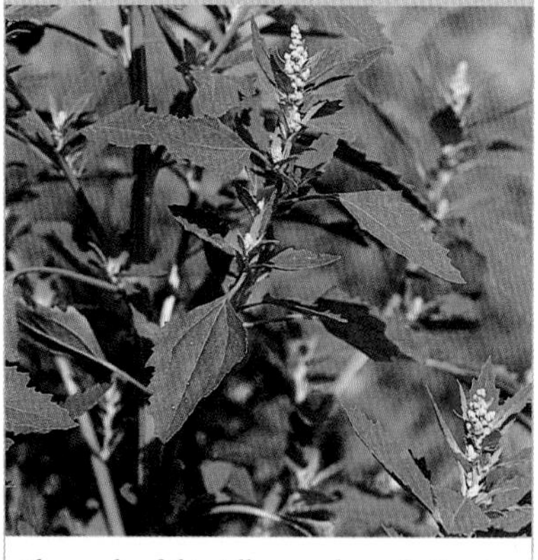

The seeds of this tall, annual weed attract several bird species, such as Collared Doves, throughout winter, either when on the plant or when dispersed on the ground.

HEIGHT 1m (3½ft) **SPREAD** 30cm (12in)

CULTIVATION Grows best in fertile soil but will also colonize bare ground. Sow seeds of the cultivated variety in spring. It flowers from June to October.

RELATED SPECIES Good King Henry (*C. bonus-henricus*) bears flower spikes.

Lemon balm

Melissa officinalis

A branching, herbaceous perennial of the mint family, grown for its lemon-scented leaves. Its seeds attract Goldfinches; other birds feed on insects that visit the flowers.

HEIGHT 80cm (31in) **SPREAD** 45cm (18in)

CULTIVATION Sow seed in autumn or spring. Plant in moist soil in partial sun. Can be grown from stem cuttings.

RELATED SPECIES *M. o.* 'All Gold' has yellow foliage. *M. o.* 'Aurea' has dark green and yellow variegated foliage.

Dandelion

Taraxacum officinale

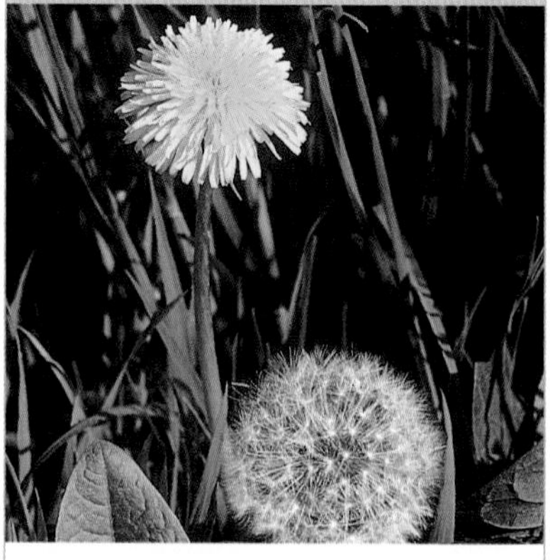

This common perennial herb and intrusive weed thrives in lawns and herbaceous borders. The seedheads are a great attraction for finches and other birds.

HEIGHT 30cm (12in)
SPREAD 15cm (6in)

CULTIVATION An invasive weed that seeds freely. Leave seedheads uncut to attract birds.

RELATED SPECIES No cultivated varieties.

Sunflower

Helianthus annuus

This tall annual bears a single, large, daisy-like flower. The seeds are eaten by many bird species, including Long-tailed Tits and Bramblings, and are a major constituent of proprietary birdfeeder mixes.

HEIGHT 3m (10ft) **SPREAD** 60cm (23in)

CULTIVATION Prefers full sun and well-drained soil, and requires staking to support the huge flowers. Hang cut seedheads for ready-made birdfeeders.

RELATED SPECIES There are a number of varieties, including dwarf forms; *H. a.* 'Teddy Bear' is suitable for containers; *H. x laetiflorus* and willow-leaved sunflower (*H. salicifolius*) suit wild gardens.

Long-tailed Tit

Golden rod

Solidago virgaurea

A herbaceous perennial with small, yellow, daisy-like flowers, followed by heads of small hairy seeds which attract birds, such as Siskins and Linnets.

HEIGHT 75cm (29in) **SPREAD** 45cm (18in)

CULTIVATION Grow in poor soil in sun or part-shade. Stake as necessary, and cut to the ground before the new growth starts. Self-seeds easily.

RELATED SPECIES *S.* 'Golden Wings' thrives in poor soil; Canadian golden rod (*S. canadensis*) has naturalized in many places.

Groundsel

Senecio vulgaris

This annual weed bears small yellow flowers throughout the year, followed by small globes of wind-blown seeds, which are eaten by finches.

HEIGHT 40cm (16in) **SPREAD** 10cm (4in)

CULTIVATION A weed that needs no cultivation and grows in any soil. It seeds freely and flourishes in flowerbeds. Cultivated varieties need moderately fertile soil in full sun.

RELATED SPECIES Cinererias, including *S. cinereria*, have silvery-green, felted leaves.

Michaelmas daisy

Aster novi-belgii

A tall, branching perennial of wet places introduced from North America. The clusters of violet flowers with yellow discs are produced in September and October. It attracts late insects and the seeds are eaten by Siskins and Linnets.

HEIGHT 1m (3½ft)
SPREAD 50cm (20in)

CULTIVATION Prefers moist soil in sun. Propagate by dividing plants or as cuttings in spring or summer. Stake taller plants.

RELATED SPECIES *A. tradescantii* bears white flowers; *A. alpinus* is suitable for rock gardens.

Siskin

Yarrow (milfoil)

Achillea millefolium

This scented, perennial herb bears flat clusters of whitish flowers that develop into heads of small seeds. Birds are attracted both to the seeds and to pollinating insects.

HEIGHT 60cm (23in)
SPREAD 60cm (23in)

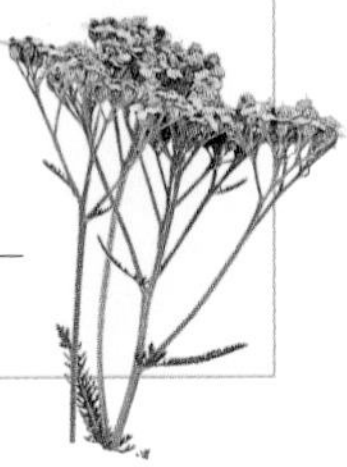

CULTIVATION Prefers a sunny, dry site. Stake stems, especially in exposed places.

RELATED SPECIES *A. m.* 'Fire King' has red flowers.

Cornflower

Centaurea cyanus

Grown for its bright blue flowers, this is an annual herb that sometimes survives the winter. The seeds are eaten by Blue Tits and Greenfinches, among other birds.

HEIGHT 1m (3½ft) **SPREAD** 30cm (12in)

CULTIVATION Sow in late summer or spring in well-drained soil with a sunny aspect. Ideal for naturalizing in grass.

RELATED SPECIES Greater knapweed (*C. scabiosa*) is a common perennial weed; perennial cornflower (*C. montana*) spreads vigorously.

Welted thistle

Carduus acanthoides

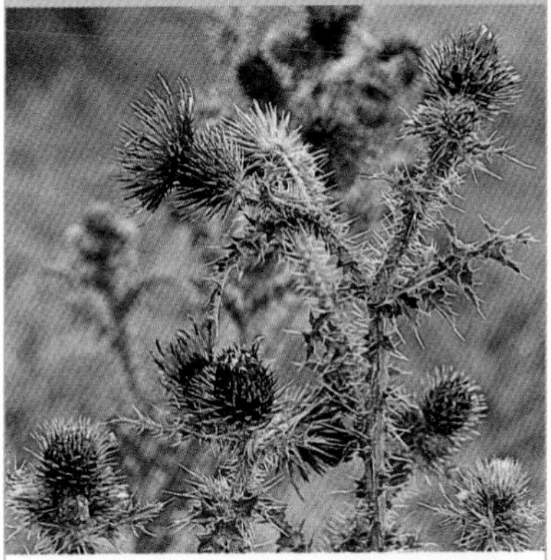

A biennial of hedges and verges that bears purple flowers. The flowers are visited by many insects, while in autumn, the seeds are eaten by many birds, including finches.

HEIGHT 1.2m (4ft)
SPREAD 50cm (20in)

CULTIVATION A weed that grows anywhere and easily self-seeds.

RELATED SPECIES Nodding or musk thistle (*C. nutans*) has red-purple flowers.

Logs are stacked *under a solar panel. As well as providing winter fuel, they are home to a variety of small animals which contribute to the ecology of the garden.*

An uncompromisingly *modern aluminium rill carries water right through the garden. It is shallow enough for birds to drink and bathe safely. Flowing water creates a relaxing atmosphere in an urban setting.*

Japanese spindle *is a hardy evergreen shrub with variegated leaves and pink fruits that yield orange seeds. It makes a good hedge or backdrop to a border, and attracts aphids and caterpillars that benefit birdlife.*

Goldfinches are *amongst the most colourful garden birds. They are drawn in by teazels and lavender, or weeds like dandelion that provide the small seeds they prefer. They also take seeds from hanging birdfeeders.*

Silver birch *is a small, graceful tree with peeling, silver-white bark. It is favoured by birds because of the insect life it supports and its edible winged seeds.*

Modern urban garden

FOR MANY PEOPLE, the garden is an outdoor room – a smart, comfortable space for leisure and entertaining. City dwellers can combine contemporary garden design and low maintenance with wildlife-friendly features that birds find irresistible.

The Chaffinch *is one of the most social urban birds.*

City gardens can be functional, modern, and beneficial to birds. Traditional, native plants may be combined to stylish effect with modern, synthetic materials and the latest environmental technologies.

Urban conservationists can use small solar panels to power their garden's lighting and water features. Burning logs in outdoor woodburners makes sitting outside viable in the autumn, while the logpiles are home to insects that in turn attract feeding birds. Water features can be given a modern spin, while still being attractive to visiting wildlife. Aluminium rills with flowing water replace traditional ponds and bird-baths, and rain-filled reservoirs dug beneath the garden keep the water flowing even in times of drought.

Recycled materials, such as glass composite and tyres, can be used for seating and to make raised beds, and bird features can have a contemporary rather than rustic tone. Feeders, for example, can be hung from glass sculptures.

PLANTING AND MAINTENANCE

Modern hard materials reflect the urban context of a garden. Specimen trees including cherry and birch provide height without encroaching too much on the small area of the garden.

Plant list

① Spindle (*Euonymus* sp)
② Silver birch (*Betula pendula*)
③ Firethorn (*Pyracantha* sp)
④ White clover (*Trifolium repens*)
⑤ Dog violet (*Viola riviniana*)
⑥ *Clematis montana*
⑦ *Cotoneaster horizontalis*
⑧ Thyme (*Thymus* sp)
⑨ *Cotoneaster dammeri*
⑩ Red dead-nettle (*Lamium purpureum*)
⑪ Ivy (*Hedera* sp)
⑫ Snowberry (*Symphoricarpus* sp)

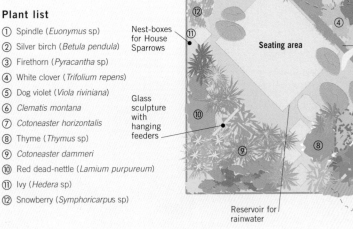

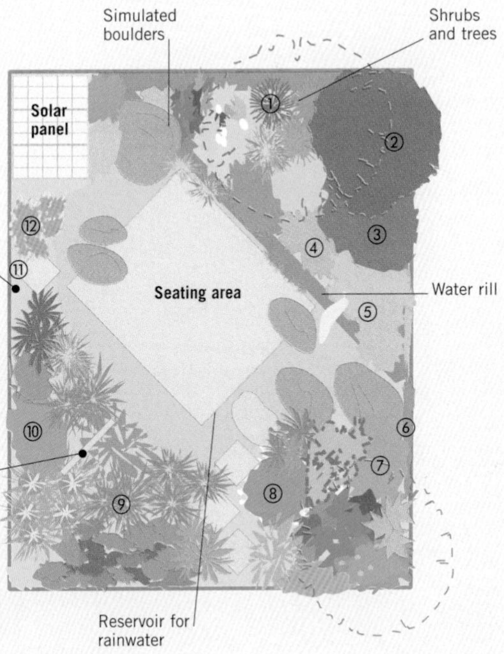

Urban terrace garden

Spotted Flycatchers
appreciate more mature gardens.

ALTHOUGH EACH GARDEN in a row of urban houses is small, a row of gardens combines to make a sizeable habitat for birds in the city centre. And because terraced houses tend to be older – often dating back 100 or more years – their gardens tend to be well-established with mature trees and shrubs that birds favour.

Diversity is the key to success when tempting birds into a smaller urban garden. A small lawn is an excellent feeding ground for Blackbirds, Song Thrushes, Robins, and Starlings, especially if you allow parts of it to grow and become weedy with clover and yarrow. Trees and shrubs provide birds with perching and roosting places, and food in the form of seeds and fruit, and while native species are preferred, ornamentals, such as crab apple, will do the job just as well.

A border planted with nectar-rich species will bring insects into the garden, and piles of organic material, such as logs and woody stems, will give homes to invertebrates, such as beetles, and will attract hedgehogs and wood mice, as well as birds. Avoiding the use of pesticides immediately increases the numbers of insects – there are many alternative, organic ways to control plant pests.

If neighbouring gardens also contain beneficial plants, the birds in the urban plot can rival those of rural gardens in number if not variety. The common tits, Robins, and Wrens may be joined by Siskins, Pied Wagtails, and Great Spotted Woodpeckers, while Herring Gulls may nest among the chimneys in coastal towns. Storms can bring almost any species into a city.

PLANTING AND MAINTENANCE

Urban gardens often have poor soil because they are sited over rubble, and surrounding buildings may cast dense shadows – factors that need to be taken into consideration when planting. They are also the hunting grounds of cats, so careful siting of birdfeeders and nest-boxes is required.

Plant list

① Cypress (*Chamaecyparis* sp)
② *Clematis montana*
③ *Cotoneaster* sp
④ Tree mallow (*Lavatera* sp)
⑤ Feverfew (*Tanacetum* sp)
⑥ Shasta daisy (*Leucanthemum* sp)
⑦ Mezereon (*Daphne mezereum*)
⑧ Yarrow (*Achillea* sp)
⑨ Loosestrife (*Lysimachia* sp)
⑩ Cherry laurel (*Prunus* sp)

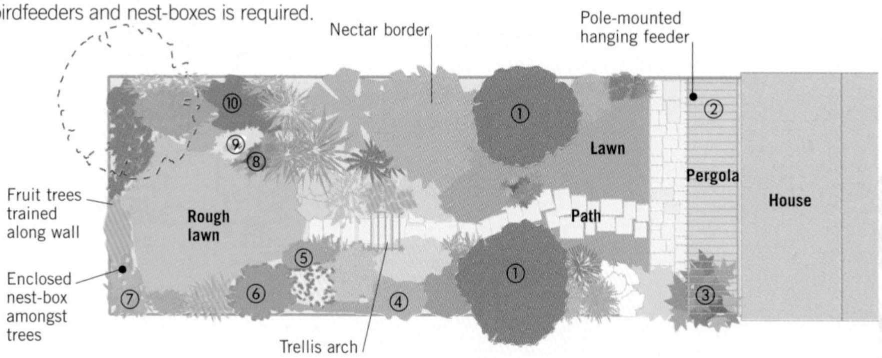

Bird cherry *is a small tree suitable for the urban garden. The fragrant flowers attract insects and the bitter-tasting black cherries are favourites of Hawfinches.*

House Martins *nest under the eaves of town houses and may be persuaded to colonize nest-boxes. They are aerial feeders, swooping over roofs, and descending only to collect mud for their nests.*

Honeysuckle *is useful for covering unsightly walls or sheds. Old growth of this scented plant provides a thick mass of stems where birds will roost and nest, and its red berries are a good source of food in late summer.*

Compost bins *are simple to erect and consume garden cuttings and kitchen waste. The rotting vegetation supports worms, insects, and other animal life that will attract birds to forage.*

Bamboos *and other grasses are grown for their sculptural effect. Their long leaves provide material for nests and their seeds may be eaten by birds.*

A peanut feeder *made of wire mesh is ideal for the roof terrace or patio. Spilled fragments of nuts are taken by birds that cannot perch on the feeder itself.*

Open-fronted *nest-boxes may attract urban species, such as Robins and Pied Wagtails. A nest-box on a trellis will become camouflaged and sheltered when climbing plants grow up round it.*

A bird-bath *will always draw birds into a rooftop garden, and can be a very attractive feature in a container garden. Metal containers add visual interest, but ensure they are not too deep for birds to enter.*

Pied Wagtails *are seen in and around towns, searching for insects on paved surfaces. They are common on roofs, usually calling before flying off. In winter they gather in large numbers to roost in town centres.*

Nasturtiums *are easy to grow and bring swathes of colour to the garden. They produce copious nectar, which attracts a range of insects that are in turn taken by birds.*

Urban roof garden

SPACE IS LIMITED in the city environment, but the pleasure of wildlife gardening is not denied to anyone who has access to an area of flat roof or even a balcony. Birds are drawn in by the oasis of vegetation to look for a good source of food and a place to nest.

Blackbirds *may nest on high window ledges.*

The diversity and number of birds in the city centre are often lower than in the suburbs, and in a roof garden the variety of species depends largely on the abundance of trees in neighbourhood parks or roadsides. However, with careful planting and supplementary feeding, it is possible to make the smallest pocket of garden into a magnet for nearby birds.

A roof garden compensates for low bird diversity by offering unusual or intimate views of certain species: Swallows and Swifts can be seen hunting from above; Starlings and House Sparrows may be observed nesting at close quarters; and Pied Wagtails can be watched for hours chasing around roofs in search of insects. In summer, there may be some unusual visitors – House Martins bask on sun-warmed tiles, and Lapwings and Golden Plovers have been known to roost on roofs.

Planting a rooftop garden presents its own challenges – not least the need to carry plants, soil, and containers up from ground level. Soil in containers or in shallow beds dries out rapidly. If possible, collect rain water in butts, and use narrow bore pipes to deliver water to the containers.

PLANTING AND MAINTENANCE

The plants in a roof garden are exposed to the elements. If they are not sheltered by walls, windbreaks of closely-woven mesh may be needed for protection. Always consult a structural engineer before building raised beds on a flat roof.

Plant list

① Honeysuckle (*Lonicera* sp)
② *Hydrangea macrophylla*
③ Corn palm (*Dracaena fragans*)
④ Ivy (*Hedera helix*)
⑤ Cotton lavender (*Santolina* sp)
⑥ *Ceanothus impressus*
⑦ Willow (*Salix caprea*)
⑧ *Begonia* sp
⑨ Myrtle (*Myrtus communis*)
⑩ *Buddleia davidii*

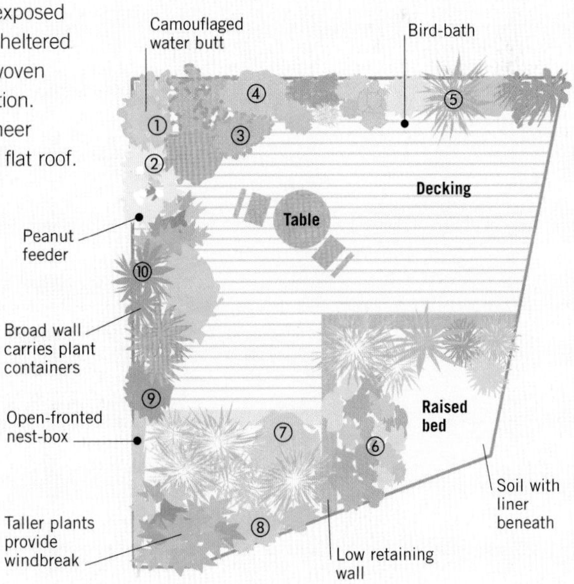

Mediterranean garden

The Greenfinch *searches for seeds in the garden.*

MEDITERRANEAN GARDENS ARE becoming more popular in northern Europe, and the warming climate is making them easier to achieve. Long, hot, dry summers and frost-free winters are set to become more common, and gardeners are adapting their planting to help wildlife in these new conditions.

Mediterranean plants are sun lovers and tolerate drought almost to the point of requiring it; many species actually flower more when given very little water. They can usually stand the cold of winter, but do not like cold combined with wet conditions. However, even with drought-resistant varieties, irrigation is important. The environmentally-friendly way is to store water from winter rains (and from rarer summer storms) in cisterns or to use waste domestic water, and to build irrigation systems that target individual plants.

Classic Mediterranean gardens are usually formal in layout, with terracing, statuary, and evergreen hedges setting the style. Lawns, which are so typical of more temperate gardens, are hard to maintain in long periods of regular drought, so are replaced by paved courtyard areas. Thick-walled pergolas offer airy, shaded places for keeping cool, and trees play an important role in providing both shade and shelter from drying winds. Some of the ornamental species – olive, date palm, fig, and stone pine – also provide useful crops. Beds can be filled with aromatic herbs and bushes, such as thyme, rosemary, fennel, and myrtle. Bulbs also flourish in the spring after the winter rains.

PLANTING AND MAINTENANCE

At northern latitudes, plenty of sand and gravel should be dug into the soil to help plants cope with damp winters. Mediterranean gardens typically require little maintenance during the blooming season. Some late summer maintenance and pruning is required to ensure full, healthy growth the following year.

Plant list

1. Yarrow (*Achillea* sp)
2. Rose (*Rosa* sp)
3. *Ixia viridifolia*
4. *Phlox divaricata*
5. Wallflower (*Erysimum* sp)
6. *Oenothera macrocarpa*
7. Lavender (*Lavandula* sp)
8. Juniper (*Juniperus* sp)
9. Broom (*Cytisus* sp)
10. Gentian (*Gentiana* sp)

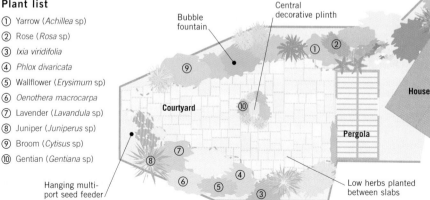

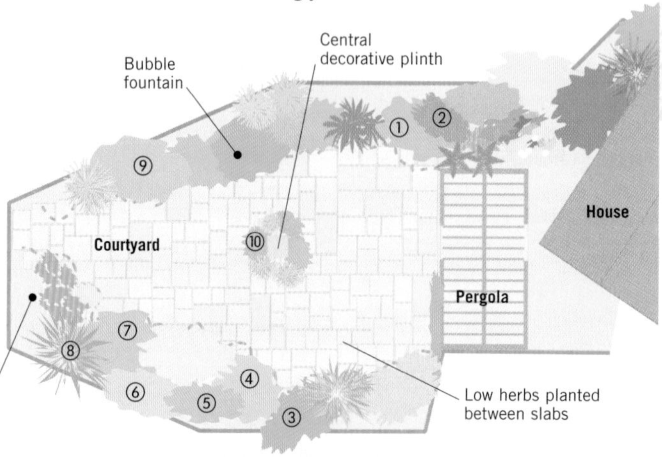

The Black Redstart *sometimes breeds in industrial parts of cities as well as suburbs. Holes and crevices in buildings provide suitable nesting places.*

Pencil cypress *is a slender tree with aromatic grey-green foliage. It grows fast when young so quickly provides shade and screening, but does not outgrow the garden. It provides cover for nesting birds.*

Rock roses *are low, spreading shrubs that thrive in rock gardens and on dry banks. As well as providing colour in the garden, their growth provides a home for many small animals that make food for birds.*

Lavender *can be grown in low hedges or mixed with other perennials. Its flowers have a high nectar content for attracting butterflies and bees and the fruits are eated by Goldfinches and Serins.*

A bubble fountain *is a low-maintenance feature that will bring passing birds into the garden. The cobbles harmonize well with the surrounding paving and walls.*

Guelder rose *thrives in full sun or part-shade, in the damp parts of the garden. It has clusters of white flowers followed by red berries that are eaten by many birds.*

Hanging feeders *provide a welcome food supplement throughout the year, even in this well-stocked garden. Decorative ironwork on the supporting poles adds character to the garden.*

Flag iris *is a shapely and colourful addition to the pond's margins. Throughout the summer months it provides cover; birds may find insects and other animals hiding around the base of the leaves.*

A Dunnock *is at home searching for food under the cover of the shrubs in this garden, although it will also come out to feed on the lawn. It is easy to overlook this drab-coloured bird, but it has a vigorous song.*

Ligularia *(golden groundsel) enhances the wildlife potential of the garden because its flowers attract insects, while slugs and snails gather under its broad leaves.*

Suburban garden

MOST LARGE GARDENS are on the edges of towns and villages, and when they are mature, birds need little encouragement to visit. Bird-friendly suburban gardens usually imitate the natural woodland habitat of many garden species.

The Great Spotted Woodpecker *is a regular in gardens with tall trees.*

Suburban gardens are usually larger than city centre plots, and their owners tend to rely more on shrubs and trees to cover the ground. The best of these gardens use foliage in all its variety of shape, colour, and texture to create architectural shapes that lead the eye from low-growing perennials to shrubs and trees behind.

Shrubs, such as barberry and firethorn, provide excellent cover for birds, while the sheer variety of plant species in a larger garden guarantees the presence of diverse herbivorous insects and other invertebrates, which themselves attract birds. Planting diversity ensures that fruits, berries, and nuts are available throughout the summer, autumn, and early winter, so maintaining wildife interest throughout the year. A selection of small flowering shrubs and herbaceous plants – such as currant bushes, mahonia, and crown imperials – offers the opportunity to watch tits and other species visiting flowers for nectar.

A pond is arguably the most important wildlife feature of a larger garden. A shallow stretch of water should always be accessible for birds coming to bathe or drink. Badgers, hedgehogs, and other mammals may also occasionally use the pond as a watering hole.

PLANTING AND MAINTENANCE

Careful cutting-back of the shrubs is required to prevent them crowding each other and shading out the low-growing herbaceous perennials. Birdfeeders are best placed on the patio where they can be seen from the windows. The pond needs regular maintenance; the plants, which are planted in pots, can be lifted out for trimming.

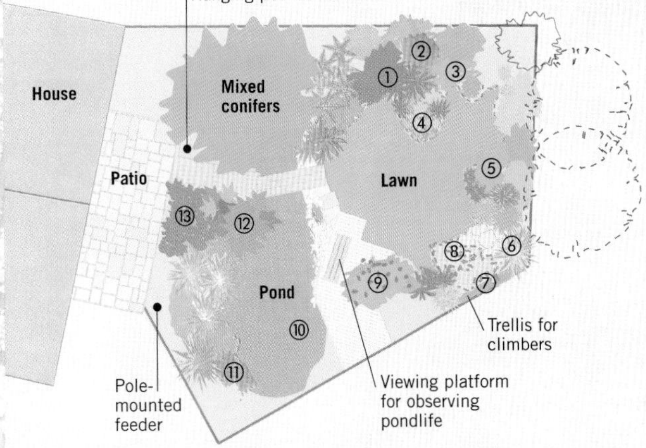

Plant list

1. *Fatsia japonica*
2. *Elaeagnus macrophylla*
3. Sycamore (*Acer* sp)
4. Lady's mantle (*Alchemilla* sp)
5. Guelder rose (*Viburnum* opulus)
6. Silver birch (*Betula pendula*)
7. Honeysuckle (*Lonicera* sp)
8. Crown imperial (*Fritillaria* sp)
9. Flowering currant (*Ribes* sp)
10. Water lily (*Nyphaea alba*)
11. Shield fern (*Polystichum* sp)
12. Gunnera (*Gunnera manicata*)
13. Groundsel (*Ligularia* sp)

Country garden

Nuthatches *come into gardens from adjacent woodland.*

A LARGE GARDEN ON THE EDGE of countryside can be managed in such a way that birds and mammals become a part of its fabric, rather than occasional visitors. Birds will include the garden in their search for food and may even find it a better place than their natural habitat.

Modern intensive farming has diminished the variety of countryside, and removed some habitats entirely. Only more traditionally farmed areas, and surviving field edges and hedgerows, still support significant populations of wild birds.

Country gardens have become vitally important bird sanctuaries, especially in the winter when natural food becomes scarce. Putting out food in feeders and creating a bird-friendly habitat by garden management will attract almost the full range of farmland birds, as well as species that are rare visitors to more urban gardens, such as the Yellowhammer and Turtle Dove.

A large garden presents the opportunity to leave "natural" patches where the plants are unkempt and weeds are left to grow. Patches of stinging nettles are good for insects, including caterpillars, while seeding weeds, such as groundsel, dandelion, and fat hen, bring in seed-eating birds. Even grass left to become hay can be valuable for seeds and for providing nest material. Hawthorn flowers on year-old stems and privet hedges become interesting wildlife features if allowed to produce tiny flowers and berries. The effectiveness of natural patches in attracting birds is proportional to their size – the larger the better.

PLANTING AND MAINTENANCE

This large country garden allows for wild areas and an extensive pond that is big enough to attract water birds as well as visitors looking for a drink and a bath. Despite the diversity and range of natural food plants in the garden, the owners have not overlooked artificial feeders, which provide essential food supplements throughout the year.

Plant list

1. *Sorbaria aitchisonii*
2. Bamboo (*Arundinaria* sp)
3. Siberian iris (*Iris sibirica*)
4. New Zealand flax (*Phormium tenax*)
5. Hawthorn (*Crataegus* sp)
6. Bird cherry (*Prunus padus*)
7. Dandelion (*Taraxacum officinale*)
8. Morning star (*Carex grayi*)
9. Candelabra primula (*Primula* sp)
10. Comfrey (*Symphytum* sp)
11. Reed (*Phragmites* sp)

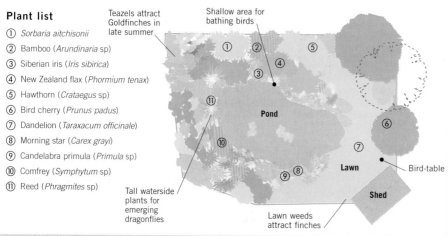

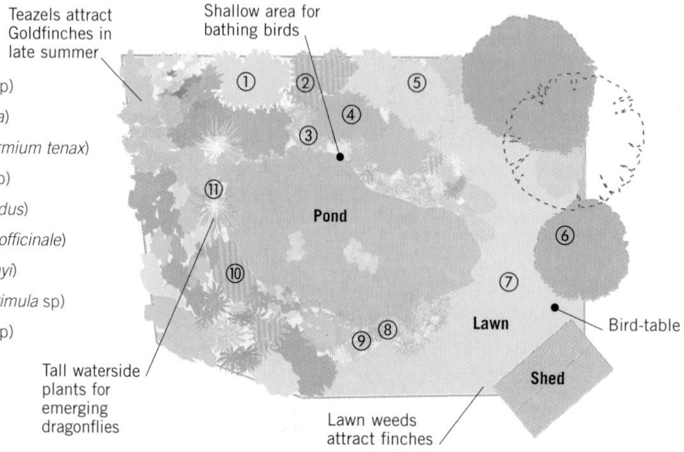

Teazels *are highly ornamental plants, and have seeds that are taken by birds. Millet seeds can be inserted into empty seedheads to extend their use.*

Shrubs and hedges *should be pruned with great care. Cutting the plants back creates dense growth suitable for nesting and roosting; conversely, allowing them to grow increases flowering and fruiting.*

A garden *with a sufficiently large pond can even attract Kingfishers. Piling up earth next to the pond creates a bank in which the birds can be tempted to nest, and perches over the water encourage feeding.*

Green Woodpeckers *come into country gardens to probe for ants' nests on the lawn. Once a nest has been discovered, the woodpecker may become a regular, though always very wary, visitor.*

Piles of rotting logs *develop into small ecosystems. Birds may nest and roost among them, and they form shelters for mice and voles, amphibians, and reptiles.*

Observing garden birds

Even the smallest of urban gardens attracts a variety of birds. An understanding of what to look for will greatly enhance your enjoyment of these visitors, and knowing what basic equipment to use will help you explore their secret lives.

How to look

BIRDWATCHING CAN BEGIN at home. While it is exciting to look for birds in wild places, the elements of observation and identification are best learned in the familiar surroundings of the garden. And because you have some control over your garden environment, it is possible to conduct simple ecological studies and experiments that reveal birds' covert behaviours.

The garden *is a good place for watching birds at close range, allowing the details of their plumage to be learned and their everyday behaviour studied.*

Home study

Your house is an ideal, ready-made hide. It is easy to watch and identify birds at close range without disturbing them, especially if you position feeders close to windows. Proximity gives you a luxury rarely afforded in the field – the time and opportunity to examine plumage, bill shape, eye colour, and other details that would normally be missed in a whir of activity.

Brief observations can be made while you go about your everyday activities, but it is worth putting aside some time for "serious" garden birdwatching. Leave a pair of binoculars by the window, ready to be used when an unexpected bird turns up or something unusual happens, or leave your telescope permanently trained on a busy birdfeeder. When observing from within your house, try standing further back in the room; wary species, such as crows, Sparrowhawks, and Grey Herons, can be scared off by the slightest movement.

Learning how to identify birds is a goal in itself (see pages 124–125), but it is limited in the garden environment, where about a dozen or so common species account for the overwhelming majority of birds seen. It is worth observing birds in more detail, recording their behaviour throughout the day, and over the year.

Using a telescope *in the garden gets you as close to wild birds as you are ever likely to be. Views, even of familiar birds, at this range can be stunning and revealing.*

A garden shed *or summer house makes a convenient hide to allow observation in remote corners of the garden.*

Ornithologists *use numbered bird rings to record the movements of birds, especially on long migratory journeys. They are also used to monitor mating fidelity, nesting place, and life expectancy.*

Investigating birds' private lives, and noting down changes in activity over time provides a fascinating dimension to birdwatching, and a means of understanding your garden as a wildlife habitat.

Studying bird behaviour is not simply about observing what is happening. You should always ask yourself how and why? You may, for example, see a bird taking food from a feeder for the first time. It could be a Blackbird or a Dunnock (both of which normally feed on the ground) or perhaps a new visitor to the garden, such as a Nuthatch or Jay. You should note how it manages the new technique. Does it struggle to cling to the feeder, with much flapping of wings, or is it naturally acrobatic like a tit?

Trying to work out why a bird behaves in a certain way is more difficult. We cannot ask it for a reason, but can merely infer its motivation from watching its behaviour as carefully as possible. For example, Collared Doves sometimes perch in the rain with one wing raised. This is the same strange action as is used for sunbathing, so we infer that this is rain-bathing and serves the same purpose as splashing in a bird-bath.

Identifying individuals

To study behaviour over time, it helps to be able to identify individual birds in the garden. They can sometimes be distinguished by details of plumage, anatomy, or chance damage. This way, you can begin to examine the dynamics of a group, and the breeding behaviour of individual birds throughout the year. Professional ornithologists often identify individuals by attaching numbered metal or plastic

KEEPING A DISTANCE

The basic rule of birdwatching is that the welfare of the birds comes first. Birds cope with everyday disturbance in the garden, but it is tempting to try to get too close to identify a rare species or move vegetation to peer into a bird's nest. The sitting parent may be driven off, but even if it sits tight, the disturbance may attract predators. It may be necessary to avoid part of the garden until the young birds leave the nest.

BIRD DETECTIVES

A diligent birdwatcher looks at the ground as well as at the skies. Birds leave many traces that reveal something about their habits and their identities. Examining traces helps to build up a natural history of garden birds.

Feathers *may be moulted or lost during an attack. If the feather has been moulted, wear on the vane is usually visible; if lost in an attack, it may be damaged.*

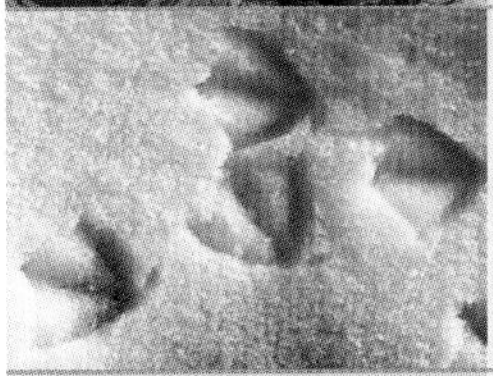

Footprints *in the snow or on mud reflect a bird's gait, revealing whether it walks or hops. They may also suggest what the bird was doing.*

A post *covered with droppings is likely to be a regular perch. It may be used as a song-post or a roost. Train your scope on the post, and wait for the visitor.*

A cone *in a rock or tree crevice is a sign of woodpecker or Nuthatch activity. Cones or nuts are wedged in before being hammered open by the birds.*

Plucking posts *are perches where birds of prey pluck and dismember their prey. They are worth checking regularly for recent activity.*

Birdsong and calls *are important clues to a bird's identity, especially when it is hidden among foliage. A tape recorder can be a useful aid for capturing the sounds and assisting your memory. A CD recording of common birdsong is a good investment – it will help you trace the identity of the singer.*

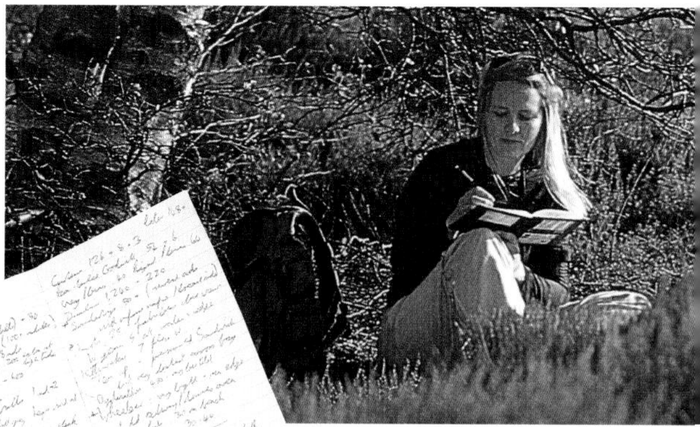

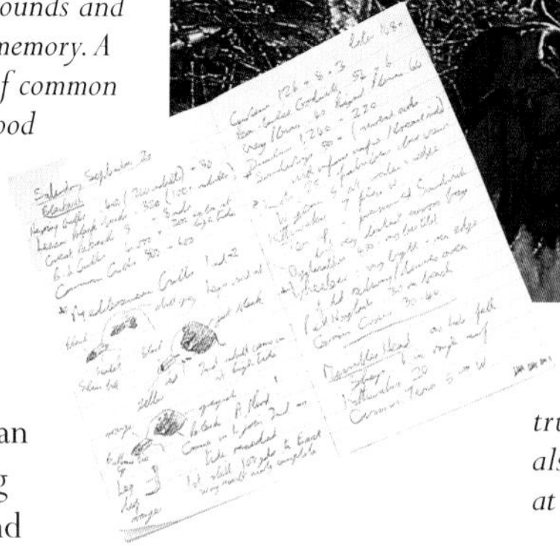

Take notes *of what you see and hear as soon as possible. Do not trust your memory. Written records also allow you to compare observations at different times and places.*

rings to their legs, using colour combinations that can be recognized from a distance. Handling and ringing birds requires a special permit, but you may well find rings on dead or injured birds. If you do, send the number and details of where, when, and how the bird was found, together with your address, to the address shown on the ring. Eventually, you will receive a history of the bird saying where and when it was ringed.

Making records

To be of much value, observations must be recorded. Use a notebook to write down numbers of birds seen, what they were doing, details of plumage, and other identification tips. Descriptions of a bird's appearance and sound in your own words are invaluable, because they will mean far more to you than the generic descriptions given in bird books. Wherever possible, use annotated sketches to record characteristics (see below). It does not matter if you cannot draw well. Work fast, and try to make several sketches before the bird disappears from view. Remember that the size and shape of the bird and the relative sizes of its body parts can be as important as colours, but try also to note down the colours of the legs, bill, and any stripes around the eyes.

HOW TO SKETCH BIRDS

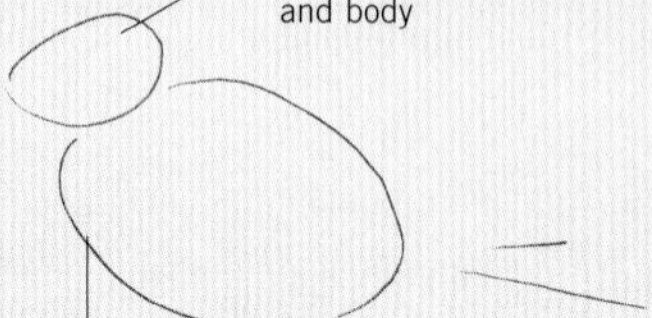
Concentrate on the outline of the head and body
Use simple shapes

❶ **Begin your sketch** *with the bird's basic shape. Two ovals show the relative size and position of the head and body and also indicate the length of the neck. The position and length of the tail and legs are also indicated.*

❷ **Pencil in** *the bird's feather patterns, and annotate patches of colours. Carefully note down any eyestripes, cheek patches, wingbars, and so on. If time allows, make separate sketches of parts of the body to highlight any details that catch your eye.*

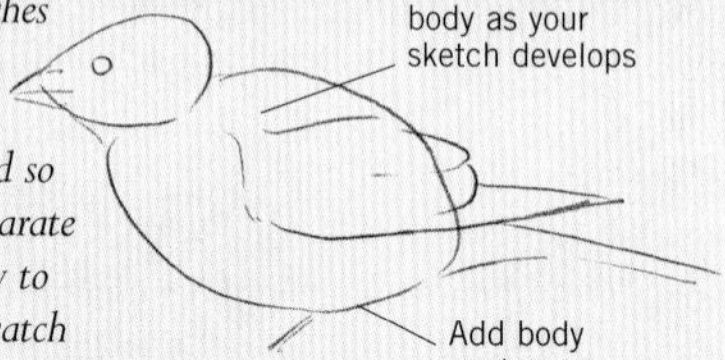
Adjust the shape of the head and body as your sketch develops
Add body contours

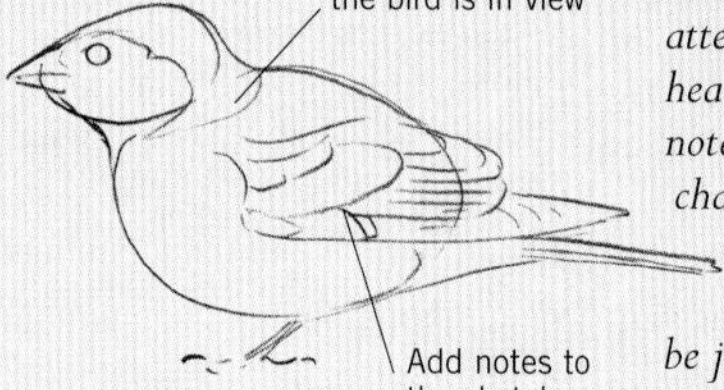
Keep building detail for as long as the bird is in view
Add notes to the sketch

❸ **By now** *the bird should be identifiable. Pay attention to details of the head and wings. Make notes of behavioural characteristics, such as gait and flight pattern – they can be just as useful as shape and colour.*

❹ **Refer to** *your sketch and notes to draw up a finished colour image. When it is complete, compare your picture with published illustrations and photos. Note how it differs, and remember to check these points next time you see the bird in the field.*

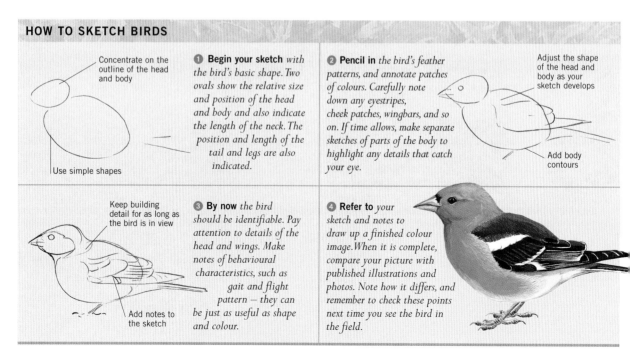

A bird's songs and calls are also characteristic, but harder to record than physical attributes. Descriptions in your notebook like "a high-pitched, clear warble" may not mean much on re-reading, but transcriptions like "*tuey*" or "*tsk-tsk-tsk*" may paint a better picture of the sound. Songs and calls are easiest to remember if they can be fitted to English phrases, like "teacher-teacher" for the Great Tit or "did-he-do-it" for the Song Thrush.

Analysing records

The simplest records are lists. These may be lists of species seen in the garden, or birds that have visited a particular feeder. Lists can be interesting in themselves, but are more valuable if you can compare them week-by-week because it becomes possible to analyse what is happening in the garden. You can answer questions like: do some birds come into the garden at certain times of year? Do Song Thrush food preferences change from spring to autumn? Did the first Blackcap arrive before the last Redwing left?

If you keep a thorough account of the numbers of birds in the garden, you may be able to detect even very subtle changes in bird populations – for example, the arrival of immigrant Blackbirds and Chaffinches in autumn, which boost the local population. You will also be able to record occurrences of rare birds – when was a Treecreeper last seen in the garden?

Some birdwatchers simply keep their observations in the original notebooks, but transcribing notes into a permanent diary allows you to organize and analyse your data in more detail. If you are thinking of making serious records, an inexpensive database program for your computer is a worthwhile investment.

Studying the behaviour *of birds nesting in your garden is amongst the most rewarding observational projects. Where possible, site nest-boxes with a good, clear line of vision to the house, so that you can watch in all weather conditions.*

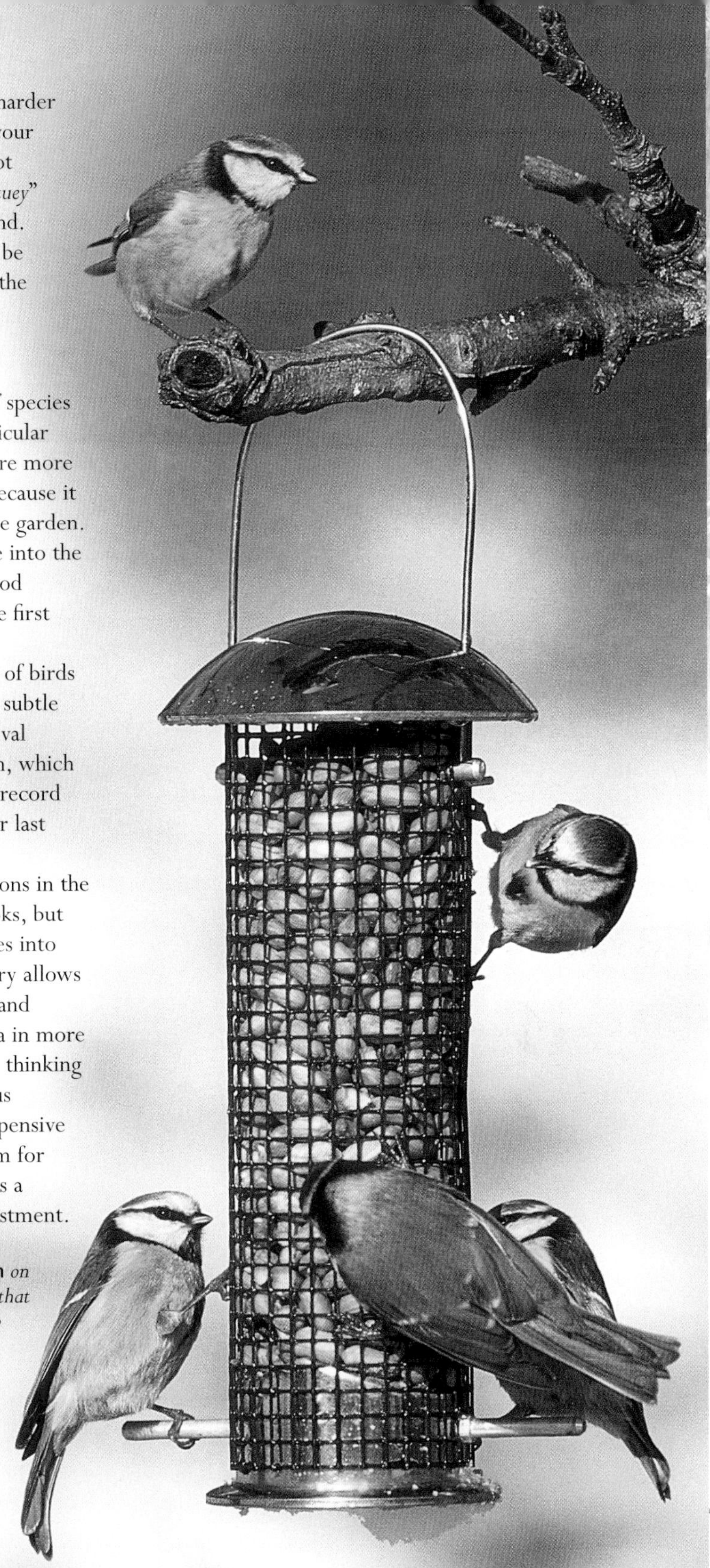

A systematic watch *on a feeder may show that some birds prefer to feed at particular times of the day or that others always feed in flocks. Sometimes the patient observer is rewarded with the sight of an unusual visitor.*

Broken snail shells *on a rock or path indicate that it is an "anvil", where a Song Thrush smashes shells to get at the soft bodies. A watch on the garden's anvils shows which species of snails are caught and when thrushes turn to hunting them.*

Ecological experiments

If observing and recording bird activity stimulates your interest in natural history, try devising a few simple ecological projects. When you next see a Blue Tit or Wren searching for food in the rough bark of a tree trunk, use a magnifying glass to see if you can find what it was eating. If a Coal Tit is flying off with whole peanuts from a feeder, try to find where it is hiding them. And keep a watch on Blackbirds and Wrens to find out where they roost at night (the position of communal roosts is given away by tell-tale accumulations of droppings).

Nesting is perhaps the most interesting and varied behaviour to observe and study in the garden. Try to see if it is the male or female parent that builds the nest and incubates the eggs. Perhaps the duties are split, or perhaps other birds assist the parents. When the eggs have hatched, record the number of visits made by each parent to the nest – which one brings the young most food? You could try to correlate breeding success with temperature and rainfall; form your own hypotheses, and use bird records from previous years to test out your ideas.

Nest investigations

In late autumn, when nests have been abandoned, they can be examined without disturbing birds. Try to identify the building materials used and look for differences in construction between species. The nest of a Blackbird, for example, is distinguished from that of a Song Thrush by the lining of grass or leaves in the mud cup. Look inside nests for addled eggs or dead nestlings, piles of berries hoarded by mice, or even bumblebee nests. To avoid possible infection, wear protective gloves, and avoid inhaling dust from the nest material.

Taking part

Systematic, year-round recording of garden birds becomes even more interesting if it is linked with local or national surveys conducted by wildlife organisations. In Britain, the

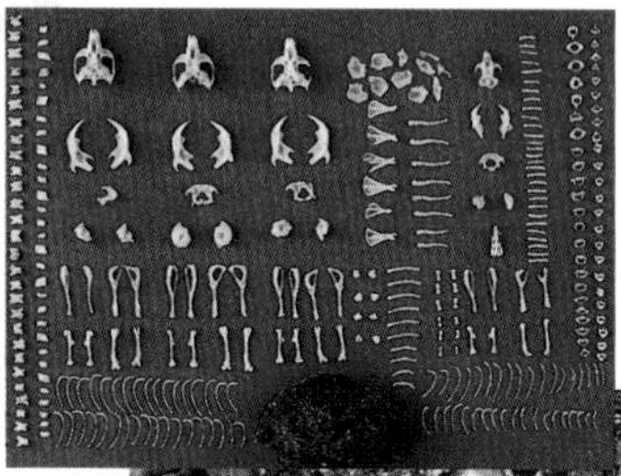

Owl pellets *(below) accumulate under owl perches. Careful dissection of the pellets (left) reveals what the owl has eaten. Skulls of small mammals and birds are easy to identify but there may also be hard parts of insects' bodies.*

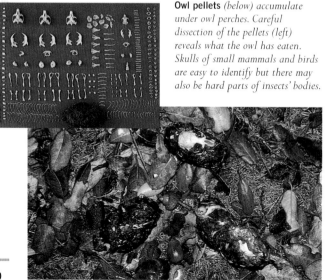

Plant life *can give valuable clues about bird activity. If birds perch regularly on a fence, they deposit seeds of their favoured food plants in their droppings. These may germinate to produce a natural and unique hedge or weed patch.*

THE RSPB BIG GARDEN BIRDWATCH

Every year, during the last weekend of January, the RSPB holds its Big Garden Birdwatch in which people are encouraged to count birds in their gardens. In 2003, counts came in from an incredible 300,000 people. They showed that Starlings are the most numerous garden birds, with an average of five per garden, followed by House Sparrows, Blue Tits, and Blackbirds. The most widespread garden bird is the Blackbird, which was recorded in 93% of all gardens, followed by the Blue Tit (87%) and Robin (85%). Because the birds have been counted in the same way since 1979, it is possible to see changes in their abundance. Starlings have decreased by two-thirds and the House Sparrow by one-half in this period. These winter numbers are reflected in changes in the nesting population. Blue and Great Tits, Chaffinches, Greenfinches, Collared Doves, and Woodpigeons have become more abundant in gardens.

Counting the birds *visiting your garden each day will reveal unexpected fluctuations in numbers. For birds that feed in large flocks, such as Starlings, a hand counter is a useful tool.*

Royal Society for the Protection of Birds (RSPB) and the British Trust for Ornithology (BTO) run surveys that depend on garden birdwatchers and do not call for specialist knowledge. The analysis of data collected from thousands of gardens across the country helps to demonstrate changes in bird populations, and reveals details of their habits. The results are important for planning conservation programmes as well as increasing our understanding of bird life.

BIRD TIMETABLES

Recording the timing of annual events in a bird's life can reveal unexpected influences on its behaviour. For example, global warming can be detected by the earlier arrival of spring migrant birds: Chiffchaffs and Blackcaps reach Britain about three days earlier for every 1°C rise in temperature. To generate your own bird calendar, simply record the first occurrence of a particular type of behaviour – arrival, nest-building, hatching of eggs, and so on – for a particular species, such as the Swallow (below). Compare the data you have collected over a number of years and try to explain any trends you observe.

| First seen 10th April | First visit to nest site 2nd May | Collecting nest material 16th May | Feeding young 21st June | Pre-migration flocks 5th September |

| April | May | June | July | August | September |

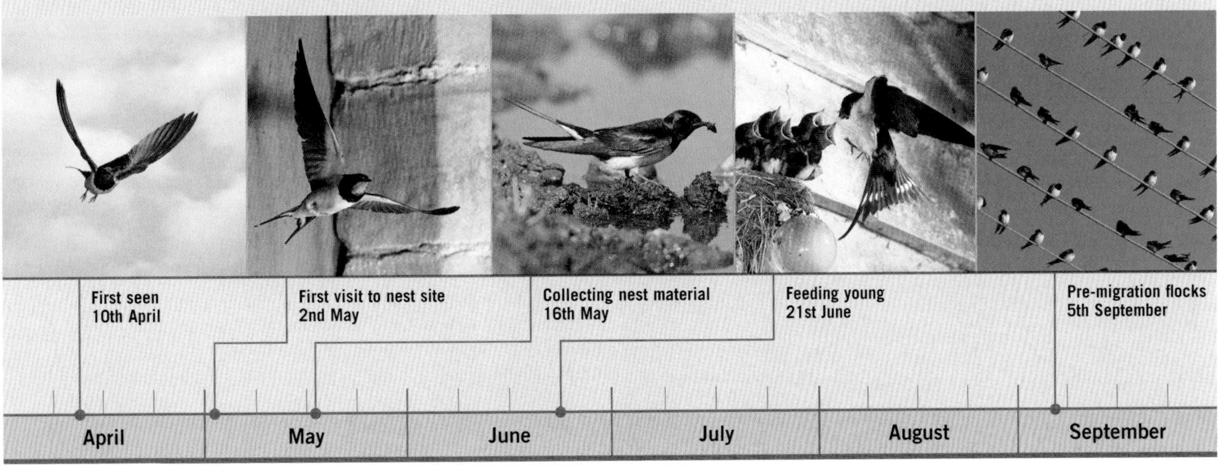

Equipment

WATCHING BIRDS AT CLOSE QUARTERS is a special pleasure, and in the garden it is possible to get great views with the naked eye. However, a good pair of binoculars or a telescope bring you even closer to the action, and provide views of fine anatomical details. It is also possible to make remarkably intimate photographs of garden birds with basic equipment.

Adjusting your eyepiece *settings according to the manufacturer's instructions ensures the crispest image.*

Choosing binoculars

Binoculars are an essential tool, especially when you get serious about your birdwatching. They do not enable you to see any further, but by magnifying what is already visible they allow you to identify and examine birds from a greater distance than with the naked eye. Binoculars come in many shapes and sizes. Generally, larger models give greater magnification, but magnifying power is not the only factor to bear in mind when choosing a pair to buy. You should also consider image brightness, build quality, ease of use, and, of course, price. Birdwatching fairs are good places to test equipment in the field before you part with your cash.

Comfort and magnification

The key specifications of a pair of binoculars are given by a pair of numbers – 10x40, for example. The first figure is the magnification, indicating how many times larger an object will appear when viewed. The second is the diameter of the objective lens; the larger this is, the brighter the

Binoculars for use *in the garden should have a short minimum focus for close-up views of birds and butterflies. Check the closest focus before buying – models vary considerably.*

TYPES OF BINOCULARS

All binoculars use reflective prisms to extend the path of light, while retaining a compact body. There are two basic designs – roof prism (right) and the simpler, and cheaper porro prism (see below). Each design has its advantages.

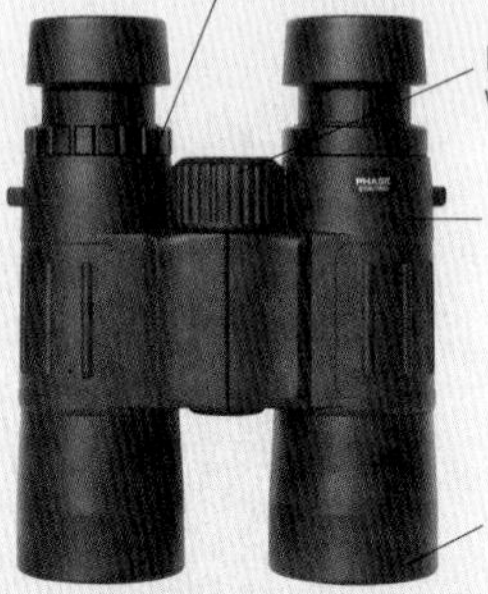

Traditional style binoculars *use a porro prism design. This simple optical arrangement is rugged and offers great value to the beginner. The widely separated objective lenses help to produce an excellent three-dimensional image.*

Waterproof optics, *a rubber-clad body, and retractable eyecups give these porro prism binoculars good all-weather performance. The lenses are made of low-dispersion glass to maintain colour accuracy. Coatings on the lenses minimize internal reflections.*

Compact models, *such as this 8x23 porro prism design, are highly portable and ergonomically designed for maximum comfort when held in one hand. The small objective lens, however, limits the brightness of the image.*

Roof prism binoculars *have a straight body. They are slender and compact, but the prisms more complicated than in porro prism binoculars, so the glass and manufacturing need to be of a higher quality, reflected in their higher price.*

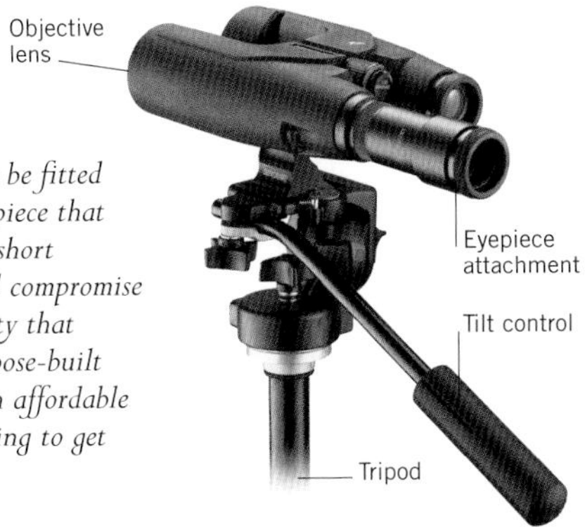

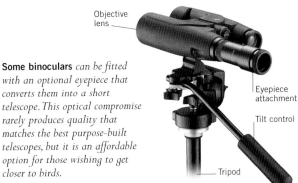

Some binoculars *can be fitted with an optional eyepiece that converts them into a short telescope. This optical compromise rarely produces quality that matches the best purpose-built telescopes, but it is an affordable option for those wishing to get closer to birds.*

image will seem. Ranges of 7x35 to 10x50 are ideal: higher magnifications may seem appealing but with a very narrow field of view they are hard to hold steady. Pay attention to comfort – the binoculars should fit well in your hands and be light enough to carry. You may have them around your neck for hours. When choosing binoculars, bear in mind that the focus wheel will be in constant use; you should be able to turn it effortlessly with a fingertip, without having to move your whole hand.

How to use binoculars

The first sign of a bird's presence is likely to be its call, or the gentle movement of leaves. Get its general bearings first by using your ears, then, facing the area, try to see the bird. The secret of keeping the bird in sight is to square yourself up to the target. Your whole body, including your feet, should turn to face the bird, and your whole head should tilt up to face the bird – not just your eyes. Now, keeping your head and body still, swing the binoculars up to your eyes, always keeping the bird fixed in view. You should find that you are looking straight at the bird.

Do not look down at your binoculars while lifting them up and then swing them around trying to find what you are looking for, because you are likely to lose the position of the bird. Wedge a finger against your forehead, or your thumb against your chin, for extra stability, or rest your arms against a window ledge or tree branch.

BINOCULARS AND GLASSES

People who wear spectacles often find that viewing through binoculars results in a poor image. This is because the eye is too far away from the binocular eyepiece and light can enter from the side. A raised finger or thumb helps block out this stray light, but the edges of the image may still appear blurred or dark. To avoid this problem, buy binoculars with eyepieces that are adjustable for spectacle wearers.

Normal eyesight | **Corrected for spectacles**

The slightest jolt is *magnified by binoculars. Leaning against a solid object, such as a tree or wall, helps to stabilize the image.*

When walking outside, carry your binoculars on a strap around your neck. Do not keep them inside a case because they need to be ready for action at all times. Clean the eyepieces often – eyelashes leave greasy smudges that blur the image. When leaving a cool room to go out into warmer, more humid conditions, get your binoculars out of their case a few minutes before you need them. This reduces the degree of fogging that occurs as water condenses on the cold lenses.

Digiscope equipment

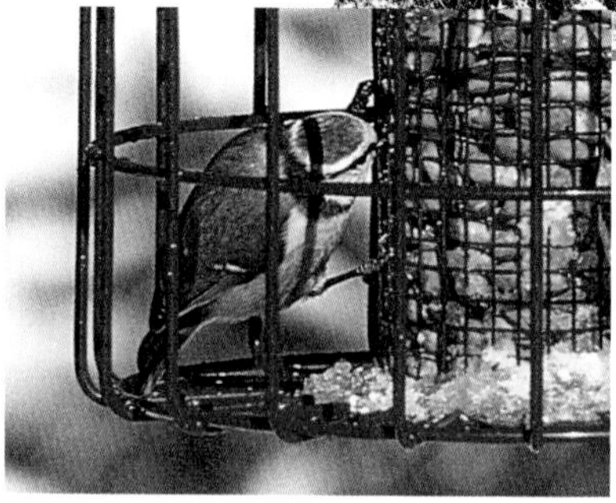

Digiscope view

Digiscoping *puts magnifications of up to 100x into the hands of amateurs equipped with a scope and a digital camera. Certain models are more suited to digiscoping than others; check on the Internet for the most up-to-date advice.*

Telescopes and tripods

Even closer views of garden birds can be achieved with a telescope. Most models targeted at birdwatchers provide a magnification of about 30x or more; however, the observed object is magnified along with any vibrations or tremors caused by shaking hands and fingers. For this reason, telescopes need to be firmly supported on a tripod, bean bag, or clamp to be of practical value.

Many telescopes have a fixed focal length, but it is worth considering those fitted with zoom lenses, which provide more flexibility. In the past, a long focal length was achieved through long physical length, and telescopes had to be made of several extendable sections for portability. Such designs are still available today, but many modern telescopes use internal prisms to reduce length; some are very compact indeed.

As with binoculars, the brightness of the image depends, in part, on the diameter of the lens, so you will have to balance light intake with bulk. Special lenses, designated fluorite or ED, increase image brightness, but add to weight and cost.

Telescopes may be fitted with straight or angled eyepieces; the former are easier and more intuitive to "aim" at a distant

All scopes come equipped *with a screw bracket that allows them to be fixed to a standard camera tripod. Angled scopes are more comfortable for low-level viewing. This position gives the greatest stability.*

bird. Angled telescopes offer other advantages: they are far more comfortable to use when mounted on a tripod, especially when keeping low to the ground; and a view of a bird is easier to share between people of different heights.

Observing with a telescope

Getting the most from a telescope takes a little practice. Lining it up with a bird presents the first challenge because the instrument has a very narrow angle of view. The most effective technique is to look along the casing of the telescope to roughly align it with the bird, and only then to bring your eye to the eyepiece.

Always keep your eye directly in line with the eyepiece; if it is off-centre, the image you see will be vignetted or in soft focus. (This is harder than it sounds, especially if using a straight telescope fixed to a tripod.) Also, try viewing through your telescope while keeping both eyes open; this will ease eye strain and you will be aware of other birds as they enter your peripheral field of vision.

CHOOSING TELESCOPES AND ACCESSORIES

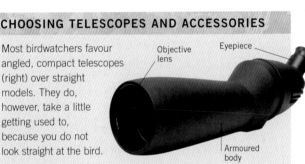

Most birdwatchers favour angled, compact telescopes (right) over straight models. They do, however, take a little getting used to, because you do not look straight at the bird.

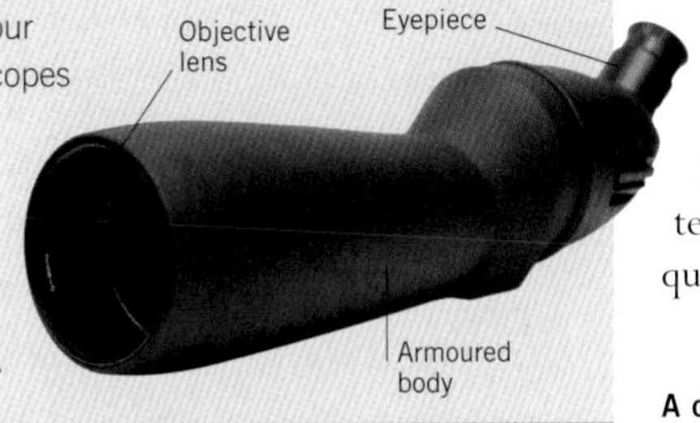

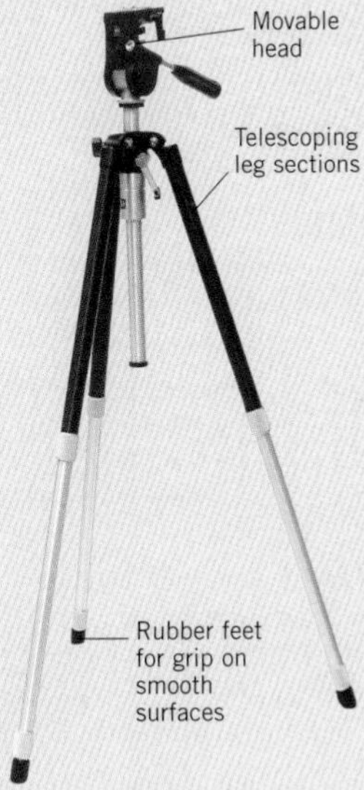

The ideal tripod *is lightweight, rigid, strong, portable, easy to set up, and tall enough for comfortable viewing. It has a "fluid head", which allows smooth movement with one control.*

Most telescopes *have changeable eyepieces. Wide-angled eyepieces of 20x to 30x are good for general use; 40x eyepieces are good for long-distance work, and zoom eyepieces give more versatility.*

MAGNIFICATION

Binoculars and telescopes magnify the image that you see with the naked eye, but will not improve the image on a dull or misty day. A standard pair of binoculars may magnify the image by eight times, while a telescope gives a far higher magnification of 30x or more. Too high a magnification, however, results in a blurred image unless the telescope can be held very steady.

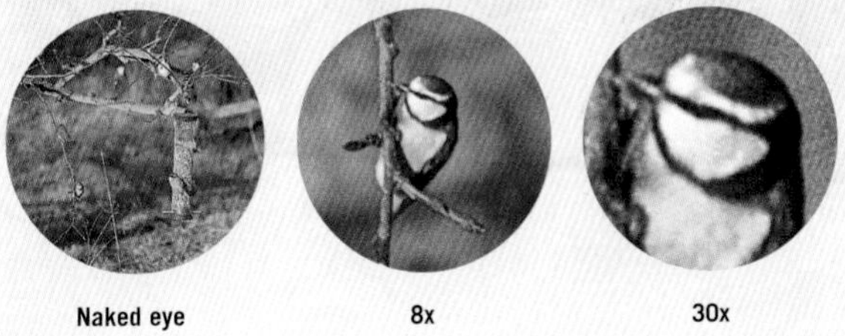

Digiscoping

The widespread use of digital cameras and digital video cameras in recent years has put still higher magnifying power in the hands of the telescope user. By attaching the zoom lens of a digital camera to the eyepiece of a telescope (see opposite), it is possible to achieve magnifications equivalent to those produced by a (very costly and cumbersome) 3,000mm lens on a conventional 35mm camera. The high quality images produced by this technique, known as digiscoping, can be viewed and edited quickly, so adding a new dimension to birdwatching.

A clamp is especially useful *for a permanent position in a hide or other observation point. The telescope can be mounted quickly when needed in a hurry and the clamp provides a very firm base.*

Setting the shutter *to a high speed (more than 1/250 second) reduces the effects of camera shake, which can be very noticeable when using a long lens. High shutter speeds also help to "freeze" the motion of birds in flight.*

Changing the aperture *(the diameter of the metal-bladed iris within the camera lens) affects the amount of light reaching the film. In tandem with shutter speed, setting the aperture gives control over exposure.*

A flashgun *can illuminate a subject in low light or complete darkness, but is just as useful in daylight, when it can light birds in deep shade, or create more pleasing effects when used to "fill in" dense shadows.*

Even equipped *with a long telephoto lens, you will need to get within a few metres of a bird to get a frame-filling shot. This will tax your field skills far more than everyday birdwatching. Sit-and-wait tactics often pay dividends.*

Exposure controls

A camera records an image when light, focused by the lens, falls on to a film (or a CCD – the digital equivalent of film). The amount of light reaching the film must be carefully controlled to achieve the correct exposure; too much light results in pale, washed out pictures (overexposure); too little light produces dark, muddy images (underexposure). Many people are content to set their camera to automatic or "program" mode and allow its onboard computer to sort out exposure and focus. In most situations this produces acceptable results, but

Photographing birds

Bird photography can become a compelling pastime, though it requires time, patience, and a little investment to achieve the best results. The key to capturing outstanding bird images is getting close. For this, you will need a telephoto lens (sometimes called a "long" lens), and a camera to which it can be fixed, or a digital camera with a long zoom range.

From the many film camera formats on offer, most bird photographers choose 35mm SLR cameras. "35mm" refers to the size of the film used in the camera, while "SLR" stands for Single Lens Reflex – meaning that you view the scene and take the photograph through one lens, so what you see in the viewfinder is (more or less) what appears in your photograph. SLR cameras are convenient because they have interchangeable lenses, so one camera body can take both wide-angle and telephoto pictures. Telephoto lenses favoured by bird photographers have focal lengths of 300 to 600mm (giving angles of view of 6° and 3°). They are capable of recording high-quality frame-filling images of birds; however, they are not only costly, but heavy and bulky.

For the photographic novice, a digital camera may be a better bet. The images it produces are visible immediately, and, with no need for film and processing, its running costs are much lower. Basic digital cameras may cost more than their film equivalents, but they put greater magnifying power at your disposal for the price.

FILM CAMERAS

35mm Single Lens Reflex cameras offer the best compromise between portability, affordability, and quality. Invest in a good long lens with a focal length of 300 or 500mm or a "long" zoom lens.

A 24mm *wide-angle lens and a medium-range zoom – say 35–105mm – plus a long telephoto will cover most photographic situations.*

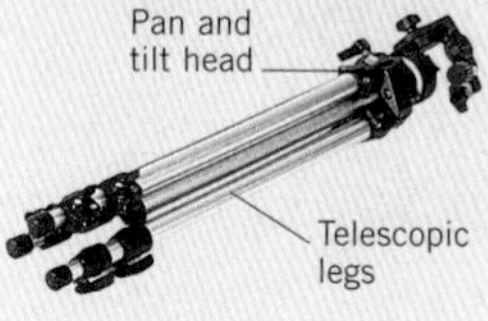

A tripod *is essential for preventing camera shake when using a long lens. Buy the heaviest and most sturdy that you can bear to carry.*

Birds will approach *a fixed hide, like this converted shed, quite boldly. Mount your camera on a sturdy tripod, and train it on a nearby feeder or bird-table.*

understanding the effects of different exposure settings on your camera will help you make more creative images. Even if you own a fully automatic camera, it is worth occasionally setting it to "manual" mode and experimenting with the exposure settings for yourself.

Making light work

Most photographs of birds are taken in natural daylight, but it is worth assessing the "quality" of the light before pressing the shutter. For example, diffuse sunlight, filtered through thin cloud or patchy leaves, is ideal for capturing a naturalistic portrait of a bird. Morning and evening light illuminates a bird from the side, adding interest (and a golden colour cast) to your pictures, while overhead light in the middle of the day tends to be less flattering.

A zoom lens *on a digital camera may magnify an object 3x, while the "digital zoom" capability adds another 4x magnification. Total zoom capacity of 12x is good enough to make frame-filling pictures of birds, albeit with some loss of quality compared to a film camera.*

Direct sunlight produces dense shadows that can appear as ugly "black holes" in a photograph; firing a flashgun set to low power can help "fill in" these shadows to produce a more balanced image. Flash can also be used to "freeze" a bird in motion.

Setting a slower shutter speed *allows a bird's movement to "paint" the scene. Used creatively, blur gives atmosphere to an otherwise ordinary image.*

Setting a wide lens *aperture gives a shallow zone of crisp focus (depth of field). This effect can help to isolate a bird against a fussy background.*

The burst of light *from a flashgun lasts as little as one ten-thousandth of a second. It freezes the fastest action and allows every feather to be seen in sharp relief.*

Understanding bird behaviour

Your garden is a behaviour laboratory. Birds visit every day, engaging in a range of activities that varies throughout the year. Keeping a close watch on these visitors reveals the complexities of their behaviour and the reasons for their sometimes odd actions.

The daily round

BIRDS ARE MOST NOTICEABLE when they are active – feeding, flying, singing, displaying, or fighting. They are especially visible in spring and summer when they must set up territories, find mates, build their nests, and tend their broods. Less regular but important behaviour includes preening and bathing. Yet even when the days are short, many birds spend a high proportion of their waking hours resting.

Birds preen *and sing in the early light of dawn. Here, a Robin scratches itself with a foot, reaching a part of its body that it cannot access with its bill.*

Cycles of activity

During a normal day outside the breeding season, a bird has two main activities. It has to feed, which it does in bouts through the day, and it must maintain its feathers in good condition by preening and bathing.

The first meal of a bird's day is particularly important because it helps replace the fat used up through the night to keep warm. However, a watch on the bird-table shows that birds are not in a hurry to start feeding in the morning. They may gather in nearby trees to preen and sing, but do not begin to feed until it is fully light. Some ornithologists think that birds delay their feeding activity because they cannot see well enough in the dim morning light to detect approaching predators, or locate food effectively.

Birds do not all become and remain active at the same times. Robins and Blackbirds, for example, are early risers, and are usually the last to disappear as dusk gathers, while gulls and Starlings leave gardens and parks early in the

A Robin, *one of the earliest risers, contributes to the dawn chorus before daybreak. A few minutes after waking up, it flies to a perch and sings for about an hour.*

Foraging is an activity *that takes up a large part of a female Blackbird's day. She does not feed continuously, but retires after each meal to rest on a perch or takes part in other activities, such as nesting, between bouts of eating.*

A Wren sunbathes *with its wings spread and body feathers raised to allow the sun's rays to penetrate. Sunbathing not only warms the body on a cold day, but is also thought to help with feather care.*

afternoon to return to their roosts when it is still light. In built-up areas that are illuminated by street and security lighting, birds may sing and sometimes even feed through the night. House Sparrows, for instance, may extend their day by catching moths attracted to street lights.

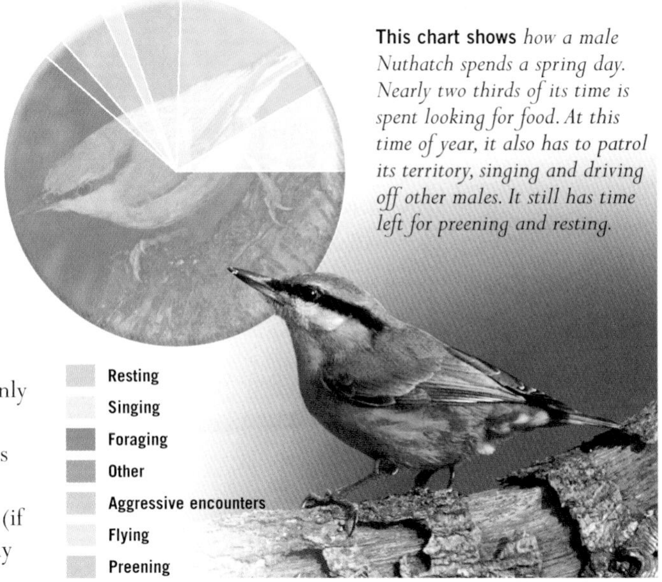

This chart shows *how a male Nuthatch spends a spring day. Nearly two thirds of its time is spent looking for food. At this time of year, it also has to patrol its territory, singing and driving off other males. It still has time left for preening and resting.*

Times of stress

A bird loses its free time twice during the year – once during the breeding season, when it struggles to feed its chicks and rear them to independence, and again in the winter, when its own survival becomes a struggle. Not only are there fewer daylight hours in the winter, but food is often in short supply and harder to find, and extra rations are needed just to maintain body temperature in cold weather. As a result, small birds may have to spend most (if not all) of their daylight hours looking for food, and many leave their roosts before sunrise in an attempt to find additional feeding time.

Keeping clean

When not feeding, birds devote much of their time to keeping their feathers in top condition. Air trapped between the feathers gives them their insulating and waterproofing qualities; when feathers are damaged, insulation and waterproofing are impaired, and flight becomes more strenuous. The barbs that hold the feather vanes together become "unzipped " by daily wear and tear, and the bird must zip them back up using its bill. Preening consists of gently nibbling or stroking the feathers one at a time with the closed bill so that splits between the barbs are zipped up. The nibbling and rubbing also removes dirt and parasites (such as feather lice and mites) and arranges feathers back into position. At intervals during preening, the bird squeezes its bill against the preen gland at the base of its tail to collect preen oil, which it spreads in a thin film over the feathers; the oil is thought to kill bacteria and fungi.

Birds dislodge external parasites from their bodies by bathing; most will ruffle their feathers in a convenient pond or puddle, but some indulge in dust baths or even "bathe" in the smoke from a chimney or fire.

This Green Woodpecker *bathes in a garden pond, but a gutter or puddle will often do. After its bath, it will fly to a safe perch and ruffle its feathers to settle them into place.*

Like other birds, *warblers set aside time every day for a thorough, systematic preen, which keeps the plumage clean and tidy. The bill – in conjunction with scratching and fluffing movements – is used to arrange the feathers.*

Outside the nesting season, *Starlings gather in the afternoon before flying in flocks to roosts where they spend the night. They also have smaller day roosts where they preen between periods of foraging.*

Annual cycle: spring

Territorial displays *are common in spring, but aggression soon subsides so that the birds can devote time to rearing their families.*

LIFE RETURNS TO THE GARDEN as the days get longer and warmer. Spring bulbs and other plants provide nectar to feed the first insects – a welcome change of diet for birds whose winter supplies of seeds are running short. The volume of song increases noticeably, signalling the start of the new breeding season.

Renewed activity

Spring is a time of change and uncertainty for garden birds. While overall air temperature rises, spells of frost and hard weather can threaten many species, especially early nesters, such as crows, pigeons, and thrushes. Without the cover of foliage, their nests are exposed to gales, highly visible to predators, and vulnerable to heavy rain, which leaves eggs and young dead in waterlogged, open, cup-shaped nests. Even nestlings in nest-boxes are not immune to cold snaps: their parents try to keep them warm by brooding for longer spells, even though they need to spend more time foraging for food for themselves just to keep alive.

Some birds that were attracted into winter gardens to feed on peanut and seed feeders begin to disperse back into the countryside to nest. The timing and duration of this exodus depends both on temperature and the availability of wild foods, particularly beech mast, and flocks of some species, such as finches and buntings, may return to the garden to feed throughout spring if wild supplies fail. Other birds migrate long distances to their summer breeding grounds, though they may linger if the weather is warm. By the end of spring, garden residents are joined by returning migrants – Chiffchaffs and Blackcaps are among the earliest to appear but they are soon joined by Swallows and martins. If the weather is poor, these birds hunt over lakes and rivers where early insects congregate, and form nesting colonies only when the weather has improved.

Throughout spring, birds are increasingly seen in pairs – arguing over territorial boundaries or in courtship. Songs and calls are used to deter rivals and establish pair-bonds, and it is the best time of year to hear the dawn chorus – not least because it is easy to be up in time for sunrise.

Birds come into *breeding condition as the days lengthen in spring, but the exact timing of egg-laying is influenced by temperature. In warm springs, Great Tits can lay as early as mid-April, but in cold years, laying may be as late as mid-May.*

WINDS OF CHANGE

Spring visitors from Africa, such as the Willow Warbler, which over-winters mainly in Ghana and the Ivory Coast, arrive in Europe from early spring. Gales can delay or accelerate their arrival. Strong southerly winds can also sweep unusual migrants into gardens – Wrynecks, Hoopoes, and Serins are all spring possibilities.

Willow Warbler

Reed Buntings *leave the winter sanctuary of the garden to nest in marshes, reedbeds, and farmland, where they are typically seen clinging to the tops of stems or low bushes.*

A few Blackcaps *spend the winter in mature, bushy western European gardens, but many more migrant birds appear in the spring, arriving from their wintering grounds in Spain, Portugal, and Africa.*

Window tapping *is an odd behaviour, most often witnessed in spring. A bird sees its reflection in a window and pecks at its apparent rival; it may return to the same spot repeatedly to investigate.*

Winter flocks *of birds, such as the Coot, break up in spring when birds pair to mate. Coots can often be seen gathering materials – large plant stems and leaves – to build their bulky nests in shallow water.*

Goldfinches *lay their eggs late in spring, by which time their neat, delicate nests of moss, grass, and spider silk are well hidden amongst the emerging leaves of trees.*

Annual cycle: summer

SUMMER SEES THE CLIMAX to the nesting season. Birds like the Starling, which lay their eggs early in the season, have completed their breeding cycle while Blackbirds, Swallows, and others are still nesting. Although insect and seed foods are plentiful, summer can be just as hard a time as winter. Heat, drought, and unseasonal weather can kill young birds and affect the ability of their parents to recover from the stresses of rearing.

A Wren returns *to the nest, laden with food. Wrens are highly active summer feeders, taking insects from low trees and shrubs.*

Times of plenty

A few Bramblings and other migrants may linger at the start of summer, but the garden now becomes the preserve of breeding populations. Sprouting foliage supports hordes of insects, spiders, and other invertebrates that most birds need to rear their young, while mown grass is a good hunting ground for thrushes and Starlings seeking earthworms and leatherjackets. If left uncut, the lawn soon becomes dotted with dandelions and clover. The flowers attract pollinating insects for wagtails, while the seeds are popular with Bullfinches and Goldfinches.

Family parties are a common sight in summer, when parents bring their broods off the nest and continue to feed them until they learn to survive on their own. Young birds, which can usually be recognized by their shorter wings and tails and high-pitched calls, may gather in conspicuous flocks. Starlings fly in tight formation and settle noisily in trees, and mixed flocks of tit species work their way through trees, often accompanied by Nuthatches and Treecreepers. Travelling in numbers gives these inexperienced birds greater safety from predators and a better chance of finding food.

As nesting comes to an end in the latter half of summer, the garden goes strangely quiet. Some birds return to the countryside while others become secretive, retiring to the undergrowth as they complete their summer moult before reappearing later with fresh winter plumage.

Nesting is timed *so that the young birds hatch when food supplies are most abundant. Different strategies have evolved in different species to maximize survival of the young. Robins lay their eggs early in the year – from March onward – so that their nestlings can be fed on the early summer flush of caterpillars from the leaves of trees.*

Spotted Flycatchers *begin laying later in the season – from late May to June. This allows their young to be fed on flying insects (expecially larger flies) that are abundant in midsummer.*

Sparrowhawks *lay their eggs in late May, but the long incubation period of up to 35 days means that the chicks do not hatch until early July. By this time, the young of other species, including tits and finches, have fledged, and they make an excellent food resource for the developing Sparrowhawk nestlings.*

WEATHER WATCH

The fortunes of garden birds are tied to the weather: a heat wave can bake the soil hard, making it difficult for thrushes to wrest worms from the ground, but hot, sultry weather is a boon for Swallows, martins, Swifts, Starlings, and gulls, which feed on swarming flies and ants. Heavy rain is disastrous for tits, which feed their young on caterpillars. The caterpillars are washed off the leaves, so parent tits are forced to search for other, less suitable, prey. This takes longer so they cannot brood the nestlings to keep them warm in the cool conditions.

Broods produced *in late summer suffer lower mortality than chicks hatching early in the season because food is more plentiful both for them and for their predators.*

Most young birds *are fed by their parents after they have left the nest. The extra food helps them complete their development and learn to feed for themselves. Their noisy begging is a common sound in the summer.*

A fledgling *Great Spotted Woodpecker accompanies its parent on the stand of a bird-table. While it is still dependent, the fledgling learns where to find food by closely observing its parent in action.*

Prolonged heat *bakes the ground hard and sends worms deeper into the soil, out of range of probing beaks. Water may also become scarce; it is essential to regularly check the levels of water in bird-baths.*

The late summer *moult, which can take several weeks to complete, is a time of stress. Flight is more strenuous and the bird needs to invest energy in the new feathers.*

Annual cycle: autumn

AUTUMN IS AN EXCELLENT TIME to observe birdlife in the garden, particularly if crops of fruit, berries, and seeds in the countryside are poor. After their summer moult, many birds are sporting new plumage, in some species making identification more difficult. A trickle of migrants passes through, and winter visitors begin to arrive, hard on the heels of departing summer species.

The size of the autumn berry *crop has a significant effect on numbers of visiting birds. Gardens with berry-bearing shrubs, such as the guelder rose, or with windfall apples, attract diverse species in years when natural foods are scarce in the countryside.*

Resumed activity

Autumn does not signal the end of the nesting season for all garden birds. Swallows, House Martins, House Sparrows, Greenfinches, and Blackbirds may have broods well into September, while Woodpigeons, Stock Doves, and Collared Doves continue nesting into October, feeding their young on "pigeon's milk" (see page 137).

Other bird activity picks up after the lull of late summer. Renewed singing by some garden species, notably Song Thrushes, Robins, Wrens, and Blue and Great Tits, builds up to a considerable chorus on fine days, while Tawny Owls are at their noisiest at this time of year. Coupled with the autumn song, there is a reappearance of courtship, territorial, and even some nesting behaviour: House Sparrows, Starlings, and Great Tits, for example, spend time investigating nest-boxes, and may even carry out some nest-building. This activity, which is more appropriate to spring, puzzles ornithologists. One theory is that it is triggered by sex hormones that begin to circulate in the blood again, after disappearing during the quiet period that follows the nesting season.

Food balance

When natural food is plentiful in woods and hedgerows, the autumn garden empties of fruit- and seed-eating birds. Beech mast attracts tits, Nuthatches, and Bramblings; conifer seeds feed Crossbills, Siskins, and woodpeckers. Thrushes, Robins, Redwings, Fieldfares, Starlings, and Woodpigeons take berries, such as haws. Trees usually produce good crops of seeds or berries only in alternate years and this affects the pattern of bird visits to the garden. In lean years, gardens fill with birds, and feeders need to be replenished frequently to keep up with demand.

Autumn provides the birdwatcher with a great diversity of species to observe, as populations of summer and winter visitors change over. One of the earliest signs is flocks of Redwings and Fieldfares flying overhead, calling to one another as they go. Stormy weather may blow migrants off course, bringing stranger sightings, perhaps of Wrynecks or Rose-coloured Starlings. Large birds, such as the White Stork or Rough-legged Buzzard, may only appear overhead but they can legitimately be added to a list of birds "seen from the garden".

Jays and other hoarding birds, *such as Coal and Marsh Tits, Nuthatches, and Great Spotted Woodpeckers, empty garden feeders extremely quickly because they cache what they do not eat on the spot.*

Swallows and House Martins *linger around gardens well into the autumn. Their departure is delayed if the weather is fine and there are plenty of flying insects to catch.*

Lesser Whitethroats *winter in Africa, south of the Sahara. They migrate south in August and September, and occasionally drop down into gardens, especially those with hedgerows and scrub, to feed on berries.*

Long-tailed Tits *return to the garden in autumn, having nested in surrounding woodland. Family parties group together to defend territories over the winter. These flocks break up again the following spring.*

Bird song returns *to the garden in autumn after the summer moult is complete. Robins are unusual because both male and female sing in defence of winter territories. Their song is a varied, melodic warble.*

By mid-autumn, *most elderberries will have been taken by birds, but blackberries, guelder rose, rosehips, hawthorn, and sloes remain until the frost softens their skins.*

Annual cycle: winter

THE WINTER IS A SEASON OF hardship for birds. The harshness of climate and shortage of food causes many birds to migrate to milder places. Within Europe, there is often a movement towards the south and west, where the oceanic climate under the influence of the Gulf Stream is less extreme than the inland continental climate. Locally, bad weather brings birds into gardens to take advantage of the food provided.

Cold and mortality

Low temperatures do not in themselves endanger birds, as long as a good supply of food is maintained. However, short winter days mean that foraging time is drastically cut, and small birds have to spend almost all of their waking hours searching for food. When supplies of food start to run short and coverings of ice and snow physically make finding food difficult, mortality rates of all birds – from Wrens to herons – can soar. This is one of the best times to attract large numbers of birds to garden feeders. Many of the incomers will be common species, but some unexpected visitors may turn up: when lakes and rivers are iced over, rare Bitterns and Water Rails may venture into gardens. Windfall apples tempt in unlikely fruit-eaters, such as as Mallards, Moorhens, and Green Woodpeckers, while the difficulty of finding prey draws Barn Owls and Buzzards closer to towns and villages.

Changing colours

A slow change comes over some birds during the course of the winter. After their late summer moult (see page 94), birds reappear with new suits of feathers – often fairly drab non-breeding plumages. Towards the end of winter, the males of some species slowly take on their courtship dress. This change does not come about through a further moult, but by the tips of the feathers wearing away to reveal brighter colours beneath. Male Chaffinches, for example, become far brighter and develop pink cheeks and slate blue heads, while their close relatives, the Bramblings, undergo an even more spectacular change when their heads and backs turn black. Starlings, of both sexes, become rather less brilliant because the pale spots decorating their non-breeding plumage wear away.

Winter Rook roosts *are organized hierarchically: the more dominant birds occupy roosts on the leeward side of trees where they get better protection from icy winds.*

RARE NORTHERN MIGRANTS

Persistent winter storms can blow coastal birds, such as the Puffin, far inland, where they can end up stranded and may even visit gardens. Disorientated and prevented from feeding (they usually catch small fish, such as sand-eels and herrings) their fat reserves soon become depleted, and the birds are too exhausted to fly. Even with assistance, their emaciated condition means that they are unlikely to survive.

Air trapped *in the feathers is a good insulator. Many birds, like this Fieldfare, fluff up their feathers in cold weather, giving them a much rounder appearance.*

Treecreepers, *along with other small birds, conserve heat by roosting in the shelter of holes and crevices. Heat losses can be cut by one-third if they roost in groups, huddling against their neighbours.*

Mistle Thrushes *and Fieldfares feed on cotoneaster berries on a snowy day. Berries are an easy and available source of winter food, but birds will lose weight if restricted to a fruit diet for long periods.*

The Reed Bunting *is traditionally a bird of reed beds and water margins. In recent years, it has begun to venture farther from water in seach of food, and can be seen in gardens at feeders and bird-tables.*

Ice prevents *water birds from feeding and allows predators to reach their roosts. In icy conditions, they often migrate to search for open water, or try to find food on land.*

Migration

BIRDS ARE ON THE MOVE throughout their lives. Every day, they may commute between their roosting and feeding grounds, and every year they may move between their summer and winter homes. These seasonal journeys vary in length. Some birds migrate from a woodland breeding place in summer to a nearby garden for winter feeding, while others travel thousands of kilometres across continents.

Swallows spend *the summer in Europe, gathering in small flocks in autumn before travelling back to their winter homes in Africa.*

Incredible journeys

Every spring, we eagerly await the return of migrant birds from their winter in warmer countries. We watch for martins, Swallows, and Swifts darting overhead, for warblers and flycatchers flitting amongst the newly opening foliage, and we listen for the first Cuckoo. Then, at the end of summer, these birds slip away again and we watch Redwings and Fieldfares arrive as they escape harsher climes.

Despite the huge expenditure of energy required to travel sometimes hundreds or thousands of kilometres, migration has clear benefits for many bird species. These mainly revolve around the need to find good supplies of food, and to exploit sources of food that are seasonally abundant. It is wrong, however, to think that they are driven to migrate by hunger. Birds prepare for migration before food runs out, eating more and laying down fat to sustain them throughout their journey. Once ready to fly, they set off when wind and weather are favourable.

Fieldfares are winter visitors *in southern and western Europe, where flocks of these large, colourful thrushes roam the countryside in search of food.*

Most small birds migrate by night and are unlikely to be seen, while larger birds travel by day. Birds leave their breeding grounds in autumn in a fairly regular order. Swifts, and other birds that rely on a healthy supply of insects, depart early, while Swallows and martins, which manage to scrape a living even when flying insects are scarce, stay longer. A change to a vegetarian diet, available when insects are in short supply, enables some warblers to delay departure for a few weeks.

In spring, birds hurry back to establish territories and make the most of the summer plenty. Swallows spread northwards through Europe as temperatures

Starlings are partial *migrants – some individuals migrate while others are resident all year round. Migrating birds stock up on berries before departure.*

increase, in a steady advance of about 40km (25 miles) per day, unless cold weather or a head-wind holds them up.

Birds are sometimes seen when they stop to rest during migration. Many of these transients or "birds of passage" are common birds, but anything may turn up, including birds from North America, central Asia, and the Arctic. Spring and autumn can therefore be exciting times of the year, offering the chance to observe bird species not usually seen in the garden. These interesting visitors may stay for a few days to feed, rest, or wait for a fair wind, before they continue on their long journeys.

In some winters, there is a sudden invasion of birds known as an "irruption". This dramatic event occurs when the food supply fails in the birds' summer homes. Waxwings, for example, irrupt from northern European forests when rowan berry crops fail, and flocks appear in more southerly gardens to eat berries or windfall fruit.

ACCIDENTAL MIGRANTS

Migrating birds can sometimes become caught up in storms and be swept far off course, appearing thousands of kilometres from their normal routes. North American species, like this Golden-winged Warbler, migrate southwards along the east coast of North America. Caught by westerly gales, they can be carried across the Atlantic and deposited on European shores.

MIGRATION ROUTES

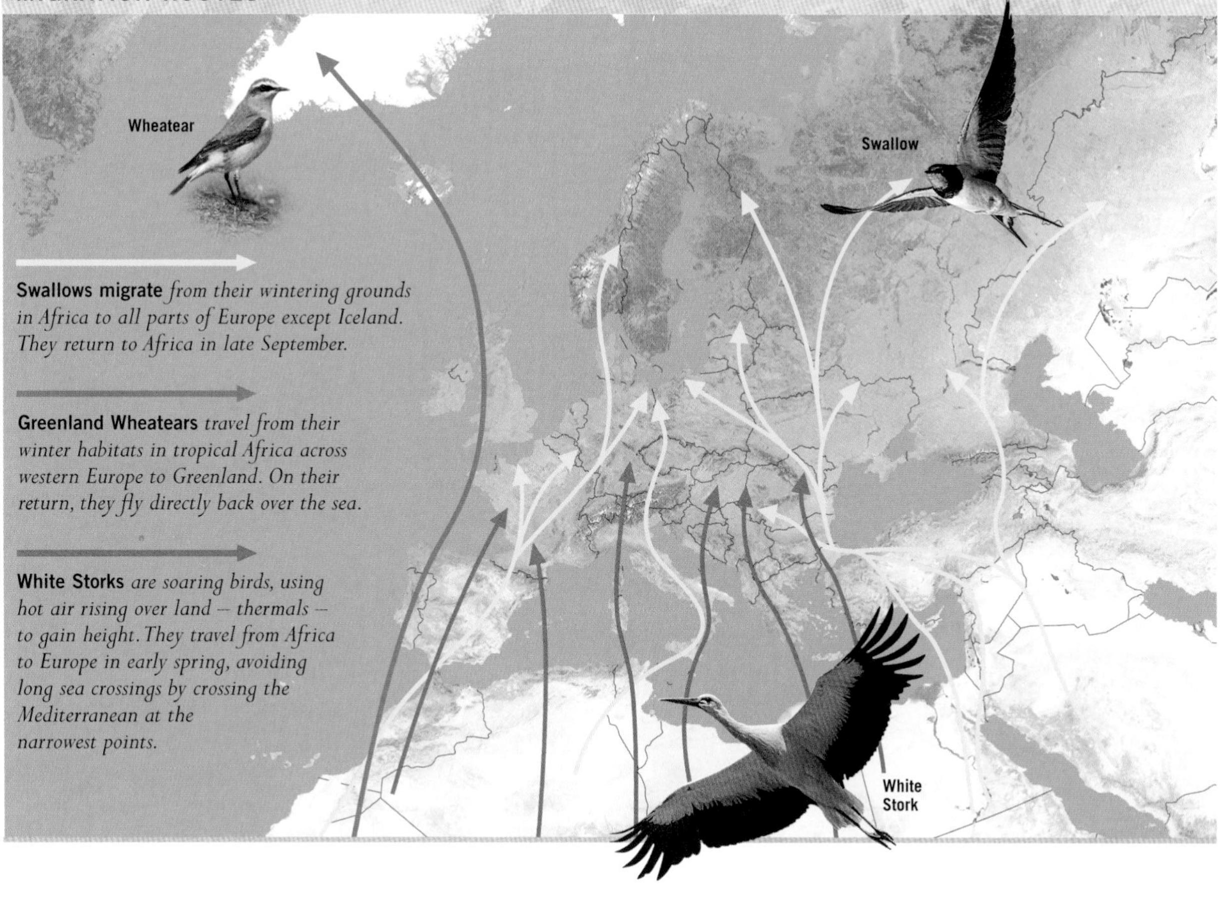

Swallows migrate *from their wintering grounds in Africa to all parts of Europe except Iceland. They return to Africa in late September.*

Greenland Wheatears *travel from their winter habitats in tropical Africa across western Europe to Greenland. On their return, they fly directly back over the sea.*

White Storks *are soaring birds, using hot air rising over land – thermals – to gain height. They travel from Africa to Europe in early spring, avoiding long sea crossings by crossing the Mediterranean at the narrowest points.*

Flying

A BIRD'S BODY is beautifully designed for flight, combining lightness with controlled muscular strength and efficient metabolism. Flight confers the great advantage of speed, but uses large amounts of energy (about 10–15 times as much as walking) so birds must find plenty of food to fuel their activity. Through evolution, the shape of the wings and tail of each species has been matched to a specific lifestyle.

Keeping airborne

Some birds, such as Wrens and Mallards, must flap their wings continuously to stay in the air, but many others reduce the cost of flight by gliding whenever possible. Economy is more important than speed when searching for food or travelling long distances, so while gulls flap regularly when flying from their roosts to feeding grounds, they glide in slow, energy-saving circles when scanning the ground for food. Rooks circle on outstretched wings in thermals – rising air found over cliffs and towns. Birds like tits, finches, and Starlings cannot glide well enough to exploit thermals, but save energy by using "bounding" flight, closing their wings completely between flaps to reduce drag.

The spread wing *and tail feathers of this Starling give maximum aerodynamic control for landing at the nest.*

AIR SPEEDS

Most birds have two or sometimes three flight speeds. A bird that normally flies at 30km/h (19mph), may average 40km/h (25mph) on migration and as much as 50km/h (31mph) when evading a predator. The table below gives average flight speeds for several European species.

Blue tit	29km/h (18mph)	**Heron**	44km/h (27mph)
Swallow	32km/h (20mph)	**Sparrowhawk**	44km/h (27mph)
Wren	32km/h (20mph)	**Carrion Crow**	50km/h (31mph)
Starling	34km/h (21mph)	**Pheasant**	55km/h (34mph)
Herring Gull	40km/h (25mph)	**Woodpigeon**	61km/h (38mph)
Swift	40km/h (25mph)	**Mallard**	68km/h (42mph)

Take-off and flight control

Like an aeroplane, a bird has to achieve a minimum speed to become airborne. From a standing start, the wings are swept to and fro to create an airflow over the flight surfaces, as the bird leaps into the air. Deep wing beats get the bird hovering just clear of the ground for a split-second before it lifts away. Larger birds, which cannot generate enough power to hover, employ a different strategy; they drop off a perch, spread their wings, and allow gravity to do the work, or, if on the ground, run a few steps to take off. When landing, the bird has to lose as much speed as possible without falling out of the air. Small birds slow down until they are hovering on whirring wings,

Barn Owls have large, *broad, rounded wings which enable them to fly at low speeds with little effort. Their special downy flight feathers result in near-silent flight.*

Large birds, such as *the Grey Heron, require huge amounts of energy to take off from the ground. Once in flight, it moves with slow, leisurely wing beats and occasional glides. The neck is retracted into its shoulders, its legs are trailing, and its broad, rounded wings appear bowed.*

Pheasants spend *most of their time on the ground. Occasionally they need to fly quickly to escape a predator. They are able to catapult straight into the air, powered by short, broad wings. Their muscles are designed for short bursts of speed.*

Small birds *can hover momentarily while foraging or feeding their young. Larger birds, such as the Kestrel, "hover" or remain in place by flying into the wind at a speed equal to that of the wind.*

and then gently touch down. Larger birds, when landing on a perch, swoop below it and then climb to lose speed. Alternatively, they land on the ground with a thump and run for a short distance to lose momentum.

A bird's flying style has important, but subtle, effects on its biology. The Swift and the Swallow, for example, are similar shaped birds. The Swift hunts for flying insects by circling around in the air, alternating bursts of flickering wing beats with long glides, while the Swallow often flies near the ground with a less economical, flapping flight. Yet the Swallow is the more agile hunter because its longer tail makes it more manoeuvrable so it can pursue and catch larger and faster insects. This explains why Swallows arrive in Europe before Swifts, depart for Africa after them, and rear more young during the breeding season.

Feeding

Knowledge of *the varied feeding strategies employed by different species allows us to attract a wider range of birds to our homes.*

A BIRD'S ENERGY REQUIREMENTS are high, and finding adequate supplies of food is vital for survival. Food is the fuel required for growth and development, movement, and keeping warm. In the nesting season, the search for food is particularly intense as males engage in energetic courtship and territorial behaviour, females produce and incubate eggs, and parents collect food to sustain both themselves and their young.

Bill shape

Different species are adapted to take advantage of a wide range of available foods. Looking at the size and shape of a bird's bill often gives the best clue as to its diet. Starlings, Blackbirds, and gulls have "general-purpose" bills that enable them to take a wide variety of foods, but other birds are equipped with specialized bills, that enable them to exploit certain types of food with great efficiency. In the finch family, for example, Siskins have slender bills for probing deep into the heads of thistles to extract seeds, while Bullfinches have short, sharp-edged bills that are effective at plucking buds, crushing and peeling seeds and fruits, and even shelling small snails. Bullfinches find picking up loose seeds difficult, however, whereas Bramblings have long bills for pecking at seeds on the ground but are unable to deal with seedheads.

The Blackbird *has a general-purpose bill, which suits its highly varied diet.*

The Blue Tit's *short bill is perfect for picking tiny insects out of crevices.*

The Reed Warbler *uses its long, fine bill for picking up caterpillars and other insects.*

The Chaffinch *manipulates seeds in its conical bill, removing the husks.*

The Mallard's *broad bill is fringed with fine plates that sieve food from water.*

Fruit-eating *species often feed in flocks, like this group of juvenile Blackbirds feasting on windfall apples.*

Spotted Flycatchers *prefer flies of bluebottle size, because they are easily caught and swallowed. Larger butterflies and bees are usually ignored because they take longer to deal with.*

The Blackcap adapts its diet *to take advantage of foods that are abundant at different times of year. Like many warblers and tits, it feeds principally on insects during the spring and summer (left), changing to fruits, seeds, and nuts from late summer onwards (right).*

The economics of feeding

A bird's aim is to get the most nutrition for the least effort, and it will change its feeding strategy to adapt to changing environmental conditions. Food that is not used to fuel activity is stored in the body as fat; these reserves are used in times of scarcity, and for energy-intensive activities, such as breeding and migration.

Typically, birds focus their attention on the best-available food at any time, feeding until this resource is exhausted. Bullfinches, for example, take the seeds of ash, bramble, dock, and nettle, and only when these crops are finished towards the end of winter will they descend upon orchards. Here, they must eat huge numbers of nutrient-poor buds – up to 30 buds per minute – just to stay alive.

Seeds and invertebrates are the food of choice for many birds because they are rich in carbohydrates, fats, and proteins. However, birds that normally rely on these foods may choose to gorge on fruit when there is a dense, easily-gathered crop. The time saved by not having to seach for food more than compensates for the lower nutritional value of the fruit. When a bird's usual foods are in short supply, it will turn to stranger alternatives: hungry Fieldfares, for example, will attack turnips and, during dry spells, Blackbirds feed their nestlings on crusts of white bread because they cannot find worms.

Some species provide for lean periods by hoarding food; this behaviour is often seen in the Coal and Marsh Tits, and the Nuthatch, all of which carry off nuts and store them in a

FEEDING STYLES

The Sparrowhawk *hunts in the air for smaller birds, such as tits. Quarry is eaten on the ground or on a stump, the hawk standing with both feet on its victim, drooping its wings to form a "tent".*

The Canada Goose *is one of few large vegetarian birds that can survive on nutrient-poor grasses, rushes, leaves, and stems. It uses its broad bill to pull up roots and crush harder vegetable matter.*

The Willow Warbler *feeds by taking insects and invertebrates from leaves and tree trunks. It favours flies, caterpillars, beetles, and midges, but it will happily take berries at the end of summer.*

The Snow Bunting *eats seeds, mainly from plants of the bistort family, manipulating them in its bill to remove the inedible husks. It takes insects too, but only in the breeding season.*

The Linnet *has a small, fine bill that can pick tiny seeds from the ground or from plants. It prefers the seeds of common weeds, such as fat hen, chickweed, dandelion, and buttercup.*

A Nuthatch *searches for a crevice to store a nut. It hammers the nut into place and covers it with moss. The crevice is also used as a vice, allowing the bird to smash the nut to get at its flesh.*

variety of hiding places. Nuts are the most usual food to be hidden because they are nutritious and keep well, but these birds also store insects, and members of the crow family may bury bread, meat, and other scraps. Hidden food may be left for weeks before the owner returns to claim it; biologists believe that a bird remembers the exact location of its food cache by reference to nearby landmarks.

New foods

The diets of many common garden species have changed over the years as birds have learned to exploit new food sources. Blackbirds, Dunnocks, and Chaffinches, which usually feed on the ground, have learned to extract food from hanging feeders by perching on them or hovering beside them. It is likely that they first discovered this new food source by trial-and-error and were later copied by their offspring and other members of the flock.

Sometimes an entirely new feeding habit crops up. The Great Spotted Woodpecker, for example, usually hunts by chiselling into wood to expose insects hiding within, but there are recent records of woodpeckers feeding flycatcher-style, by picking flying insects from the air. Perhaps the most famous example of birds adapting their diet to changing circumstances is that of cream-stealing from milk bottles. Milk bottles with cardboard or foil tops are pierced by Blue and Great Tits, Magpies, and even Great Spotted Woodpeckers, which add the cream to their diet. This habit probably started at several places independently as the birds punched through the caps using the same technique as they apply to hammering open nuts.

Birds and fruit

Many gardeners become despondent when their prize crop of fruit is raided by birds just as it begins to ripen, but the fact is that fruit is designed precisely to be eaten by birds. From cherries and elderberries in summer to holly and ivy in winter, fruits provide birds with food for a large part of the year, and in return, birds provide fruit trees and bushes with an excellent means of dispersing their seed. The fleshy pulp of each fruit contains starchy sugars that protect the seed within. A glossy, colourful coat makes the whole package more visible and attractive to birds – such as thrushes, warblers like the Blackcap and Garden Warbler, Starlings, and members of the crow family – which eat the fruit and then disperse the undigested seeds in their droppings. In most cases, the relationship between birds and plants is mutually beneficial, but co-operation breaks down in the case of tough-billed species, such as finches, tits, and Woodpigeons. These birds break open and destroy plant seed, as well as taking the fruit. Not to be outsmarted, plants like the hawthorn produce seeds tough enough to withstand the digestive system of almost any bird, while yew seeds are coated with an unpalatable poison that causes the bird to spit out rather than swallow the seed.

Specialist feeders *need special consideration in the garden. Planting teazel will attract Goldfinches (above), while mature conifers, such as pine, larch, and spruce will draw in Crossbills (left).*

FOOD AND HUMAN ACTIVITY

Refuse tips *provide Herring Gulls with easy pickings. Hundreds gather every day, sometimes having flown many kilometres from their roosts. These huge supplies of food have caused populations of gulls, and other scavengers, to increase dramatically. Some become pests when they turn to other sources of food and create a nuisance by fouling.*

Commercial fishing *activity has increased dramatically since the end of the 19th century. The intestines of gutted fish from a catch are discarded in enormous quantities, providing many scavenging opportunities. The rapid increase in populations of Fulmars, Gannets, and several gull species is often attributed to this artificial source of food.*

Earthworms and other insects *are a major part of the Blackbird's diet. Originally a woodland bird, this versatile species adapted its natural foraging behaviour on woodland floors to exploit food sources in new habitats, such as gardens. It hops alongside gardeners, for example, to pick off insects unearthed by their spades and forks.*

Fruits, and especially berries, are an important source of winter food for many birds, and one of the most delightful sights of the season is to see a crowd of Fieldfares or Blackbirds at work in a holly tree or dotted along a hawthorn hedge. Irruptions of Waxwings can be equally spectacular, as these birds can strip 500 cotoneaster (or similar) berries apiece in the course of a single day. Sometimes a Mistle Thrush or Fieldfare attempts to defend its private fruit tree against all comers. The effort is worthwhile because the bird stands to keep its secure food supply, but it may be overwhelmed if a flock of fruit-eaters invades. Then the "owner" has no option but to join them in stripping the tree of its fruit as fast as possible.

Taking on water

Although birds do not sweat and their excretory systems are designed to conserve fluid, they constantly lose water through respiration and in their droppings. Some water is released when metabolizing or "burning" fat, so birds can survive for a while on dry seeds; and insectivorous birds take in water with their juicy food. Nevertheless, all birds need regular topping-up with water and, in warm weather, they may need to drink several times a day. Most garden birds employ one of two drinking techniques (see below). Swallows, however, are an exception; they drink at ponds and lakes by swooping over the surface and taking a mouthful of water without landing.

Birds like the Thrush, *which feed on juicy foods, such as earthworms, only need to drink water in the hottest conditions.*

Most garden birds, *such as this Starling, drink by taking a sip from a pool and then tilting their heads back to swallow.*

Pigeons and doves *drink by dipping their bills in a pool and sucking up the water, as if through a straw.*

Voice

VOCAL COMMUNICATION between birds of the same species is often surprisingly sophisticated. They use sometimes astonishingly intricate songs to establish territories, deter rivals, and attract mates, the subtleties of which are largely indistinguishable by the human ear. Many birds also have an extensive "vocabulary" of basic calls, used especially when they are living together in flocks or as families.

Nightingales are seldom *seen, preferring to hide in dense cover, but their presence is betrayed by their distinctive, rich song.*

The meaning of song

Song varies greatly between birds, from rich and varied repertoires to sequences of simple notes, but all species use it to broadcast one of two basic messages: "Go away!" (to repel rivals) or "Come here!" (to attract a mate). Singing is largely a male activity, and is most intense at the start of the breeding season, when birds are setting up territories. Song is used by males to establish boundaries and to defend their spaces, and they sing vehemently if a stranger or potential threat approaches. When a bird's territory is part of the garden, this behaviour can easily be observed. You may see a male Starling in spring, for example, singing loudly from a corner of your roof to broadcast his presence.

For many species, song is not only important for defending a territory, but is also the principal method used to attract a mate. Ornithologists believe that females of some species, such as Robins and Dunnocks, select their mates on the quality of their songs. This may perhaps be because the songsters with the largest repertoires are the healthiest males or those with territories with plenty of food, so they promise to be the best providers for a family. A rich and varied song may also be the sound equivalent of elaborate plumage – like the peacock's train – designed to dazzle the female and induce her to accept the male. For some species, singing reduces or stops completely once a pair has formed, while others continue as a means of strengthening the pair-bond.

The Skylark *delivers its warbling song while in special "song-flights". After take-off, it spirals steeply upwards, singing loudly. It descends more slowly, gliding down in larger, slower spirals.*

Some species adopt *a characteristic pose when singing, which can be a useful aid to identification. The Wren, for example, stands upright, with its tail held rigidly cocked, to deliver its powerful, trilling song.*

The Greater Spotted Woodpecker's *"song" is not made vocally but by repeatedly striking a tree trunk or branch with its bill. It "drums" in a series of short bursts, each lasting less than a second, to announce its presence in spring.*

A Mallard duck *keeps her brood together with quiet quacks, which the young learn to recognize before they hatch out of the egg. The ducklings utter high-pitched cheeping to keep in touch with their mother.*

Rooks and crows *can be hard to distinguish at a distance and both call with loud caws. To tell them apart, watch as they call: Rooks bow and raise their tails while cawing, while crows raise and lower their heads.*

A bird's song is partly inherited from its parents but is also learnt from other birds that it hears, sometimes even while still in the nest. A bird grows up listening to the males of its species singing in neighbouring territories and uses the memory of their notes to compose its own song.

Communicating with calls

Bird calls are distinct from song. They are simple sounds, used throughout the year, that are delivered by a bird to coordinate the behaviour of others by communicating intentions or feelings. The Great Tit, for example, has over a dozen different calls, all of which convey different meanings and are used in different contexts. The simplest calls are the notes used by a bird to broadcast its position, so that individuals in a flock can keep in touch. As a small flock of tits make their way along a hedge searching for insects, for example, they deliver shrill notes to keep members of the flock together while they are out of each other's sight.

Alarm calls are used to alert others to a potential threat. When a cat tries to sneak up on a bird-table, its attempt to catch a feeding bird is often frustrated by a simple, harsh "*chat*" call from a vigilant neighbour. Birds of all species recognize this sound and, as soon as the call is uttered, they fly up to safety, thus ruining the chances of the cat reaching its prey. This early-warning system is sophisticated, and takes into account the nature of the threat. If a hawk approaches, birds retreat into foliage and deliver a different alarm call – a thin "*seee*" – that warns of danger overhead. Unlike the warning given in response to the cat, this alarm call is a type of sound that is hard to pinpoint, so birds sounding it do not give away their positions and put themselves in danger.

SONG-POSTS

The Song Thrush has a musical, penetrating song, consisting of a variable combination of short, repeated phrases. The male advertises his territory by delivering this complex song from prominent, high vantage points, such as the tops of trees or the corners of rooftops. He returns regularly to the same spots, or "song-posts". By observing the birds singing in your garden over a few weeks and recording where you see each bird singing from, you will gradually be able to build up a rough map, like the one below, of the song-posts around your garden.

By singing *from prominent perches around the garden, the Song Thrush defines the borders of its territory.*

Territory

A TERRITORY IS A PATCH OF GROUND that a bird defends against intruders to preserve a precious commodity – typically food or a place to breed. Territories are usually held only for the duration of the breeding season. The Tawny Owl, however, defends its territory throughout its adult life, while a wintering Fieldfare defends a bush-sized territory only as long as it carries a crop of berries.

A male Great Tit *shows off his broad, black breast-stripe to threaten an intruder.*

Size and survival

Defending a territory costs time and energy. Yet many birds are prepared to make the investment because having exclusive rights to a feeding and nesting area is invaluable – indeed personal survival and successful breeding may be impossible without it. Territorial behaviour also improves survival rates by helping birds to avoid predators. Consider a nest robber, such as a Magpie: when it locates a nest, it will take eggs and then search nearby for more of the same; it is far less likely to be successful if birds hold territories that separate their nest sites.

The territories held by many garden birds tend to be large in area, simply because they need to contain sufficient food for the breeding pair plus their offspring. A pair of thrushes, tits, or Wrens, for example, holds an area that covers several suburban gardens (this explains why there are fewer birds to be seen in a garden during the breeding season than at any other time of year). Other species hold smaller territories, and must venture beyond their boundaries in search of food. Some hole-nesting species, including Starlings, and colonial birds like gulls, defend only small areas in the immediate vicinity of their nests.

The sizes of territories held by birds of one species are similar, but their exact extent depends on the abundance of food. In years of plenty, birds need less space and so defend smaller territories, with the result that more birds can squeeze into a given area. When food is scarce, territories must be larger, so fewer birds are able to breed.

Many species conduct *territorial "song fights", matching the song of their rivals for several minutes; these help to set the boundaries of the territories.*

Setting up a territory

Competition for breeding space is fierce amongst birds, so males begin to stake out their territories as soon as the weather improves after winter. Among migrant species, the males return before the females in order to claim their space. Territories are usually defended by the male alone,

TERRITORY SIZE

The extent of a territory varies greatly between species, and is elastic within a species, depending on habitat quality.

	25–30 ha (65–75 acres)	**Tawny Owls** *hold their large territories for life. They become familiar with the terrain and move with ease in darkness.*
	1–1½ ha (2½–3½ acres)	**Male and female Robins** *have separate territories in winter, but meet to establish a mutual breeding territory.*
	½–1 ha (1–2½ acres)	**Blackbirds** *defend territories that meet all their needs in the breeding season, but relinquish them in winter.*
	1 sq. m (1¼ sq. yd)	**Starlings** *defend the immediate area around the nest, but remain sociable when feeding in large flocks.*
	Nest only	**Pairs of Swifts** *defend a small area around their nesting cavity. It is impossible for them to defend a feeding territory in the air.*

Two Redwings dispute *the ownership of some windfall apples. If more birds arrive to feed, they will discontinue their argument and join in the group feeding.*

Two Greenfinches *fight for dominance. A junior bird recognizes its inferiority and retreats before a fight starts, but fights between birds of equal rank can be fierce.*

A Barn Owl *surveys its territory from the entrance to its nest. It defends a small area around its nest and roost but its hunting ground overlaps those of its neighbours.*

but the female may occasionally help. The male deters rivals through territorial singing, aggressive displays, and sometimes by fighting. Physical contact between birds is most common when they first assert their ownership of a patch; after a short period, neighbours recognize one another, and warning songs and displays are sufficient to deter intruders.

Maintaining boundaries

It is possible to map the boundaries of bird territories in your own garden. Keep a look out for song-posts (see page 109), which are typically located on the borders, and make a note of locations where you spot disputes between neighbours. Sometimes, however, the extent of a territory is not clear. Late in the breeding season, once a territory has been established for some time, the resident bird often becomes tolerant of neighbours encroaching on his space. This is why two male Blackbirds can be seen gathering food for their nestlings on the same patch of lawn. In other cases, there may be a "no-man's-land" between widely-spaced territories.

Non-breeding territories

Most territories are abandoned at the end of the breeding season but non-breeding birds will also defend space. Robins, Wrens, Pied Wagtails, and Kestrels, for example, hold feeding territories in the winter, and Fieldfares, Redwings, and Mistle Thrushes may defend trees or bushes containing crops of fruit. Roosting territories are defended by Starlings outside the breeding season. These birds can be seen jostling for space when they line up on buildings as night falls.

Flocks

WHILE SOME BIRDS are seen only in ones or twos, others live or feed in large flocks. Vast groups of many millions of Bramblings have been seen feeding on beech mast in German and Swiss forests, for example, while Long-tailed Tits form extended family groups to search for food and to roost. Co-operation confers distinct advantages, but living in flocks also has its drawbacks.

Starlings space out *evenly along a roof and chimneys. The distance between birds prevents them pecking at one another and preserves harmony.*

Keeping a distance

All birds maintain a clear personal space around themselves – the "individual distance" – that prevents collisions when a flock takes to the air and minimizes conflict and disturbance when feeding. Starlings, for example, space themselves out on a lawn when hunting so that each bird can creep up on worms undetected. The extent of a bird's individual distance depends on its circumstances and lifestyle, and on its place in the pecking order, established through a series of skirmishes. Individual distance is sometimes reduced to allow contact, such as when mating or huddling for warmth in a roost, and species that are normally solitary sometimes group together for specific purposes; Redwings, for example, feed singly, but form loose flocks when migrating.

Avoiding predators and finding food

In some ways, flocks can be thought of as a single organism, feeding, moving, and surviving together. There are many advantages to communal living. For a start, a bird in a flock is less likely to be taken by a predator than a solitary individual. Many pairs of eyes can keep careful watch for approaching danger, and flocks have been shown to take off fractionally sooner than single birds when threatened. Flocks confuse and deter predators. A diving hawk knows that it could get damaged in a collision with birds in a flock, and it is hard for the hawk to concentrate its attack on a single target if surrounded by many others.

Another advantage of living in a flock is economy in feeding. Birds need to spend less time scanning their surroundings for danger and so can devote more energy to the important task of feeding. Finding food also

A flock of Chaffinches *feeds on fallen seeds. The birds keep their distance from one another so they can feed peacefully, but dominant birds make sure they get the lion's share.*

becomes more economical, because rather than wasting precious time searching for food singly, it is far easier to keep an eye out for neighbours who have a good supply, and simply fly over to join them. Flocking is a particularly useful strategy in winter when food is especially hard to find. Mixed flocks of tits, Goldcrests, and Treecreepers are often seen foraging together. If one bird finds an aphid skulking in the foliage, others will search nearby leaves, so making the most of highly localized food sources.

Where food *or feeding space is limited, higher ranking Greenfinches displace their rivals.*

Flocks on the move

Many birds form flocks in order to migrate, but the exact advantages of travelling in a group are unclear. Avoidance of predators is an unlikely explanation, because most birds migrate at night, but travelling in flocks may make it easier for juvenile birds to find their way, particularly if experienced "pathfinder" birds are in the group. Another explanation is aerodynamics; individual birds expend less energy when moving in a group than singly because aerodynamic drag is reduced.

Living alone

Under some circumstances, living and feeding alone is better than being part of a flock. If food is thinly but evenly spread, for example, it is more efficient to be alone, getting to know the best places to search and defending good feeding grounds against rivals. Some birds benefit from both strategies, switching from flocking to living alone as their circumstances change.

House Sparrows *are gregarious birds that live in small, loose colonies. Here, a group of sparrows settles down to roost in an urban tree on a winter's night.*

Collisions are rare *as a tightly packed flock of Starlings circles before going to roost. The birds are alert to the slightest movements of others. The flock wheels in precision when one or two birds decide to alter course, and a wave of movement passes along the mass of birds.*

Courtship

PARADOXICALLY, COURTSHIP AND PAIR-FORMATION have much in common with territorial behaviour – the songs and displays used in defending territories are often the same as those used to attract a mate. Courtship involves more than bringing birds of two sexes together. It allows birds to select the best partner, and, by feeding their mate during courtship, males demonstrate their ability to provide for the family.

The size of a male sparrow's *black "bib" indicates his status. Females look out for this marking when selecting a mate.*

Prepared for parenting

Birds normally maintain a certain amount of space between one another in order to prevent conflict (see page 112). But for breeding to take place, a male and female must come into intimate contact, first to fertilize the eggs and then to feed and care for their eggs and nestlings. Courtship is the very necessary process that breaks down the barriers between the birds by reducing their natural aggression towards one another.

Behaviour related to courtship is very distinctive. For most of the year, birds keep a deliberately low profile to avoid predators, but when courting, males make themselves obvious to attract females. This is a risky strategy, but one that brings a rich reward – successful reproduction.

At the beginning of the breeding season, males typically start by attacking females, simply because their instinct is to drive intruders from their territories. Females overcome this aggression by holding their ground and acting submissively, so gradually establishing their presence. The males switch to courtship behaviour and the bond between the pair begins to form: in some species, this is almost instantaneous, but in others, it may take more than a week.

Choosing a mate

One of the functions of courtship is to let a bird choose the best possible mate. The selection is, as a rule, carried out by the female birds. They assess males according to several criteria – including quality of song and display ritual, size, and colour – that indicate individuals with good genes and parenting skills. One of the attributes that a female bird looks for in a potential mate is age: an older, more experienced male has already proved his ability to survive hard times and find food efficiently, so is likely to make a good father. Mature males may signal their age with a more elaborate song than younger birds; and older males tend to display more vigorously and pursue females with more determination than younger birds. An older male Chaffinch will, for example, chase a female across neighbouring territories in order to entice her to come back to his territory.

Female Swallows assess the suitability of males by the length of their tail

Collared Doves *pair after the male advertises his presence to a female, and then impresses her with his display flights.*

feathers, while for a female Wren, the main factor for choosing a mate is his skill at nest-building, and she prefers a nest that is hidden from predators.

A female bird does not necessarily choose to stay with the first male to court her; she may visit several before making a choice. If the female pairs with a male in one breeding season, it is likely that she will pair again with him in the next, if only because the two birds return to the same place to nest and so meet again. Familiarity and experience with last year's partner help courtship to proceed rapidly and nesting to start early. This is an advantage in some species, such as tits, because the earliest clutches of eggs yield the most young.

Courtship feeding

Male birds of diverse species present females with gifts of food. Some ornithologists believe that this "courtship feeding" helps to strengthen the bond between the pair, but it is also another way for a female to assess the qualities of a prospective mate – a male that brings her plenty of food will almost certainly also be good at feeding her young.

Courtship feeding has another, very practical, function: providing the female with the extra food she needs for breeding. A female tit, for example, requires 40 per cent more food than normal in order to form her eggs, so the extra meals provided by her mate are a vital supplement to her diet. Courtship feeding continues during incubation, when it helps to reduce the time that the female has to spend away from the nest to find food herself. In this way, it helps prevent the eggs from losing valuable heat.

PAIRING UP

Some birds pair for a single season, while others seek out the same mate, year after year. Dunnocks have two or three partners simultaneously, while Mute Swans pair for life. In most species, once the birds have paired, they are inseparable before egg-laying; they feed and roost together, and male songbirds follow their mates while they are collecting nest material. This is not so much a sign of devotion as of jealousy. The male guards his mate to ensure that no other male can court her and that he alone will be the father of her eggs. On the other hand, he will take advantage of any lapses in his neighbour's vigilance to cuckold him.

The Black-headed Gull *is monogamous, at least for one season, and birds frequently pair with last season's mate.*

After pair formation, *but before egg laying, the male Mallard follows his mate closely, never letting her out of his sight.*

A male Starling *sings from a perch to attact a mate, slowly beating his wings. In intense courtship song, his throat feathers are puffed out.*

A female Robin *accepts an offering from her mate. Courtship feeding begins a few days after the female's completion of the nest and continues through laying and incubation.*

Mutual preening *(also called allopreening), seen here in a pair of Moorhens, helps to maintain the pair bond as well as serving a necessary grooming function.*

Nesting

NESTING AND RAISING OFFSPRING are key events in the life of a bird. Acting by instinct, it must make a nest, incubate the eggs, and then rear its family until they become independent. As a rule, birds that leave the nest shortly after hatching – such as Mallards and Pheasants – have simple nests, often no more than a scrape in the ground, while those that remain in the nest until they can fly have more elaborate structures.

Male tits check out *potential nest sites from autumn onwards. The female eventually chooses one of the several alternatives her mate has found, and roosts in it for some time before she starts to build the nest.*

Site selection

In late winter and spring, garden birds can often be seen hopping from twig to twig along hedges or among bushes and climbers. Most of these birds are foraging for food, but some will certainly be prospecting for nest sites.

In the majority of species, choosing the nest site and building the nest are the responsibilities of the female. For hole-nesting tits, Starlings, Pied Flycatchers, and Redstarts, however, it is the male that chooses the nest site, and with Wrens, males carry out much of the nest construction.

Wrens usually nest under overhangs in banks or above streams, while Robins build their nests in low vegetation or in hollows in thickets. However, how a bird selects its nest site remains something of a mystery. It probably looks out for a suitable configuration of twigs or some other foundation that will give a solid base to the nest. Protection from predators and shelter from the elements are other considerations, although birds often nest in surprisingly exposed places (Blackbirds, for example, may nest on bare window ledges). This may be either because the builder is inexperienced or because there is a shortage of suitable sites – a situation that occurs in gardens where overzealous pruning has removed undergrowth and tangled foliage.

The nest *of the Long-tailed Tit (right) is a ball of moss, hair, and lichen, bound with spiders' web. The nesting pair shares the task of collecting more than 1,000 feathers (above), which are used to line the nest. The result is a well-insulated nursery that is elastic enough to accommodate the growing brood.*

Nest construction

Nests come in all shapes and sizes – from the bulky stick structures of Rooks and Herons to the intricate balls of lichen, cobwebs, and feathers built by Long-tailed Tits. Most common garden birds build cup-shaped nests, but several kinds prefer to nest in holes. Nests are built using only the bill (sometimes assisted by the feet) as a tool, and can take up to three weeks to complete. As a rule, building a nest takes longer at the start of the season because work may have to be suspended in cold weather.

The most difficult part of nest construction is making the foundation – providing a firm anchor for the nest. When a female Chaffinch starts building a nest, she first makes secure anchor points by wrapping strands of spiders' web around twigs. She then adds moss and grass, until she has built up a firm cushion. Sitting on this pad, the bird works still more material into place before forming the cup shape of the nest by pushing with her breast and scrabbling with her feet until the materials become felted together.

Considering the time and energy invested in building a nest, it is surprising that very few are used for more than one brood, even if subsequent broods follow in the same year. Each brood gets a brand new nest, probably to minimize the problems caused by fleas and other nest parasites, or simply because the nest is squashed by the first set of nestlings.

Most nests do not survive the wind and rain of winter, although Rooks and House Martins regularly refurbish their old nests in spring.

A Lesser Spotted *Woodpecker makes a nest hole in a dead tree. Male and female excavate the cavity, which is 21cm (8in) deep, with an entrance hole roughly 3.5cm (1¼in) in diameter.*

Eggs and laying

Formation of the eggs inside the female's body starts several days before laying. The fertilized eggs, consisting mainly of yolk, move down the oviduct where they are coated in albumen (the egg white) and the shell is added. Producing eggs places great demands on the female: so much calcium is required to build the shell that the bird has to "borrow" some of the precious mineral from her bones. It is not surprising that females of some species become less active before laying and roost at night in the nest so that they use less energy to keep warm.

Usually, a few days pass between building the nest and the start of egg-laying, during which time the female concentrates on feeding. Most garden birds lay their eggs in the morning at 24-hour intervals, but herons, owls, and

NEST DESIGNS

A Wren's nest *fits snugly into a cavity. It is a domed structure of grass, leaves, and moss built by the male and lined with feathers and hair by the female. The site of the nest varies from the inside of a shed, a hole in a wall, the fork of a tree, or, as here, inside the pocket of an old coat.*

The outer *foundations of a Rook's nest are made of large sticks. Inside is a layer of pliable twigs and a lining of leaves and soil. The sticks are gathered from the ground or broken off trees or stolen from other nests. The birds must guard their nest to deter nest material thieves.*

House Martins *build their nests under the eaves of a roof. The pair spend days collecting hundreds of balls of wet mud from the edges of a pond or puddle and sticking them together over a framework of grass stems. Nests are liable to collapse if the material is not strong enough.*

A female Dunnock *fits neatly into her nest. She both builds the nest and incubates the eggs. The nest is a cup made of leaves, twigs, and roots, warmly lined with moss and wool. Occasionally a Dunnock will use the old nest of another species.*

Swifts lay at longer intervals. If the clutch is lost, through predation or the nest being blown down, most birds are able to lay a replacement clutch.

The numbers game

Some birds, such as pigeons and gulls, lay a consistent number of eggs in each clutch, but for most garden species, clutch size depends on how well the females have fed, their state of health, and environmental conditions. In bad weather, the Swift lays two, rather than three eggs, while the Tawny Owl and Kestrel may not even attempt to lay if there is a shortage of mice and voles. There is also variation with geography and climate. Birds in northern countries lay more eggs than those in the south. For example, Scandinavian Robins lay, on average, one more egg per clutch than Spanish birds; and German tits are more likely to lay a second clutch than British tits. It is also interesting to note that some birds lay fewer eggs in gardens than they do in their natural habitats, suggesting that gardens are a "second-best" habitat for certain species.

The number of clutches laid in one season also depends on food supply. Tits, which depend on the spring flush of caterpillars to feed their young, usually manage a single brood in one year, while Blackbirds, which have a wide diet of worms and insects, can rear several broods. However, if the ground becomes too hard to dig for worms, Blackbirds will lay fewer clutches. Chaffinches stop nesting by midsummer when swarms of insects dwindle.

An incubating female, *like this Robin, will often slip off the nest if a predator approaches. It is better to lose the eggs and start again than to risk injury.*

Incubation

Birds are warm-blooded animals, and the chicks developing inside eggs need to be kept warm by their parents. Shortly before the eggs are laid, the parent bird sheds feathers from its breast to leave a patch of bare skin, known as the brood patch; ducks pluck their breast-feathers to provide a warm nest lining. The rich supply of blood vessels to the brood

Hatching begins *a few days before the nestling eventually emerges. The nestling hammers a hole in the shell using its bill, protected by a horny, white egg-tooth. Several hours later, it punches a ring of holes in the shell to weaken it and forces the cap off.*

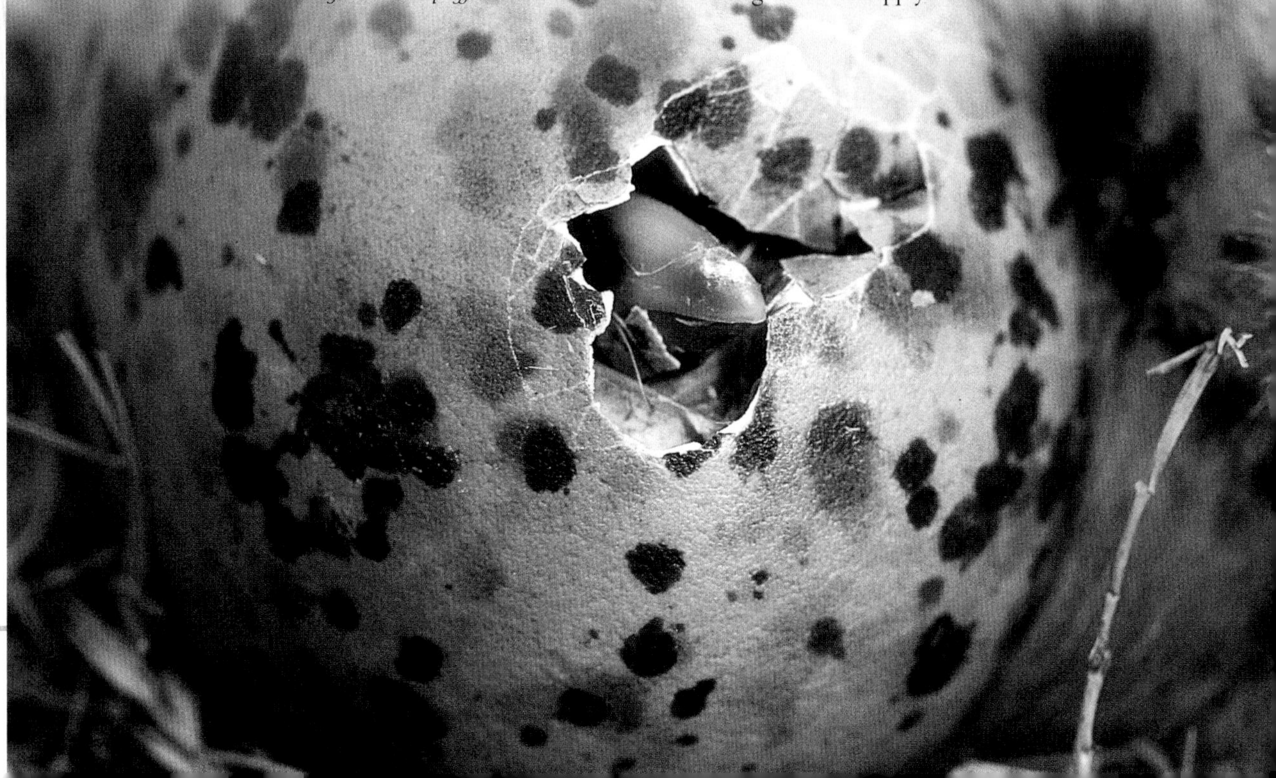

EGGS AND NESTS

Just as the type of nest, size of clutch, and number of broods varies for sound adaptive reasons from species to species, so too does the size, shape, and colour of the eggs. For example, the eggs of birds that use open nests are often well spotted or streaked for camouflage, while the eggs of hole-nesters are white for visibility.

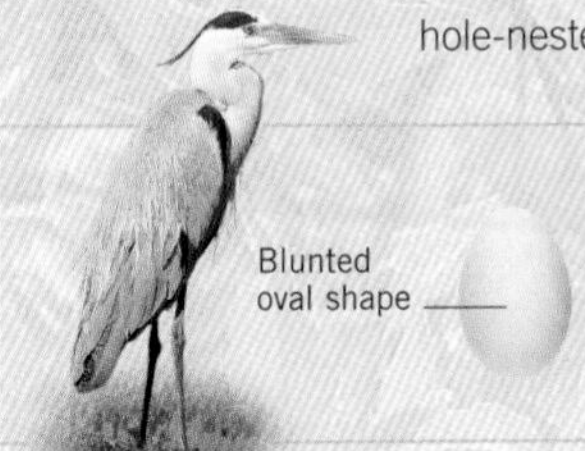

The Grey Heron *raises one brood each year, building its large, stick nests in tall trees. There are 3–5 white eggs in a single clutch.*

The Swallow *builds its mud nest on small ledges against vertical surfaces. The eggs are elongated and strongly tapered in shape.*

A Blackbird's *nest is a cup of grass, twigs, and plant material. It usually raises 2–3 broods per year, or up to 5 in exceptional years.*

House Sparrows *build untidy, domed nests from dry grass or straw. Clutch size is four eggs on average, and they lay 2–4 clutches per year.*

Herring Gulls *nest on open ground and roofs, where their nests are little more than mounds of vegetation. They lay a clutch of 2–4 eggs.*

Chiffchaffs *raise two broods per year across most of Europe. Their grassy, domed nests with a side entrance are concealed in taller vegetation.*

Jackdaw nests *are messy structures, made of sticks, mud, and dung. The birds lay a single clutch of up to eight eggs in one year.*

A Mallard's *nest is a shallow dip in the ground, lined with down from the female's breast. It lays one large clutch of up to 18 eggs per year.*

patch enables it to serve as an efficient hotpad for transferring body heat to the eggs.

For most garden birds, incubation is carried out by the female alone, but in species such as the Starling, where the male shares in the work, he also develops a brood patch. Most birds do not remain on the nest continuously when incubating, but take regular breaks to feed, defecate, and indulge in bouts of preening.

Before settling to incubate the eggs, the adult ruffles its feathers to expose the brood patch. At intervals, it stands up and pokes the eggs with its bill to shuffle them. This has several functions: it allows air to circulate so the embryos inside the eggs can breathe (air diffuses through the egg shells), and rearranges the eggs so they are evenly warmed to within a few degrees. Turning the eggs is also thought to be necessary for the embryonic tissues to develop correctly into the organs of the young birds.

The sitting bird has to monitor the temperature of the eggs and regulate it accordingly. The amount of heat needed to keep the eggs warm depends on the nest insulation and the weather, so incubating birds can stay off the nest for longer on warm, sunny days than on wet, windy, and cool days.

Timing

The eggs in a clutch are laid at a rate of about one per day, but the adult birds do not begin incubation in earnest until the clutch is complete. This results in the eggs hatching simultaneously. Owls, birds of prey, and a few other species are exceptions to this rule; incubation starts as soon as the first egg is laid, and they consequently hatch in sequence at the same intervals as they were laid.

Soon after hatching, *parents remove egg shells from the nest, perhaps to prevent infection, dropping them away from the nest so as not to attract predators.*

Growth and independence

THE YOUNG OF SONGBIRDS, pigeons, woodpeckers, and birds of prey (known as nestlings) hatch in an almost helpless state and stay in the nest until they are ready to fly, while the young of gulls, Coots, and Moorhens (known as chicks) leave the nest soon after hatching. Even under the protection of their parents, these inexperienced birds face the most hazardous time of their lives.

A fledgling's ability *to fly is instinctive, even if it has never fully extended its wings in the nest before its first flight.*

Early days and parental care

When nestlings hatch, they are weak and unable to maintain their body temperature, so they must be brooded almost continuously by their parents. As they grow stronger, they are left alone in the nest for longer periods while the adults forage for food. Brooding resumes at night and in bad weather until the nestlings are well developed.

Faecal sacs of *newly hatched birds are removed from the nest by a fastidious parent Nuthatch.*

Feeding the family keeps the parents busy all day, and even males that played no part in nest-building or incubation now help their mates by bringing food. The favoured food for many young birds is insects and other invertebrates, such as spiders, snails, and worms. Even the vegetarian finches give their young some animal food, because it contains more of the protein, calcium, and other nutrients needed by growing bodies. Animal food is also rich in fluids, so the young birds do not need to drink. However, collecting insects is hard work for the parents, particularly in bad weather. It takes an estimated 10,000 caterpillars and a hundred times as many aphids to raise a family of Blue Tits.

Fledging and flight

By the time the nestlings grow feathers and are ready to fly, they have grown to a size at which they are almost bursting out of the nest. Leaving the nest is a priority, because the young birds are less vulnerable to attack when out in the open than when confined in the nest. The time taken to

At first, nestlings *cannot open their eyes or direct their gape. They raise their heads and open their beaks when they detect vibrations in the nest. The parents simply push food into their brightly-coloured gaping mouths.*

Older nestlings *are able to open their eyes. They respond to the sight of their parents by directing their gaping mouths towards them. The fittest and strongest nestlings in the brood get a larger share of the food.*

Most birds *continue to feed their young after they have left the nest. The fledglings follow their parents and so learn how to find different kinds of food and rich feeding grounds.*

fledge varies between species, but in general birds raised in open cup-shaped nests fly at an earlier age than those raised in the greater safety of nests sited in holes. Even within a species, fledging time depends on the abundance of food and the number of mouths that the parents have to feed.

For the first few days after leaving, most fledglings do not fly much but rest quietly in a secluded spot, such as a dense hedge or bush, where they wait for their parents to bring food. The fledglings are easily recognized on the ground, because their tails and wings look stumpy and they lack the effortless grace of their elders.

As their feathers complete their growth, the young birds become more confident. They follow their parents and save them the effort of flying to and fro with every beakful of food. Young Starlings, for example, can often be seen following their parents as they forage on the lawn; the adults have only to turn to push the food into a waiting mouth. The time taken for young to reach independence from their parents varies considerably between species (see right). Swifts, for example, are independent from the moment they fly, while Tawny Owl young remain with their parents for three months after leaving the nest.

Survival of the fittest

Many young, inexperienced birds die shortly after leaving the nest, especially in times of food shortage or bad weather. In Great Tits, for example, for every 1,000 eggs laid, only 500 fledglings will leave the nest, and just 120 will survive to the next spring. Fledglings are more vulnerable to predators and are at a special disadvantage when competing with older birds, which always occupy and dominate the choicest feeding spots.

TIME TO INDEPENDENCE

The chart below shows the times taken for a selection of garden birds to reach independence after leaving the nest.

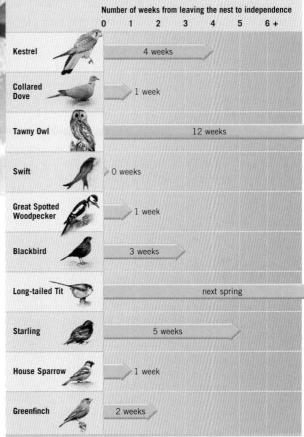

Bird	Number of weeks from leaving the nest to independence
Kestrel	4 weeks
Collared Dove	1 week
Tawny Owl	12 weeks
Swift	0 weeks
Great Spotted Woodpecker	1 week
Blackbird	3 weeks
Long-tailed Tit	next spring
Starling	5 weeks
House Sparrow	1 week
Greenfinch	2 weeks

UNWITTING CARERS

Cuckoos are renowned for laying their eggs in the nests of other species, and fooling the foster parent (here a diminutive Dunnock) into rearing their young. However, Cuckoos are not the only brood parasites: Starlings occasionally lay eggs in the nests of other Starlings, removing one of the rightful eggs so the owner cannot tell what has happened.

Bird profiles

Identification is an essential skill for any garden birdwatcher, and learning bird characteristics is a satisfying end in itself. The directory on the following pages profiles the most common garden visitors, and describes their typical feeding and nesting habits.

Recognizing birds

BIRD IDENTIFICATION IS A SKILL that can be honed by study and experience, but which can take a lifetime to master. Appearance and song give the most immediate clues to a bird's identity, but location, season, and habitat are also important factors to consider. In time, and with patience, you should be able to identify birds with the ease that you recognize old friends.

A flash of white *on the rump and wing of a Jay identifies the bird as it takes off.*

Feathers are *arranged around well-defined feather tracts. It is useful to be familiar with the names of the main tracts.*

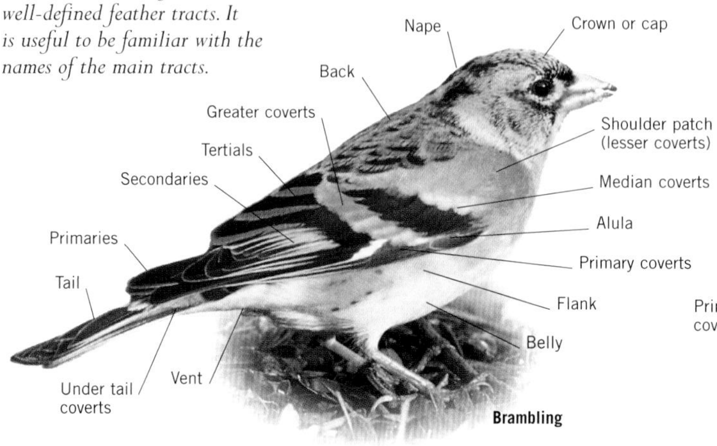

Brambling

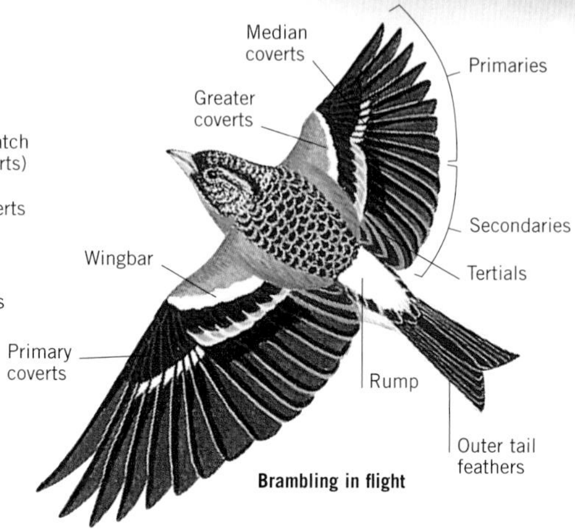

Brambling in flight

Reliable signs

Most species have "absolute" characters that will identify them – a Robin's red breast or the stumpy tail of a Wren, for example. However, birds rarely present themselves in textbook poses that afford us good views of their diagnostic markings. Also, relying on a single characteristic to identify a bird can be unreliable. A bird's colour and plumage pattern may change over the course of a year and its size is difficult to judge in the absence of objects to provide a sense of scale. Shape is trickier still, because a bird can fluff or sleek its feathers, extend its neck, or spread its wings and tail to change its profile.

Rather than focusing on single characteristics, seasoned birdwatchers talk about the "jizz" of a bird, which is an amalgam of its basic physical appearance, its behaviour, and its personality. It allows them to identify birds just as we recognize

To assess a bird's *size, it is useful to compare it to other, familiar "reference" species.*

RELATIVE SIZES

A Nightingale may *be hidden from sight in a tree but its identity is betrayed by its distinctive, musical song.*

Cuckoos can sometimes *be mistaken for Sparrowhawks, but they winter in Africa, ruling them out for at least part of the year.*

our friends – from their walk, the way they hold their bodies, or from some small but characteristic mannerism.

Studying books and articles, and listening to birdsong on CD, will help familiarize you with a bird's features, behaviour, and sounds, but there is no substitute for hours of observation in the field (or your garden). Soon, you will learn to differentiate the fluent swooping flight pattern of a Swallow from the flickering, jerkier wingbeats of a House Martin, and the liquid cadence of a Willow Warbler from the staccato song of a Chiffchaff. Learning about plumage terminology (see opposite) is useful because it helps you compare your own observations and notes with books, and allows you to share your findings with other enthusiasts.

Behaviour is an *excellent clue to identity, especially from a distance, when details of plumage or anatomy cannot be seen. Even from afar, this Nuthatch can be distinguished from a Treecreeper because it is walking down a tree trunk (Treecreepers only walk upwards).*

ABOUT THE BIRD PROFILES

The following pages describe 64 of the most common European garden birds, giving details of their size, shape, colour, voice, and behaviour. Distribution maps (see below for key) show the seasonal range of the species; the letters below the maps indicate the months during which the bird can be seen in the UK.

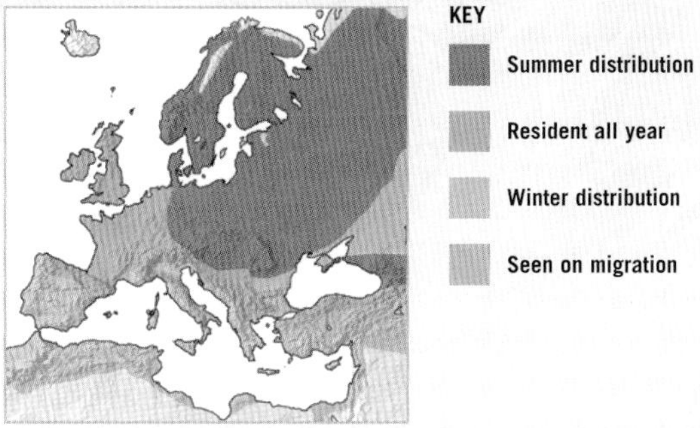

Grey Heron

GREY HERONS ARE WARY BIRDS, not often seen in gardens because they visit in the early morning. These visits are to feed on fish and other pond animals; the clear water and colourful fish of a garden pond make a good hunting ground. Once a heron has discovered the source of an easy meal, it is likely to return many times.

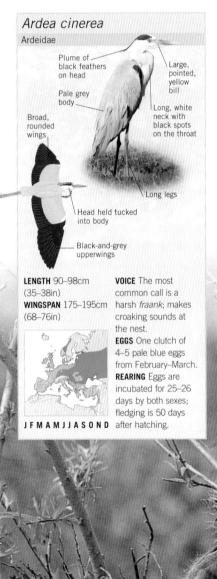

Juvenile birds *have less white on the head and neck than adult Grey Herons, and lack the black plume.*

Ardea cinerea

Ardeidae

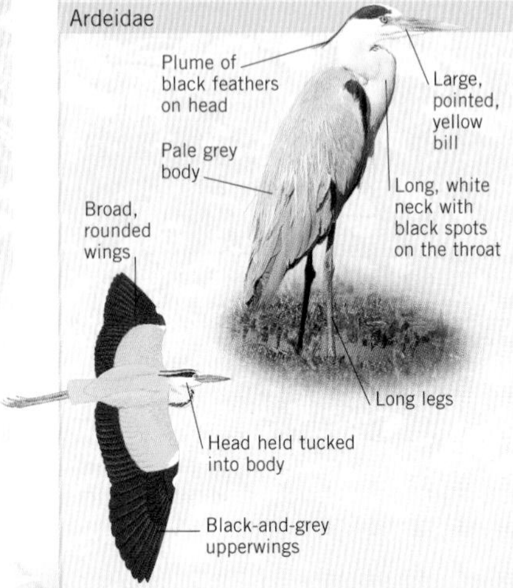

LENGTH 90–98cm (35–38in)
WINGSPAN 175–195cm (68–76in)

J F M A M J J A S O N D

VOICE The most common call is a harsh *fraank*; makes croaking sounds at the nest.
EGGS One clutch of 4–5 pale blue eggs from February–March.
REARING Eggs are incubated for 25–26 days by both sexes; fledging is 50 days after hatching.

Pond visitor

The Grey Heron is an unmistakably large, grey bird with long legs, a long, slender neck, and a dagger-like bill. The bill changes from yellow to reddish in the breeding season. In flight, the large size, broad wings, and slow wingbeats are also obvious.

Herons nests in tall trees (rarely on buildings) in traditional heronries, which may be hundreds of years old and are often also used as communal winter roosts. Both sexes help to build the nest, with the male collecting the material. They often reuse nests from previous years, with the addition of fresh lining material.

The diet of the Grey Heron mainly consists of a variety of fish, but also amphibians, large water insects, insect larvae, snails, and worms. They occasionally also eat some small mammals and birds.

The Grey Heron's nest *is a large platform of twigs and sticks lined with grass and leaves, usually built at the top of a tree.*

IN THE GARDEN

Grey Herons sometimes visit garden ponds to take frogs and fish. Protect the fish by covering the pond or stretching fine nylon line round the edges.

Mallard

THE MALLARD IS THE ANCESTOR of almost all domestic ducks. These familiar birds visit gardens near lakes and rivers, and may nest in large gardens with plenty of cover. A Mallard duckling's early life is hazardous, and large broods may be reduced to only one or two by predation, harsh weather, and accidents.

Mallard ducklings *can swim and feed soon after hatching, but the mother cares for them until they are fully independent.*

A common duck

An amazing range of peculiar colour schemes can be seen where Mallards have interbred with domestic ducks, but curled feathers on the tail of a drake confirm its Mallard ancestry. Female Mallards have brown plumage with darker streaks and spots. After mating, the male moults into the eclipse plumage, which is similar to the female but with a darker crown.

Mallards form pairs while still in their winter flocks. The male accompanies the female to the nest and leaves her when she is incubating the eggs. The nest of leaves and grasses lined with down is placed under dense vegetation, sometimes in a tree or on a building. The female covers the nest when she leaves to feed. The eggs hatch together and the ducklings depart the nest before they are a day old. After breeding, Mallards moult all their flight-feathers at once, and become flightless for about four weeks.

Mallards eat a wide range of plant and animal food on land and water. On land, they graze on lawns and eat acorns, while in the water, they hunt for water-snails, caddis fly larvae, frogs, and small fish, and eat plant material. The ducklings feed mainly on insects.

IN THE GARDEN

Mallards take bread, potatoes, and grain from the ground. They nest in large, enclosed boxes with entrance holes of 15cm (6in) – position boxes on a raft or island. They also use special nesting baskets.

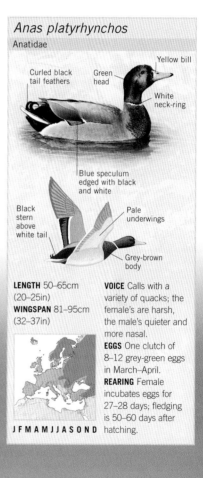

A familiar figure *on village ponds, pestering visitors for food, the Mallard is also a truly wild species, with large numbers that never interact with humans.*

Anas platyrhynchos

Anatidae

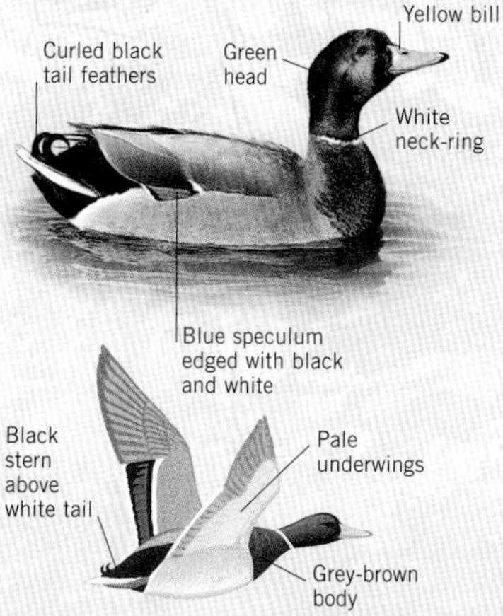

LENGTH 50–65cm (20–25in)
WINGSPAN 81–95cm (32–37in)

J F M A M J J A S O N D

VOICE Calls with a variety of quacks; the female's are harsh, the male's quieter and more nasal.
EGGS One clutch of 8–12 grey-green eggs in March–April.
REARING Female incubates eggs for 27–28 days; fledging is 50–60 days after hatching.

Sparrowhawk

THIS STEALTHY PREDATOR became scarce in the 20th century because it was badly affected by pesticide poisoning. Populations have revived in recent decades as a result of changes in agricultural practice, and this solitary hunter is now regularly seen in suburban gardens, where its ability to turn at speed and dive into trees after its prey always makes for a thrilling spectacle.

Accipiter nisus

Accipitridae

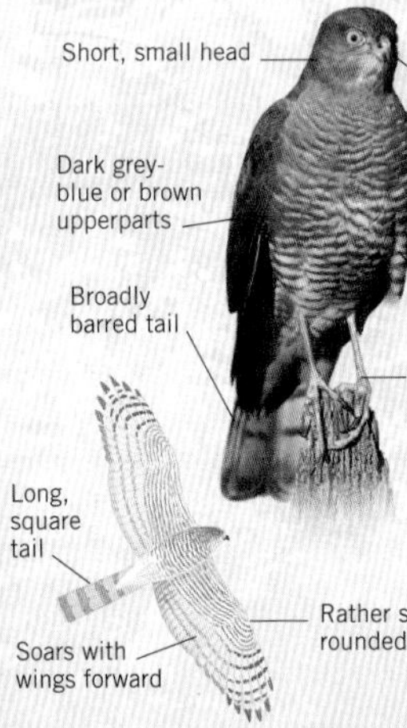

LENGTH 28–40cm (11–16in)
WINGSPAN 60–80cm (23–31in)

J F M A M J J A S O N D

VOICE A shrill, chattering *kek-kek-kek* usually near the nesting place.
EGGS One clutch of 4–6 grey-green eggs in April–May.
REARING Female incubates eggs for 32–36 days, and is fed by the male; fledging is 24–30 days after hatching.

Primarily a bird *of woodland margins, the Sparrowhawk has adapted well to larger gardens that contain hedgerows, thickets, copses, and taller ornamental plantings, which allow room for flight within and below the canopy.*

Prey is typically carried *to a well-covered spot, such as a tree stump or sturdy branch, before the Sparrowhawk begins to eat. Clusters of discarded feathers, larger bones, and bills on the ground often betray the presence of these "plucking posts".*

Plumage and size variety

Sparrowhawks display marked differences between the sexes. Mature females are up to 30 per cent larger and twice as heavy as males, and have duller plumage. While male birds have blue-grey upperparts, pale underparts with orange bars, and distinctly orange faces, females and juveniles are brown above with grey-brown barring below. In flight, the Sparrowhawk's barred breast and broad, rounded wings help to distinguish it from the similar Kestrel. Sparrowhawks do not defend their hunting territories, with the result that several individuals may be seen in the same area, though not at the same time of day.

An immature Sparrowhawk *is attracted to bathe at a garden pond. The young bird has a distinct pale line over its eyes and is barred grey rather than brown-orange beneath.*

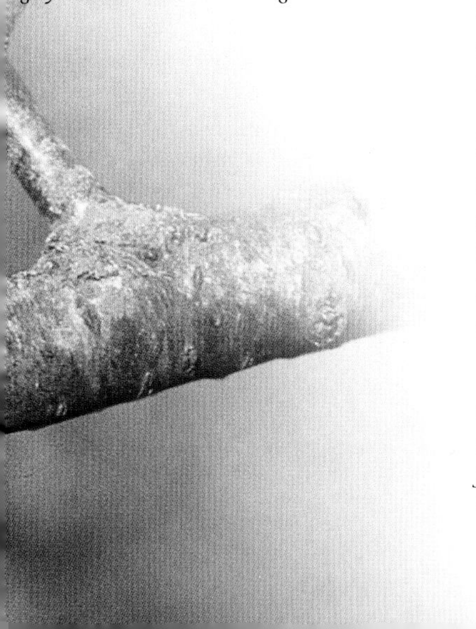

Display and breeding

At the beginning of the breeding season, Sparrowhawks display over the nesting area, circling slowly and calling with a shrill, chattering *kek-kek-kek*. They may chase one another noisily through trees to cement the pair-bond. Sparrowhawks are monogamous, the pair remaining together through the breeding season.

The nest is a cup of twigs built in the fork of a tree, sometimes on an abandoned pigeon's nest, and the Sparrowhawk lines this structure with fine twigs and leaves. Laying is timed so that the birds are hunting for their hungry nestlings when their prey species' own young have left the nest – so ensuring a plentiful supply of food. The eggs hatch at intervals, rather than together as with the clutches of most birds. If food is short, the youngest and weakest nestlings die and the adults concentrate on raising the older, stronger nestlings.

Stealth predators

Sparrowhawks hunt by waiting on a perch for prey to approach or by flying swiftly round trees, hedges, houses, or other cover to catch victims unawares. They commonly follow regular flight paths when out on hunting sorties and the prey is almost entirely small birds, such as tits, sparrows, and finches. Larger species, including thrushes, Blackbirds, Stock Doves, Jays, and even small mammals may be taken by the stockier females. The victims are taken from perches or snatched in flight – sometimes after a protracted chase.

Most often seen *in low, darting, predatory flight, Sparrowhawks also soar over wooded areas and scrubby margins, diving suddenly with closed wings.*

IN THE GARDEN

Sparrowhawks occasionally nest in trees in larger gardens, and are attracted to garden feeders where they prey on small birds. To provide small birds with a means of escape, create obstacles for the larger bird of prey by placing trellises or dense bushes around feeding stations.

Conifers, located *near clearings that allow for easy flight access, are the preferred nest sites for Sparrowhawks.*

Kestrel

THE KESTREL WAS the most common bird of prey around rural gardens until the recent increases in Sparrowhawk numbers. Without a good look, it is possible to confuse the two species, but the Kestrel can be recognized by its habit of floating on outstretched wings in a stiff breeze or hovering in still air with rapidly whirring wings.

Female Kestrels *have browner, more uniform plumage than males, with a black terminal bar on the tail.*

The Kestrel *can be distinguished from the Sparrowhawk by its more pointed wings and the spotted, rather than barred, breast.*

A familiar raptor

The Kestrel has long, pointed wings, typical of the falcon family. The male is slightly smaller and more colourful than the female, with a grey head, chestnut back, and a grey tail with a bold, black terminal bar.

Kestrels are most likely to be seen in rural gardens, but a few settle and nest in cities, where nests may be found on window sills. No nest as such is built, but a lining of sticks and straw may be added to a hole in a tree, a deserted bird's nest, or a ledge on a cliff or building. Both parents provide food for the young.

Garden and urban Kestrels are most likely to prey on small birds, but some catch mice attracted to seeds spilt from feeders. In the countryside, the main prey is rodents, large insects, and earthworms. Kestrels hunt from prominent tree perches or wires, or hover, allowing them to scan a wider area of terrain. Hovering is less likely to be seen over a garden, however – it is a strenuous activity, only used when there is no convenient perch.

IN THE GARDEN

Kestrels are rare visitors to gardens, catching small birds and mammals. They sometimes nest in urban areas, building their nests in large open next-boxes or near the tops of mature trees.

Falco tinnunculus

Falconidae

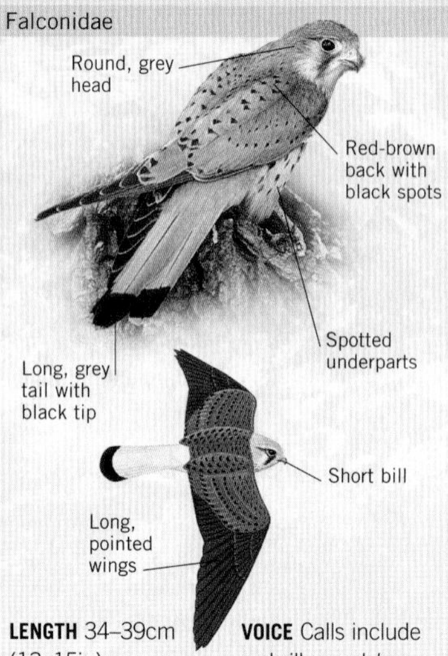

LENGTH 34–39cm (13–15in)

WINGSPAN 65–80cm (25–31in)

J F M A M J J A S O N D

VOICE Calls include a shrill, nasal *kee-kee-kee* during the breeding season.

EGGS One clutch of 4–5 brown-blotched, white eggs in April–July.

REARING Female incubates eggs for 27–29 days; fledging is 27–32 days after hatching.

Pheasant

First introduced into Europe from Asia by the Romans, the Pheasant is now a common bird in most areas. Although many are reared on shooting estates, they also live freely in the wild. Pheasants enter gardens, including suburban ones, usually in autumn and winter, and especially in hard weather.

The female Pheasant *is much plainer than the male, with a brown body flecked with black.*

Brilliant colours

The male Pheasant is a colourfully marked gamebird, with a green head and neck, red wattle, and often a white neck-ring. In contrast, females and juveniles are smaller and drab brown. Male Pheasants are more often seen in gardens than females, and can often become quite tame.

As with other bird species in which the male is colourful and the female dull, the female is wholly responsible for raising the family. She builds the nest in a shallow depression, under a hedge, or in long grass or bracken. The chicks leave the nest shortly after hatching, and can fly short distances when about 12 days old. They do not become fully independent, however, for a further ten or eleven weeks.

Pheasants mainly forage for food by scratching on the ground, but they also clamber in trees for buds and fruit. They eat a wide range of foods, especially grain and other seeds and acorns, but also insects, snails, worms, and occasionally small mammals and lizards. In winter, they eat grass, leaves, and roots.

The male's song – *a loud* kork-kok *accompanied by wing-flapping – may attract several females, each of which mates with him.*

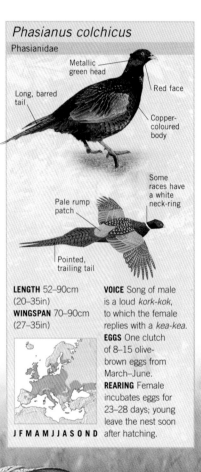

Phasianus colchicus

Phasianidae

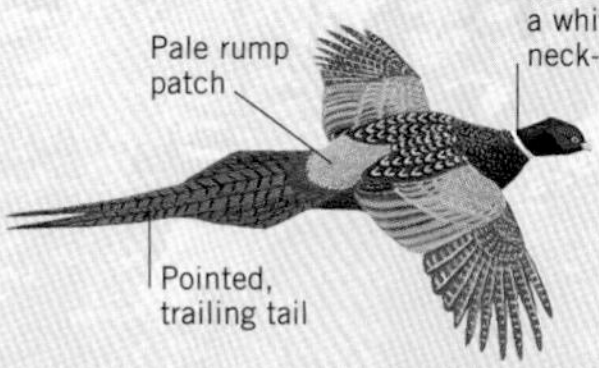

LENGTH 52–90cm (20–35in)
WINGSPAN 70–90cm (27–35in)

J F M A M J J A S O N D

VOICE Song of male is a loud *kork-kok*, to which the female replies with a *kea-kea*.
EGGS One clutch of 8–15 olive-brown eggs from March–June.
REARING Female incubates eggs for 23–28 days; young leave the nest soon after hatching.

IN THE GARDEN

- Pheasants sometimes visit rural gardens to take grain, bread, and kitchen leftovers.

Coot

A COMMON SIGHT IN PARKS and on urban reservoirs, Coots sometimes visit gardens nearby, but prefer larger ponds and lakes, and even slow-flowing rivers. Watch for conflicts between rivals, in which one Coot races after another over the water or fights by sitting back on its tail and kicking and clawing.

A familiar waterbird

Larger than a Moorhen, with a plump body and short tail, the Coot has black plumage and a characteristic white bill and shield on the face. The grey legs have long toes with fleshy lobes to aid swimming. Male and female are alike, while the juvenile has paler grey-brown plumage, a yellowish bill, and lacks the white facial shield.

Coots build their nests in shallow water, often amongst reeds or other wetland vegetation. Both sexes contribute to the construction of the nest, which is a pile of plant stems and other vegetation. The male collects most of the material, while the female works it into place. After the eggs hatch, the female broods the nestlings for the first few days; after this, the male builds a platform where he broods the young at night.

Omnivorous diet

Coots spend most of their time on the water, feeding on a variety of water plants, fish, and invertebrate animals. They find food at the surface, or by diving to the bottom of ponds, and steal food from swans and ducks. They also feed on land, grazing on grass, and sometimes taking small mammals and birds. In winter, they regularly form large feeding flocks, often mixed with other wildfowl.

Male and female *Coots feed their young for up to nine weeks after they hatch, dividing their brood between them.*

IN THE GARDEN

Coots are rare visitors to gardens near water, taking scraps, bread, and grain.

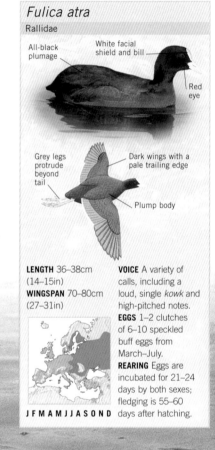

Fiercely territorial, *Coots lower their heads and raise the feathers on their backs in threat displays, as a warning to potential intruders.*

Fulica atra

Rallidae

LENGTH 36–38cm (14–15in)
WINGSPAN 70–80cm (27–31in)

VOICE A variety of calls, including a loud, single *kowk* and high-pitched notes.
EGGS 1–2 clutches of 6–10 speckled buff eggs from March–July.
REARING Eggs are incubated for 21–24 days by both sexes; fledging is 55–60 days after hatching.

Moorhen

THE MOORHEN IS MOST OFTEN seen in parks, where it stalks daintily across the grass around lakes, but a garden pond, especially near other water, is always an attraction; it betrays its presence with sharp *purruk* calls. Moorhens are surprisingly agile and regularly roost or nest in bushes and amongst tree branches.

Fed by their parents *until they fly at about six weeks, Moorhen young are able to feed themselves after only three or four weeks.*

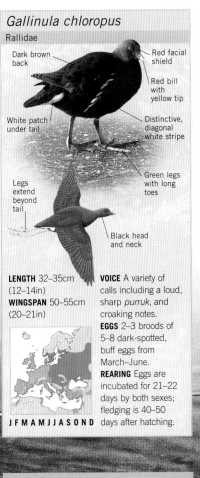

Gallinula chloropus

Rallidae

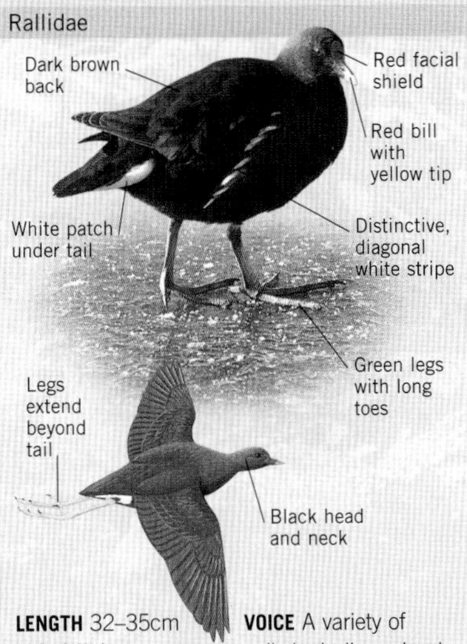

LENGTH 32–35cm (12–14in)
WINGSPAN 50–55cm (20–21in)

VOICE A variety of calls including a loud, sharp *purruk*, and croaking notes.
EGGS 2–3 broods of 5–8 dark-spotted, buff eggs from March–June.
REARING Eggs are incubated for 21–22 days by both sexes; fledging is 40–50 days after hatching.

J F M A M J J A S O N D

Town-park regular

A Moorhen resembles a small, black, long-legged chicken. Its black plumage has tinges of grey, brown, and blue when seen close-up. Adult males and females, which are alike, have a red bill and shield, absent in the young. The Moorhen is easily told apart from the Coot by its smaller, slimmer body, the patches of white under its tail and edging the wing, and the red bill and shield. It also constantly flicks its tail, both when swimming and on land.

Moorhens build their nests among water vegetation, and also in hedges or trees. Both sexes help to construct the nest of twigs and dead reeds, lined with finer plants, and they also share the task of incubating the eggs. If a pair has more than one brood in a season, the young of the first brood stay with their parents and help feed their younger siblings.

Moorhens eat a wide variety of small animals, including worms, snails, insects, spiders, and small fish, and also various leaves, seeds, and berries. They occasionally also eat the eggs of other birds. They feed while swimming, picking food from the water surface and foraging in waterside vegetation, and also on land, but they rarely wander more than about 200–300m (660–990ft) from the water's edge.

As the breeding season *approaches, Moorhens start to collect nesting material, such as twigs, plant stems, dead reeds, and grasses.*

IN THE GARDEN

Moorhens enter gardens to feed and may nest in or near large garden ponds if there is enough cover. They eat bread and fat scattered on the ground.

Herring Gull

A FAMILIAR BIRD of the coast, the Herring Gull also comes inland to feed in towns and countryside outside the breeding season, and regularly nests in seaside towns. Large feeding flocks are a common sight on refuse tips, where they take advantage of the large amounts of readily available food.

Larus argentatus

Laridae

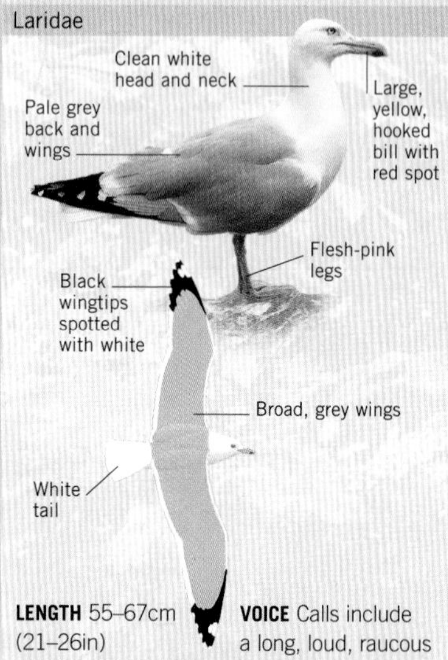

LENGTH 55–67cm (21–26in)
WINGSPAN 130–160cm (51–62in)

J F M A M J J A S O N D

VOICE Calls include a long, loud, raucous *kyee-kau-kau-kau*.
EGGS One clutch of three olive to brown eggs with dark brown markings, in April–June.
REARING Eggs are incubated by both sexes for 28–30 days; fledging is 35–40 days after hatching.

Seaside regular

The Herring Gull is a large gull with an all-white body, except for a grey back, and grey wings with black-and-white wingtips. Its hooked bill is yellow with an orange-red spot. Adult male and female Herring Gulls are alike; juveniles are grey-brown, and gradually assume adult plumage over the course of two or three years.

Herring Gulls are social birds, nesting in colonies and roosting and feeding in huge flocks in winter.

Herring Gulls *are easily confused with other, less common gulls; look for the pink legs and a red spot on the yellow bill.*

Herring Gull *chicks are well camouflaged, with brown spots on their downy white plumage, to protect them from predators.*

Their natural nest sites are on open ground and sea cliffs but colonies have become established in towns, where the birds nest on buildings. The nests are piles of vegetation gathered by both sexes, shaped into a cup and lined with fine material. The nestlings leave the nest when they are two or three days old, but they stay within the territory until they can fly. Food is brought to them until they can follow their parents.

A versatile scavenger

Herring Gulls are predators and scavengers with an extremely varied diet. At sea, they catch fish and shellfish, and flocks follow fishing boats to feed on the discarded fish. When inland, they scavenge for anything edible, from earthworms, small mammals, and ducklings, to discarded food and carrion.

IN THE GARDEN

- Herring Gulls sometimes visit gardens, especially in coastal areas, to take kitchen scraps.

Black-headed Gull

ALTHOUGH A SEABIRD, the Black-headed Gull started to move inland about 100 years ago. Initially only a winter visitor to towns, returning to the coast to breed, it began to nest inland in small numbers. Inland gulls roost and nest in gravel pits, reservoirs, and sewage works and commute daily to feed on farmland and in city parks and gardens.

Larus ridibundus

Laridae

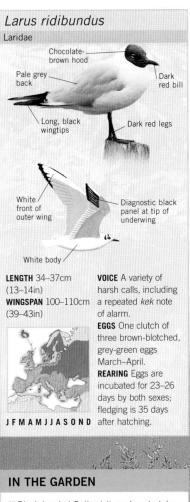

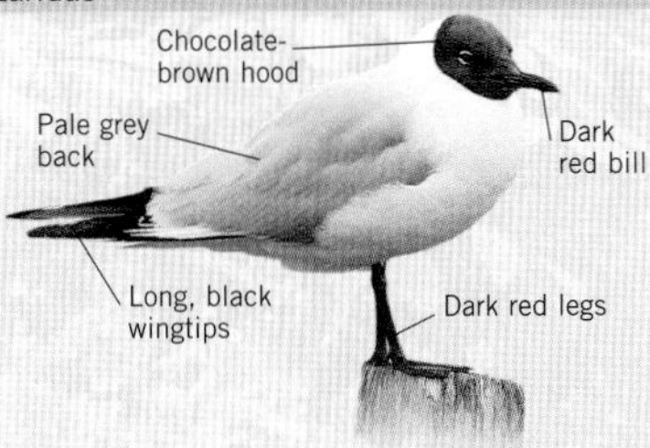

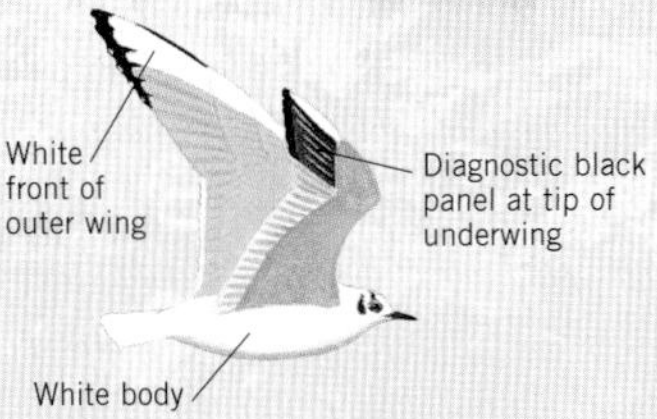

LENGTH 34–37cm (13–14in)

WINGSPAN 100–110cm (39–43in)

J F M A M J J A S O N D

VOICE A variety of harsh calls, including a repeated *kek* note of alarm.

EGGS One clutch of three brown-blotched, grey-green eggs March–April.

REARING Eggs are incubated for 23–26 days by both sexes; fledging is 35 days after hatching.

A distinctive gull

The Black-headed Gull has a characteristic chocolate-brown "hood", which is lost after the nesting season except for marks behind the eyes. Juveniles are a mottled, pale brown; by the time they are one year old, their legs and bill are orange, but they still retain some brown on the wings.

Black-headed Gulls build simple nests of grass on the ground or, rarely, on buildings. Both parents share the duties of incubation and caring for the chicks. The male feeds his mate before egg-laying and during incubation, but concentrates on feeding the chicks after they hatch.

The diet of the Black-headed Gull mainly consists of animal material, especially insects and worms seized from the ground or stolen from other birds. Gulls also circle in upcurrents to catch flying ants, pick berries while airborne, and scavenge for scraps.

In winter, *the Black-headed Gull's head is white, with a dark spot behind the eye, rather than dark brown.*

Black-headed Gulls *mate for life and breed in colonies with nests usually only a few metres apart.*

IN THE GARDEN

Black-headed Gulls visit gardens to take kitchen scraps, and sometimes become bold enough to take food from the hand.

Collared Dove

NOW A FAMILIAR GARDEN BIRD, the Collared Dove is a relative newcomer. About 100 years ago, it started to spread westwards from southeastern Europe and reached Britain in the early 1950s, breeding for the first time in 1956. Collared Doves prefer to live in towns and villages, or near farms, where they can find plenty of food. They are frequent residents in gardens, nesting in trees and hedges.

IN THE GARDEN

Collared Doves feed on the ground and enjoy grain, seeds, bread, and scraps. In autumn, they will sometimes feed on berries, such as those of elder. They nest in trees and tall hedges.

Streptopelia decaocto

Columbidae

LENGTH 31–33cm (12–13in)
WINGSPAN 47–55cm (18–21in)
VOICE Calls with a repeated, monotonous *coo-COO-cook* and a nasal *whurr-whurr* when excited.
EGGS 3–6 clutches of two white eggs, mainly from March–November.

REARING Eggs are incubated for 14–18 days by both sexes; fledging is 17 days after hatching.

Collared Doves *are a common sight on lawns and open spaces, and may visit garden ponds to drink and bathe. Like other pigeons, they do not raise their heads as they drink, but suck up water in a continuous draught.*

Muted colours

A pale grey dove, the Collared Dove is dark on the wings, with a pinkish tinge to the face, neck, and breast. It has a narrow black collar round the back of the neck, edged with white. Similar in appearance to the smaller, more distinctly patterned Turtle Dove, the presence of a Collared Dove is often advertised by a gentle, repeated cooing, although sometimes, when it gives only two coos, it can be mistaken for a Cuckoo. Collared Doves often form mixed feeding flocks with Feral Pigeons and Woodpigeons.

During courtship, *Collared Doves engage in a number of ceremonial rituals, including mutual feeding and preening.*

Breeding and diet

If the winter is mild and there is plenty of food, Collared Doves may breed all the year round. The male advertises his territory with a dramatic display flight. He flies up steeply from a perch and then circles on outstretched wings while uttering a nasal call. The female builds the nest – a loose platform of twigs, stems, and roots – while the male gathers the material. Both adults incubate the eggs, with the female taking the night shift. The nestlings are fed on pigeon's milk – a cheesy secretion from the crop, rich in protein and fat – for the first ten days after hatching. Parent doves fiercely protect the nest, trying to drive away Jays, Magpies, and even humans. They also perform "injury-feigning" displays – flapping their wings or limping across the ground – to lure predators from the nest.

The diet of the Collared Dove consists largely of seeds, and the recent spread of the species was helped by the availability of spilt grain in farmyards as a food source. Largely vegetarian, it also eats some leaves, buds, and fruit, and occasionally feeds on caterpillars, aphids, snails, and other small animals.

Juvenile Collared Doves *are duller in colour than the adults and lack the characteristic black-and-white collar.*

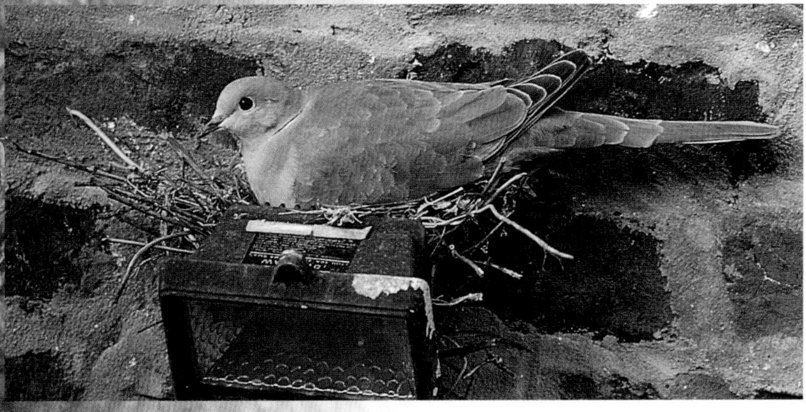

The flimsy nest *is usually built in a tree, bush, or tall hedge, but occasionally a convenient ledge on a building is chosen.*

With one wing *raised, a Collared Dove sunbathes on a warm day. This is thought to mobilize feather parasites. As they crawl around, they are easier for the bird to spot and remove.*

Feral Pigeon

FERAL PIGEONS ARE THE DESCENDANTS of domestic pigeons that have become wild, and these domestic breeds are, in turn, descendants of the wild Rock Dove. Pigeons were traditionally kept for the table, especially to provide fresh meat in the winter, and as "carrier pigeons" or "homing pigeons" for carrying messages. They still continue to be bred for racing and for show.

IN THE GARDEN

■ Feral Pigeons are regular visitors to garden feeding stations, taking grain, bread, and scraps. They will nest in a garden in large, enclosed nest-boxes with entrance holes 10cm (4in) in diameter.

Columba livia

Columbidae

LENGTH 31–35cm (12–14in)
WINGSPAN 63–70cm (25–27in)

J F M A M J J A S O N D

VOICE The low, cooing *ooor-ooor* or *o-roo-coo* is a familiar sound in city parks and streets.
EGGS 2–3 clutches of two white eggs, mainly from March–September.
REARING Eggs are incubated for 17–18 days by both sexes; fledging is 35 days after hatching.

City dweller

Few birds are more easily recognizable than the Feral Pigeons that live in our towns and cities in such large numbers, even though their plumages vary so considerably. Some individuals more closely resemble their wild Rock Dove ancestors; these birds are blue-grey with two distinctive black bars on each wing. Plumage colours range, however, from all-black to all-white, with a myriad of shades of brown and grey. All variants have a large, white fleshy patch – the cere – at the base of the bill. Wild Rock Doves are now mostly found in isolated colonies (see map, left), but

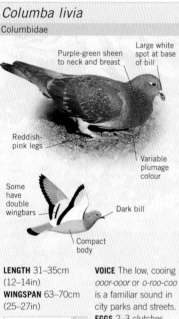

Feral Pigeons *breed freely with domestic pigeons and wild Rock Doves, creating a wide range of plumage variations. This inter-breeding will eventually threaten the existence of wild Rock Doves.*

their feral cousins are widespread throughout most of Europe, especially around areas of human habitation.

Feral Pigeons are often very tame in parks and city squares where they are fed, and can become a problem because they foul buildings and may spread disease. Despite attempts by authorities to restrict numbers, the easy pickings in towns allow pigeon populations to quickly build up.

Paired for life

Young Feral Pigeons spend their time in flocks, but pairs retain their nesting territories and often live together all year round, even when not breeding. Feral Pigeons, like wild Rock Doves, usually mate for life, and pairs may nest at any time of year if conditions are favourable, although fewer nest during the winter months.

The male courts the female by driving her away from the rest of the flock and performing bowing-displays, or by flying close behind her when she takes off. The nest of twigs or grasses is built by the female, with the assistance of the male. The chosen site is often on a ledge or in a hole in a building, within easy reach of an available source of food. Both parents help to incubate the eggs and feed the nestlings, continuing to do so for ten days after fledging. Like other pigeons, Feral Pigeons feed their nestlings entirely on "pigeon's milk" (see page 137) for the first ten days.

When courting *a female, the male bows with feathers fluffed and tail depressed, and calls with a cooing* ooor-ooor *or* o-roo-coo.

Flocks of Feral Pigeons *gather for feeding, roosting, and flying long distances, and they also breed in loose colonies. The large flocks that are seen in cities are random gatherings.*

Indiscriminate scavenger

City-dwelling Feral Pigeons scavenge for any edible litter, and also eat grain, seeds, and bread. In rural areas, they feed on the seeds of some crops and plants, and on green leaves, buds, and invertebrates. At one time, grain from the nosebags of horses was an important food for Feral Pigeons, but litter from fast-food outlets now provides the most readily accessible supply. Many urban pigeons take at least some of their food from handouts in city squares and parks, and some birds even learn to recognize the individuals who provide food regularly and approach these people when they appear.

Dominance hierarchies *exist in Feral Pigeon populations, and an individual bird's ranking is established through minor skirmishes. This "pecking order" allows higher-ranked birds to have first access to food and perches.*

Woodpigeon

LARGE WOODPIGEON FLOCKS are a dramatic sight in the countryside, but can sometimes be a problem for the farmer because they feed in the fields in winter, eating cereals, root crops, and legumes. Wild and shy birds in this habitat, they become tame in residential areas, where you may see them walking on lawns with a typically "pigeon-toed" gait – with toes pointing inward.

IN THE GARDEN

■ Woodpigeons are unmistakable garden visitors, taking bread, seeds, and vegetable scraps from ground feeders. These large pigeons also visit the garden for a drink at a garden pond or bird-bath.

A handsome pigeon

The bulky Woodpigeon can look uniformly grey from a distance, but on closer inspection the pinkish breast and browner back are obvious. It can easily be distinguished from other pigeons, even at a distance while in flight, as it has unique, white, crescent-shaped patches on the midwing.

With deep, even wingbeats, *the Woodpigeon is powerful and direct in flight and uses bursts of wingbeats and swerves to evade predators. It takes off with loud, clattering wings when disturbed.*

Display and nesting

Outside the breeding season, Woodpigeons gather in large flocks for feeding and roosting. When these flocks break up, male Woodpigeons take up territories. The male often advertises his presence in the territory, which may be no more than a single tree, simply by sitting conspicuously in the bare branches. At intervals, he makes a display flight, which is a steep climb and glide. At the top of the arc, one or two loud wing-claps can be heard; these are whip-cracks made by a forceful down-stroke rather than by the wings clapping together.

Woodpigeons breed in farmland, woodland, and, increasingly, urban areas. Both parents assemble the nest, which is such a flimsy platform that the eggs can be seen through its floor. It is usually built in a tree but sometimes a building is chosen. If an old nest is reused, more twigs are added to make it bulkier. In much of northern Europe, the nesting season is very long, lasting from early spring until late autumn; this is because Woodpigeons, like other pigeons, do not feed their young on insects – available only over a limited season – but on "pigeon's milk" (see page 137), which is rich in protein and fat.

Vegetarian fare

The Woodpigeon's diet mainly consists of plant material: leaves, berries, seeds, and flowers. Unlike other European pigeons, they have hooked bills for tearing leaves and they eat grit to enable them to grind food in their gizzards. They occasionally feed on small insects, such as beetles.

Frequent visitors *to garden ponds in summer, Woodpigeons need to drink regularly, especially in hot weather, because they do not get sufficient moisture from their diet.*

During courtship, *the male Woodpigeon makes soft cooing notes, and performs a bowing display before the female, with his plumage puffed out and tail fanned.*

The juvenile Woodpigeon *(right) is generally duller in colour than the adult, and lacks the striking white patches on each side of the neck. Like the adult, it is easily identified by its dark tail band.*

Sometimes seen *individually when perched or preening (left), Woodpigeons are more often seen in pairs in summer, or in large feeding flocks on farmland in winter. City dwelling birds may hold their territory all year round.*

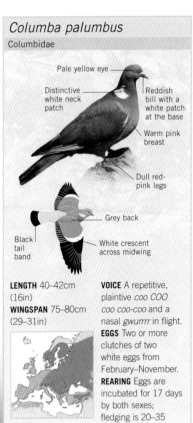

Columba palumbus

Columbidae

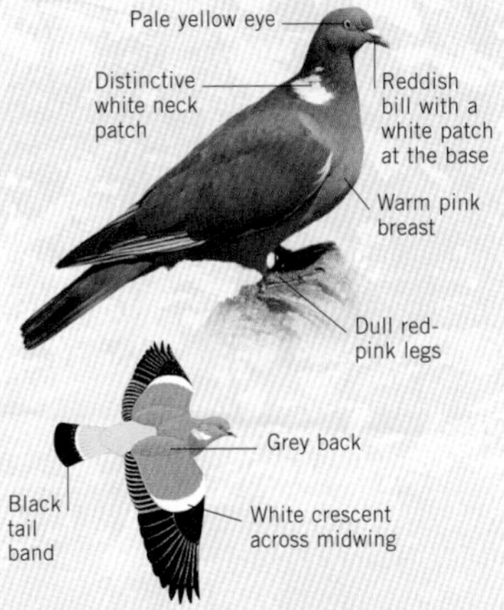

LENGTH 40–42cm (16in)

WINGSPAN 75–80cm (29–31in)

J F M A M J J A S O N D

VOICE A repetitive, plaintive *coo COO coo coo-coo* and a nasal *gwurrrr* in flight.

EGGS Two or more clutches of two white eggs from February–November.

REARING Eggs are incubated for 17 days by both sexes; fledging is 20–35 days after hatching.

A Woodpigeon *pecking at a garden lawn or in an open field is a familiar sight, but they also forage for food in trees.*

Cuckoo

A SUMMER MIGRANT to all parts of Europe, the Cuckoo is famous for laying its eggs in the nests of small birds. The unmistakable sound of the Cuckoo's call is one of the first signs of spring, but its appearance is less familiar, and it is easily mistaken for a Sparrowhawk. This brood parasite only rarely comes into gardens to find a host for its eggs.

When perched, *the Cuckoo is distinguished from a small bird of prey by its horizontal stance and drooped wings.*

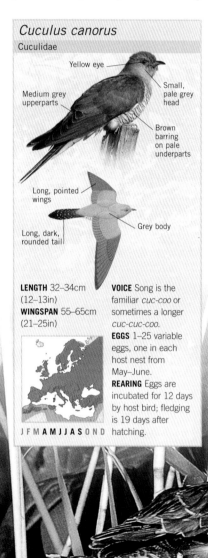

Cuculus canorus

Cuculidae

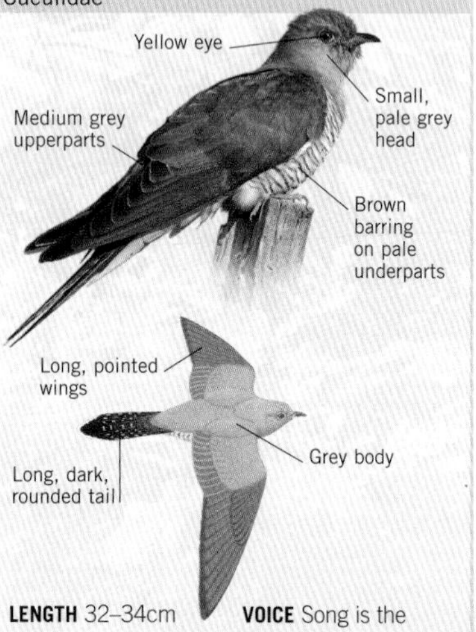

LENGTH 32–34cm (12–13in)
WINGSPAN 55–65cm (21–25in)

J F M **A M J J A S** O N D

VOICE Song is the familiar *cuc-coo* or sometimes a longer *cuc-cuc-coo*.
EGGS 1–25 variable eggs, one in each host nest from May–June.
REARING Eggs are incubated for 12 days by host bird; fledging is 19 days after hatching.

Brood parasite

The Cuckoo is roughly the size of a Collared Dove and has pointed wings and a rounded tail. It is grey above, darker on the wings and tail, and white underneath with fine brown bars. The sexes are alike, but the juvenile is either grey or rufous, with barring above and below and a white patch on the neck.

The female Cuckoo lays her eggs in the nests of another bird species. She keeps watch for a bird that is in the process of laying its eggs and sneaks in to lay an egg while it is away.

The appearance of the Cuckoo's egg often mimics the eggs of the host bird. The nestling Cuckoo hatches first and throws the other eggs out of the nest so that it gets the undivided attention of its hosts. When the young Cuckoo leaves the nest, it continues to beg for food from its foster parents with squeaking calls, and also entices other birds to stop and feed it. Young Cuckoos grow up on the diet of their hosts, but adult Cuckoos specialize on caterpillars and beetles.

The host parent, *like this Reed Warbler, feeds and cares for the giant Cuckoo fledgling as if it were its own. The most likely hosts in gardens are Robins and Dunnocks.*

IN THE GARDEN

■ The Cuckoo is an unusual visitor to all but the most rural gardens. Juveniles are more often seen than adults, especially in late summer when they call loudly for food.

Long-eared Owl

LONG-EARED OWLS HUNT AND NEST in more open country than Tawny Owls, but are inhabitants of parks and suburbs in some parts of Europe. In winter, they gather in traditional communal roosts, where a dozen or more owls may perch one or two metres apart. They return to their breeding territories before the end of winter.

The Long-eared Owl's *favourite daytime roosts are pine trees and dense thickets, from which they rarely move until dusk.*

A distinctive owl

The Long-eared Owl is slightly smaller than the similar Tawny Owl, but is easily identified when perched because it reveals characteristic long ear tufts. Its plumage is buffish brown with darker streaks, with very little difference between back and front. From close range, its bright orange eyes are striking.

Expert hunter

The male Long-eared Owl attracts a mate with courtship displays. He flies slowly, sometimes clapping his wings and calling with a drawn-out hoot. The nest is usually in an old Magpie, crow, or squirrel nest, and nest-boxes are also used. The female incubates the eggs and feeds the young, while the male feeds the female.

The main food of the Long-eared Owl is voles, and sometimes other mammals and roosting birds, which it hunts from a perch or in flight over open ground. Hunting is mostly done at night, although it sometimes continues by day when there are hungry young to feed.

IN THE GARDEN

■ A very rare visitor to gardens. The owl may occupy old nests of other species or wicker baskets placed high in trees.

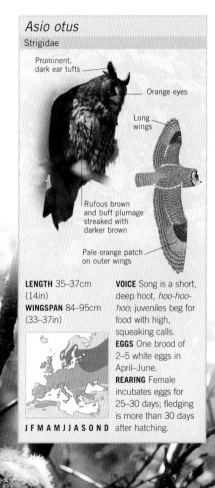

The young are fed *by the female Long-eared Owl. They can fly after about four weeks, but continue to be cared for by their parents for a further four or five weeks.*

Asio otus

Strigidae

LENGTH 35–37cm (14in)
WINGSPAN 84–95cm (33–37in)

VOICE Song is a short, deep hoot, *hoo-hoo-hoo*; juveniles beg for food with high, squeaking calls.
EGGS One brood of 2–5 white eggs in April–June.
REARING Female incubates eggs for 25–30 days; fledging is more than 30 days after hatching.

Tawny Owl

A BIRD OF MATURE WOODLANDS, the Tawny Owl has been able to adapt to city life wherever there are enough large trees to provide places for roosting and nesting. It is a common resident in many parts of Europe, but is almost completely nocturnal and is rarely seen by day. The Tawny Owl is perhaps best known for its song, often heard on autumn evenings – a familiar, hollow *hooo hoo-hoo-hoo-ooooo*.

Juvenile Tawny Owls *have barred, downy plumage, but are otherwise fairly similar in appearance to adult birds.*

Distinctive shape

The Tawny Owl has a characteristic large, round head with "facial discs" like huge spectacles, and its plumage is brown with dark streaks. The stocky body shape and large head make it unmistakable when in flight. Male and female Tawny Owls are similar in appearance.

Courtship and breeding

Tawny Owl pairs remain on their territories all year, and throughout their lives, giving them a vital, intimate knowledge of their hunting grounds. The male attracts a female with a hooting advertising-call. The female lays the eggs in a hole in a tree or building, or in an abandoned squirrel or Magpie nest. Once they can fly, the owlets remain in their parents' territory, hiding amongst tree branches, and can often be heard calling with a hissing *ke-sip* on summer nights. They are fed by their parents until they are driven away when about three months old, and they must then find a territory of their own if they are to have any chance of survival.

The female *Tawny Owl remains with the nestlings for the first 15 days, while the male hunts for food for the family.*

Expert hunters

Tawny Owls prey mainly on small mammals (such as voles) and birds, but also catch fish, amphibians, reptiles, worms, beetles, and moths. Earthworms are easy to find on damp, warm nights when they come to the surface – the owl lands, listens intently, then hops over the ground to seize the worm. Although owls have good eyesight, prey is detected mainly by ear, and consequently rain and wind hamper hunting because the owls cannot hear movements.

In country gardens, Tawny Owls mainly catch mice and voles, but town birds are more likely to feed on birds, up to the size of pigeons. Garden birds are killed mostly at dawn or dusk when they are just active, but Tawny Owls have also been seen taking birds from their roosts. They sometimes attack nests, dragging away the sitting adult and stealing the contents. The birds are plucked first, and remains from plucking and pellets regurgitated after a meal accumulate on the ground under a roost.

The Tawny Owl *carries any prey that is too large to swallow whole to a convenient perch, where it dismembers it.*

IN THE GARDEN

■ Tawny Owls visit bird-tables at dusk to catch small birds while they feed. They may use specially designed owl boxes, particularly if natural sites are scarce.

The contents *of a Tawny Owl pellet can reveal the owl's last meal – this pellet contains the bones and skull of a small mammal.*

At its daytime roost, *the Tawny Owl perches in a tree, with eyes closed and plumage ruffled. It is surprisingly difficult to see amongst the foliage, despite its large size, but its presence is sometimes revealed by its white droppings or when it is mobbed by small birds.*

Strix aluco

Strigidae

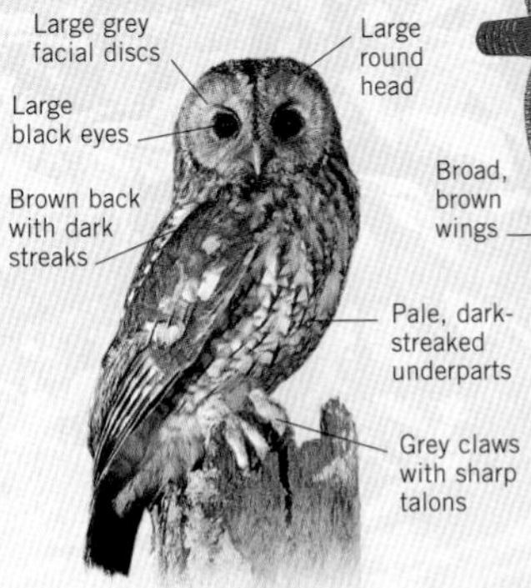

LENGTH 37–39cm (14–15in)
WINGSPAN 94–104cm (37–41in)
VOICE Song is a hollow *hooo* followed by a wavering *hoo-hoo-hoo-oooooo*; call is a sharp *ke-wick*, used for keeping in contact with other birds.
EGGS One brood of 3–4 white eggs in February–May.
REARING Female incubates eggs for 28–30 days; fledging is 32–37 days after hatching.

J F M A M J J A S O N D

Little Owl

WIDESPREAD THROUGHOUT MOST OF EUROPE except the north, the Little Owl is a bird of open countryside, but parkland with trees, even in towns and cities, is also a favourite habitat, and it may stray into gardens. It is more visible than the Tawny Owl and is often seen perched on a tree or fence-post during the day, perhaps because it is on guard near the nest.

Hunting only after dusk *and before dawn, the Little Owl catches small mammals, birds, amphibians, and a variety of insects.*

Daytime perches

This small, long-legged, short-tailed owl is often seen by day. The plumage is brown with spots above, whitish with streaks below. The sexes are alike, but the juvenile is paler with fewer markings. Its bounding flight, in which flapping alternates with wing-closing, is unique among owls. It is easily distinguished from the similar Tawny Owl by its smaller size and yellow rather than dark eyes.

The eggs are laid in a hole in a tree or building, or sometimes in nest-boxes. There is no nest material, but the female scrapes a clear patch on which to lay her eggs. The young may leave the nest before they can fly, to explore along branches or vegetation. Warning calls from their parents send them scuttling back to safety. The owlets continue to be fed for a month after they leave the nest, while they are learning to hunt for themselves.

When hunting, the Little Owl drops from its perch or runs across the ground to prey on earthworms and insects, such as beetles, as well as small mammals and birds. It chases craneflies and other flying insects, and raids compost heaps for worms.

Athene noctua

Strigidae

LENGTH 21–23cm (8–9in)
WINGSPAN 50–56cm (20–22in)

VOICE The male's song is a plaintive whoop, which the female answers with a scream.
EGGS One brood of 2–5 white eggs in April–June.
REARING Female incubates eggs for 27–33 days; fledging is 30–35 days after hatching.

Perched on a post, *the Little Owl has a distinctive round, short-tailed shape, but if alarmed, it stretches its body upwards and has a more elongated profile.*

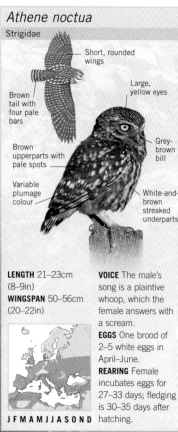

IN THE GARDEN

- Little Owls nest in large, enclosed nest-boxes with a 7cm- ($2\frac{3}{4}$in-) diameter entrance hole, placed in a dark, shaded spot in mature, country gardens.

Swift

NO OTHER BIRD SPENDS as much time in the air as the Swift. After nesting, a Swift may not land again until it returns to its nest the next spring, after mating on the wing. On summer evenings, flocks gather, then circle skywards. They spend the night in a semi-slumber, drifting with the wind, and descend at dawn.

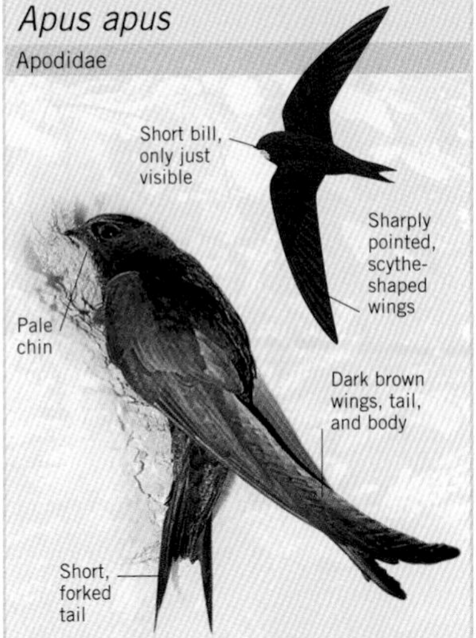

LENGTH 16–17cm (6–6½in)
WINGSPAN 42–48cm (16–19in)

VOICE Calls include a loud, screaming *sree* from flocks and a chirping when at the nest.
EGGS One brood of 2–3 white eggs in May–July.
REARING Eggs are incubated for 18–22 days by both sexes; fledging is 35–56 days after hatching.

Distinctive in flight

In flight, the Swift has an arrow-shaped silhouette, with slender, curving wings and a short, forked tail. Its plumage is wholly dark except for a white chin, distinguishing it from the Swallow and House Martin, both of which have pale or white underparts. Juveniles look similar to adult birds, but have a more obvious, pale throat and subtle, whitish edges to their wing feathers.

Swifts site their nests in holes in walls or under eaves, and will use special, purpose-made nest-boxes. The nest is a shallow cup of grasses, leaves, and feathers collected in the air, and is cemented with saliva. Unusually, the young become fully independent as soon as they leave the nest.

Swifts feed on a wide variety of small flying insects, including aphids, beetles, ants, and flies, which they catch in a slow, gliding flight. They gather over lakes to feed on swarming midges and will fly over 500m (⅓ mile) high to catch small insects and spiders floating on gossamer carried up in turbulent air. In cold, wet spells, flying insects are difficult to find, and Swifts have to travel long distances to locate food.

Nestlings put on weight *rapidly and, by becoming torpid, can survive for long periods without being fed.*

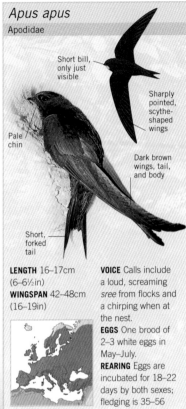

Most often seen *in flight, Swifts rarely perch, but sometimes cling to walls or rooftops. If grounded, they can have great difficulty in taking off again.*

IN THE GARDEN

Swifts nest in special nest-boxes designed with the entrance hole underneath. Fit these horizontally under the eaves of a building.

Green Woodpecker

BOLD COLOURS AND LARGE SIZE make the Green Woodpecker an exciting visitor to the garden. With a diet consisting mainly of ants, its distribution depends on short turf grazed by sheep or rabbits, which create a suitable ant habitat. In the garden, it is ants' nests in lawns that may attract one of these striking birds. Once a nest has been found, a woodpecker may return several times and can find it again even through a layer of snow.

In the breeding season, *the Green Woodpecker excavates a nest-hole in a suitable tree. Its bill is not very strong, however, and this may take up to two or three weeks.*

Picus viridis

Picidae

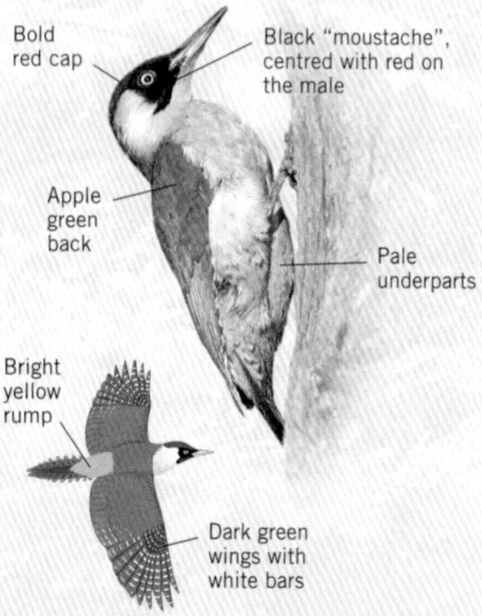

LENGTH 30–33cm (12–13in)

WINGSPAN 40–42cm (16in)

VOICE Loud, laughing calls; the song is a ringing *kleu-kleu-kleu-keu-keu.*

EGGS One clutch of 5–7 white eggs in April–June.

REARING Eggs are incubated for 17–19 days by both sexes (male at night); fledging is 23–27 days after hatching.

Colourful plumage

The Green Woodpecker is a large, striking bird with bright green and yellow body plumage and a red crown and black eye-patch. Distinctive in flight, it has an undulating motion and reveals a bright, yellow rump. The male has a black-edged, red "moustache", which is wholly black in the female. The juvenile is speckled and lacks the characteristic crown and "moustache" markings.

Tree dweller

The Green Woodpecker uses its bill to excavate soft wood when searching for insects or making a nest-hole. Unlike other woodpeckers, it rarely "drums" on tree trunks, but both sexes advertise themselves with loud, ringing, laughing calls that earned this woodpecker the name "yaffle".

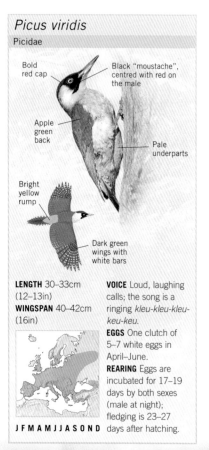

Green Woodpeckers *mainly feed on the ground, moving with short hops across the grass in search of ants. Looking quite hunch-backed, they quickly stand upright if alerted.*

Green Woodpeckers may nest in some large gardens if there are suitable trees in which to excavate holes; they are especially attracted to oak, birch, and ash. The nest-hole is mainly excavated by the male, and has a depth of up to 50cm (20in) and an entrance 6cm (2½in) in diameter. The nest site may be reused in successive years, but is often taken over by Starlings.

Ant eater

The diet of the Green Woodpecker consists mainly of ants, although it occasionally also preys on other types of insect. To reach the ants in a nest, it tears the turf or digs characteristic conical holes, 2cm (¾in) wide at the top, in the soil. It then pushes its 10cm- (4in-) long tongue, which is sticky with saliva, into the nest and wipes up the ants and their pupae,

IN THE GARDEN

- Green Woodpeckers very rarely visit feeders, but may take fat and mealworms. They also forage for ants on garden lawns, making holes in the nests, then using their long tongues to extract the ants. They may sometimes make their nest-holes in mature trees in large gardens.

Juvenile birds *have duller plumage than adult Green Woodpeckers; the green upperparts are heavily spotted with white, while the pale underparts have dark barring.*

larvae, and eggs. If undisturbed, it will feed at the nest for an hour or more, although it may have to stop occasionally to shake the ants off its plumage.

Although it mainly feeds on the ground, the Green Woodpecker sometimes excavates soft wood for insects or forages for them on tree branches. In winter, when insects are particularly hard to find, it is at its most resourceful, excavating insects from telegraph poles and the wooden walls of houses and sheds. This habit can sometimes make this colourful woodpecker unpopular, particularly where it has attacked the cedar shingles of churches and houses.

Female Green Woodpeckers *can be distinguished from males because they have an all-black rather than a red "moustache". Both sexes feed the young while in the nest.*

On fleeting glance, *the Green Woodpecker can be mistaken for the much rarer Golden Oriole because, although it looks bright green while perched, it displays a bright yellow rump when it flies away.*

Great Spotted Woodpecker

A REGULAR AND INTERESTING VISITOR to many gardens, the Great Spotted Woodpecker is not always entirely welcome, because it sometimes raids nest-boxes to eat the eggs and young inside. Like other woodpeckers, it has a stiff tail and an unusual arrangement of toes – two facing forwards, two backwards. These enable it to climb up (and occasionally down) trees and also provide a firm base when the bird chisels wood to search for insects and excavate nest-holes.

The diet of *the Great Spotted Woodpecker consists mostly of insects, but in autumn and winter it relies on a variety of seeds, fruits, and nuts. To prise the seeds from a pinecone, the woodpecker wedges the cone into a cleft in a treetrunk (an "anvil") – it can then be hammered open and the seeds extracted.*

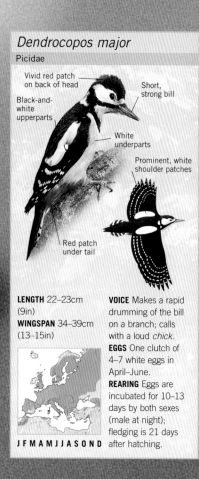

Dendrocopos major

Picidae

LENGTH 22–23cm (9in)
WINGSPAN 34–39cm (13–15in)

J F M A M J J A S O N D

VOICE Makes a rapid drumming of the bill on a branch; calls with a loud *chick*.
EGGS One clutch of 4–7 white eggs in April–June.
REARING Eggs are incubated for 10–13 days by both sexes (male at night); fledging is 21 days after hatching.

Striking colours

The Great Spotted is a medium-sized woodpecker with bold black-and-white colouring on its back, white underparts, and red under its tail. The male has a crimson nape, while the juvenile is duller and has a red crown. In flight, the Great Spotted is recognized by the fast, undulating, flapping and gliding flight and its barred wings with white patches. In regions where several woodpecker species overlap, careful observation of these characteristics is vital to ensure accurate identification.

The juvenile, *easily distinguished by its bright red cap, accompanies and is fed by its parents for about one week after fledging.*

Great Spotted Woodpeckers *are solitary outside the breeding season, and it is rare to see more than one at a time at a feeder.*

Wooden notes

The woodpecker's "song" is a rapid (20 times per second) drum on a trunk or branch, which produces a far-carrying sound like a snore. The note produced varies according to the size and type of branch. To protect the bird's brain from the effects of these repeated impacts, it is cradled and cushioned inside a strong skull.

Male and female Great Spotted Woodpeckers live in separate home ranges until late winter, when pairing takes place and the male's drumming "song" can be heard. The pair-bond may last for up to three years. It takes two or three weeks for both sexes to excavate the nest chamber in a treetrunk, usually 3–5m (10–17ft) above the ground; once made, the chamber is used for several years, unless usurped by Starlings. Both parents incubate the eggs, with the male taking the greater part, and both feed the nestlings.

The selected "anvil" tree *is often repeatedly used throughout winter, the emptied cones dropping to the ground below.*

Seasonal diet

Great Spotted Woodpeckers have a very broad diet. In summer, they feed mostly on a variety of insects, ranging from woodboring beetles to flies caught in the air. They are so well-known for feeding on insects living in timber, chipping away wood with hammer-blows of the pointed bill, that it is surprising to see them eating peanuts in the garden. They extract soft-bodied grubs in timber by impaling them on a 4cm- (1½in-) long tongue; smaller insects stick to the mucus-covered bristles at the tip.

In winter, Great Spotted Woodpeckers feed on the seeds of pine, larch, spruce, birch, and other hardwood trees, as well as on nuts, fruit, and fungi. In parts of Europe, but rarely in Britain, they also drill holes in the trunks of trees, drinking the sap that oozes out.

Female Great Spotted Woodpeckers *can easily be distinguished from males because they lack the distinctive, red nape patch.*

IN THE GARDEN

- Great Spotted Woodpeckers take peanuts and suet from garden feeders or log-feeders. In mature gardens, they will sometimes nest in holes in old trees.

House Martin

IN THE DAYS BEFORE BUILDINGS provided nesting places, the House Martin occupied cliffs and rock outcrops, where colonies can still be seen. Nests are now more often built under the eaves or on the window frames of houses. While many people welcome these charming birds, some complain about soiled windows and paths – a problem that can be solved by fixing a "splashboard" under a nest.

IN THE GARDEN

- House Martins nest under the eaves of buildings, and use artificial nests placed high on a wall. Always leave old nests in place as they may be re-used, and will attract birds back in future years.

Summer visitors

Elegant visitors to most of Europe, House Martins are a welcome sight in summer, visible high in the sky or in their mud nests under the eaves of buildings. They migrate south in autumn to over-winter in Africa. House Martins can easily be distinguished from the similar Swallows, because their forked tails lack long tail-streamers. They have blue-black upperparts, with white underparts and a white throat. In winter, the white underside is mottled with brown-black. When seen in flight, House Martins reveal a bright white rump; this is duller and browner on juvenile birds, and juveniles also have some white mottling on the nape.

House Martins collect *mud from the edges of puddles or ponds to build their nests. In warm, dry summers, they may struggle to find enough material; gardeners can help by watering patches of soil to provide a source of mud.*

Social throughout the year, *House Martins form large flocks for migration and in their winter habitats, while in the breeding season, they build their nests in small colonies.*

Group dynamics

Soon after they return to their breeding grounds in spring, House Martins prospect for suitable nest sites, usually returning to a previous year's nest or selecting a new site near old nests. They breed in colonies averaging five nests, although sometimes numbering tens or even hundreds. Colonies that have been stable for years can sometimes suddenly go into decline, partly because new housing allows the martins to spread out, but also perhaps as a result of a general decline in House Martin numbers. The siting of artificial nests can be very successful, as House Martins will readily use them, and this in turn attracts others to nest nearby.

A cup-shaped nest *is built from pellets of mud, and lined with feathers and grasses collected in the air. Both sexes help to build the nest, although the male takes the major role in choosing the site.*

A pair of House Martins usually spends some time in the nest before the start of egg-laying. Both parents are involved in incubating the eggs and feeding the young.

When the nestlings are nearly fully grown and are ready to leave the nest, their heads appear at the entrance. As the time approaches for them to leave the nest, the parents, with other unrelated birds also joining in, try to lure the young martins out by hovering in front of the entrance and calling. Eventually an adult bird, usually the mother, lands at the nest, and a youngster emerges and flies away with her. Later, the fledglings are fed by their parents in midair.

Aerial hunter

House Martins feed on the wing, catching a variety of flying insects, including flies and aphids. They may sometimes also pick prey from the ground or while perched in trees. Typically, while in flight, a House Martin will suddenly climb steeply on rapidly beating wings, grab an insect, then glide down. House Martins usually fly higher than Swallows and catch smaller insects.

House Martins are *most often seen in flight or perching on wires or rooftops. They do not spend much time on the ground except when collecting mud for nest-building.*

Delichon urbica

Hirundinidae

LENGTH 12cm (4½in)
WINGSPAN 26–29cm (10–11in)
VOICE Soft, twittering song; contact calls include quick, chirping notes.
EGGS 1–3 clutches of 2–5 white eggs from late May–August.
REARING Eggs are incubated for 15 days by both sexes; fledging is 22–32 days after hatching.

J F M **A M J J A S O** N D

Swallow

SWALLOWS SPEND THE WINTER in Africa, returning to nest in much of Europe. The precise timing of their return in any year depends on the weather – they move north through Europe as the air warms up, and a cold snap or adverse winds will slow their progress. Before nesting, and again afterwards, Swallows roost communally in reed beds and scrub, and occasionally in buildings.

IN THE GARDEN

■ Swallows make saucer-shaped nests inside barns and other buildings. Leave a window open for access to a shed or garage. In very dry weather, water a patch of soil to provide mud for nest-building.

The nest is constructed *with pellets of mud collected from the edges of ponds and puddles. The male Swallow collects the nest material while the female builds the nest.*

Distinctive in flight

Shiny blue-black above and white below, the handsome Swallow has a red face and throat with a broad blue-black band across the breast. Long tail streamers and more pointed wings distinguish the adult Swallow from its close relatives, the Sand and House Martins. The male has longer tail streamers than the female.

Display and nesting

Unlike House Martins, Swallows do not nest in colonies, but build solitary cup- or half-cup-shaped nests of mud and grass, lined with feathers. The male circles above his chosen site, singing to attract a female. Buildings have almost entirely replaced cliff ledges and hollow trees as the favoured sites, and nests are usually placed on a beam or a shelf, or anchored to a vertical surface. A light fitting or a protruding nail is sufficient foundation. Old nests are often used, especially by experienced pairs.

The female is responsible for incubation but the male assists with feeding the young. Both mob predators, such as cats, Magpies, birds of prey, and even humans, swooping over them and sometimes making contact. Other unrelated Swallows may also join in the attacks.

On the wing

The Swallow forages for insects in the air, either swooping low or circling overhead in graceful movements that are punctuated by swift, jinking turns. The long tail-feathers provide great manoeuvrability in flight and make the Swallow more efficient at catching prey than Swifts or martins.

Swallows generally choose larger insects than House Martins. Bluebottle-sized flies are the preferred choice, but bees, butterflies, moths, and other large flying insects are also caught. In colder weather, when larger insects are in short supply, they also catch greenfly and other tiny insects, and may take insects from leaves or the ground if there is a shortage of flying insects.

After arriving from *their long migratory journeys in early summer, Swallows delay the start of nesting if there is a spell of colder weather.*

Swallow young *leave the nest after about three weeks, but continue to be fed by both of their parents for a further seven days.*

Hirundo rustica

Hirundinidae

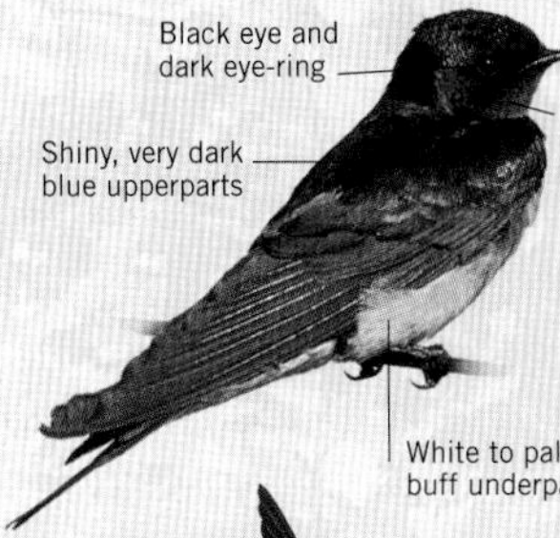

LENGTH 17–19cm (6½–7½in)
WINGSPAN 32–35cm (12–14in)

J F M A M J J A S O N D

VOICE Pleasant, twittering song; calls with a repeated *swit-swit-swit.*
EGGS 2–3 clutches of 4–5 red-spotted, white eggs from May–August.
REARING Female incubates eggs for 14–15 days; fledging is 19–21 days after hatching.

Before migration, *Swallows gather in huge flocks, creating an impressive sight as they perch in long, tight rows on overhead wires.*

Elegant in the air, *the Swallow flies with shallow wingbeats, often interspersed with graceful swoops and glides as it hunts for flying insects.*

Swallows swoop *down to the water to drink on the wing; they also hunt for insects over areas of open water, especially in early spring.*

Pied Wagtail

ORIGINALLY A WATERSIDE BIRD, the Pied Wagtail has adapted well to man-made habitats. It visits gardens, parks, car parks, and rubbish tips for feeding, and nests and roosts in buildings. Always on the move, with tail bobbing up and down, this active bird walks or runs after insects that it catches on or near the ground.

The White Wagtail *is a race of* Motacilla alba *that breeds in Europe; it looks similar to the Pied Wagtail except for its pale grey back.*

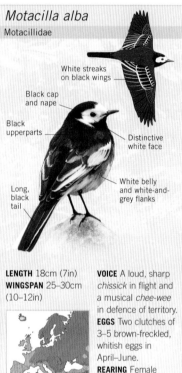

Motacilla alba

Motacillidae

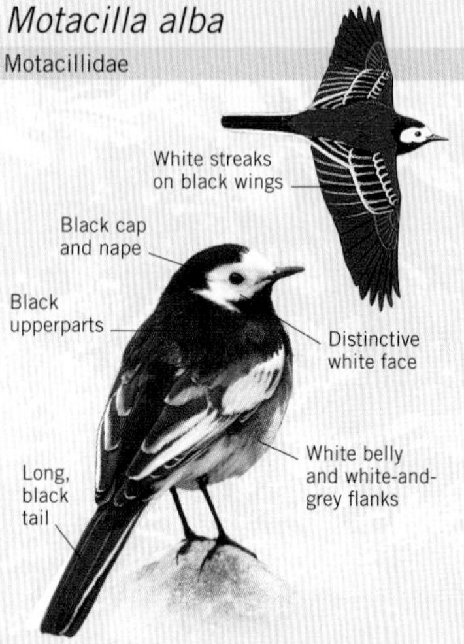

LENGTH 18cm (7in)
WINGSPAN 25–30cm (10–12in)

J F M A M J J A S O N D

VOICE A loud, sharp *chissick* in flight and a musical *chee-wee* in defence of territory.
EGGS Two clutches of 3–5 brown-freckled, whitish eggs in April–June.
REARING Female incubates eggs for 14 days; fledging is 14 days after hatching.

Stark colours

With its striking black-and-white plumage and long, bobbing tail, the Pied Wagtail is an unmistakable character often found in urban areas. In winter, the black throat turns white. The female has a greyer back than the male, while the juvenile looks "dirtier" and its tail is shorter.

Many Pied Wagtails gather in flocks for the winter, and roost communally in warehouses, glasshouses, city trees, and other warm, safe sites. They disperse into nesting territories in spring. The cup-nest of grass, roots, and mosses is built in a suitable hole in a bank, cliff, wall, or building. Old nests of larger birds may also be used. Nesting females can sometimes be identified because their tails become bent while incubating in a small space.

Pied Wagtails are energetic in their search for food, typically picking up food while walking, but also pursuing moving insects with darting runs and jumps, or with short bursts of flight to catch them in the air. They have successfully moved into urban areas to take advantage of the wealth of insect life that human habitation attracts.

IN THE GARDEN

- Pied Wagtails take stale crumbs, grated cheese, and mealworms from the ground. They sometimes use open nest-boxes, especially if placed amongst ivy or other thick vegetation.

Flies and other small insects *are the Pied Wagtail's main food, but it also eats spiders, snails, earthworms, and small seeds.*

Waxwing

THE WAXWING TAKES ITS NAME from the red, waxy spots, like blobs of sealing wax, on its secondary wing feathers. Waxwings breed in northern Europe, and each year some migrate southwards, reaching northern Germany, Belgium, and the Netherlands. A few get as far as Britain, especially when food supplies are scarce.

The female Waxwing *incubates the eggs, but both sexes feed the young, providing a mixture of insects and berries.*

Striking plumage

The Waxwing is an eyecatching, colourful, pinkish-brown bird, with a dramatic, pointed crest, a bold, black bib, and bright red markings on the wings. Its tail has a band of yellow at the tip, and males also have yellow markings on their wings. Male and female are difficult to distinguish, although the markings on the female's wings and the black bib are slightly duller than the male's. Juvenile birds also have a duller plumage than the male, and lack the black bib.

Outside the breeding season, Waxwings form flocks for migration, feeding, and roosting. Every few years, a shortage of food forces nomadic behaviour, when large numbers travel to areas, such as Britain, that are outside their normal winter range.

Waxwings nest in conifer and birch forests. The cup-shaped nest of twigs, grass, and lichen, lined with fine grass, is built by both male and female, usually close to the trunk of a tree, up to 15m (50ft) from the ground.

IN THE GARDEN

- Waxwings feed on the fruits and berries of a range of shrubs in winter, including those of rowan, apple, pyracantha, cotoneaster, and rose.

In summer, the Waxwing's diet chiefly consists of insects, especially mosquitoes and midges. As the weather gets cooler towards autumn, and insects become increasingly hard to find, they switch to fruit and many kinds of berries.

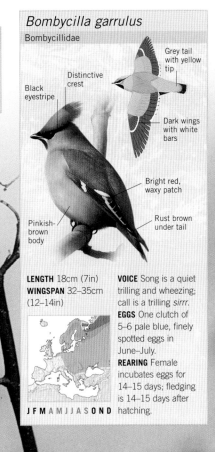

Berries and fruits *are an important part of the Waxwing's diet in winter; it picks berries from trees and bushes, or forages for fallen fruits on the ground.*

Bombycilla garrulus

Bombycillidae

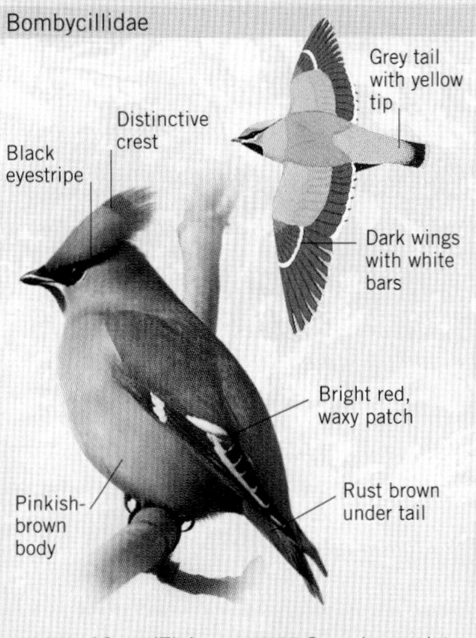

LENGTH 18cm (7in)
WINGSPAN 32–35cm (12–14in)

J F M A M J J A S **O N D**

VOICE Song is a quiet trilling and wheezing; call is a trilling *sirrr.*
EGGS One clutch of 5–6 pale blue, finely spotted eggs in June–July.
REARING Female incubates eggs for 14–15 days; fledging is 14–15 days after hatching.

Dunnock

ONCE KNOWN AS the Hedge Sparrow because it looks rather similar to the House Sparrow, the Dunnock is in fact a member of the accentor family. Common in British gardens, it is a shy woodland bird in continental Europe, and is easily overlooked because of its skulking, mouse-like habits. It keeps near cover, spending much of its time under bushes.

Dunnocks *may visit gardens in search of food and nest sites. They are particularly attracted to dense shrubs that provide cover for nesting.*

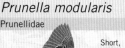

The Dunnock's warbling *song is similar to that of a Wren. The male Dunnock sings from early spring throughout the breeding season, usually from a prominent perch in a tree or bush, although sometimes in flight.*

Prunella modularis

Prunellidae

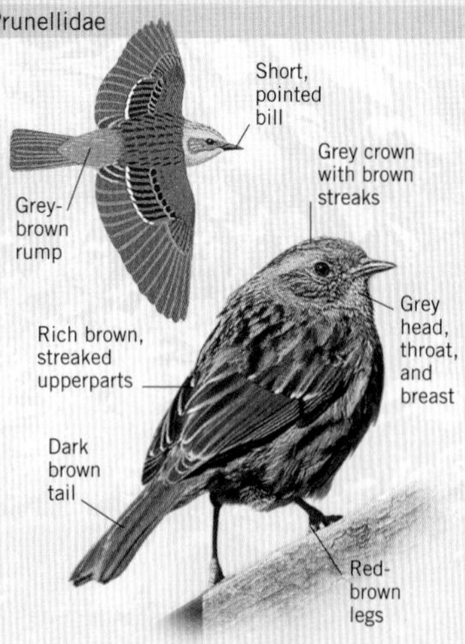

LENGTH 14cm (5½in)
WINGSPAN 19–21cm (7½–8in)

J F M A M J J A S O N D

VOICE Song is a rapid warbling, similar to the song of a Wren; calls include a sharp, shrill *tseep*.
EGGS 2–3 clutches of 4–5 blue eggs in April–July.
REARING Female incubates eggs for 14 days; fledging is 12 days after hatching.

IN THE GARDEN

■ Dunnocks feed on nyjer seed, peanut hearts, oatmeal, and grated cheese scattered on the ground, and also forage for fragments under bird-tables. They will sometimes visit a quiet bird-table.

Both parents *care for the young, and additional males may also provide help. The fledglings remain with their parents for 2–3 weeks after they fly the nest.*

Subtle markings

At first sight, a Dunnock looks uniformly brown, but on closer inspection, sparrow-like, brown, streaked upperparts and a grey head, throat, and breast are revealed. The sexes are alike, but juveniles are browner and more striped than the adults. Although similar in size to the House Sparrow, it is easy to tell them apart because the Dunnock has a very thin bill and its legs are orange.

Unusual breeding habits

Individual Dunnocks maintain separate ranges through the winter, but several may come together to take advantage of good feeding places. They advertise their presence in their winter ranges with repeated *seep* calls, and display aggression by raising and quivering one wing (the "shufflewing" display).

Dunnocks have been discovered to have a complex and unusual mating system. Males and females hold separate, but overlapping, territories. A single male may consort with one or two females, one female may share two males, or occasionally, two of each sex associate together. The advantage to a female of having extra males is that each male helps to feed the nestlings of each female with which they have mated.

The female builds the nest of twigs and moss, lined with moss and hair, low-down in thick hedges and shrubs. She incubates the eggs on her own. Dunnocks are favourite hosts to Cuckoos, which occasionally visit gardens to find a nest in which to lay their eggs.

The juvenile Dunnock *lacks the grey markings of adult birds, and has more brown in its plumage, with more prominent streaks.*

Resident in western Europe, *Dunnocks are migrants in other parts, with many travelling south from northern Europe in winter.*

The daily grind

A large proportion of the Dunnock's day is spent feeding, and in winter, the search for food may take up almost all available daylight hours. It hops along the ground, pecking continuously to pick up small items of food. The diet consists mainly of small insects, spiders, snails, and worms in summer, which are found among vegetation as well as on the ground. The winter diet is mostly seeds picked from the ground.

Flicking their wings *and calling with shrill "tseep" calls, two Dunnocks perform their unique, pre-mating courtship display.*

Wren

The Wren's powerful voice *belies its tiny size; its warbling song can be heard all year round, except in late summer and early autumn.*

THE TINY WREN IS SECRETIVE in its habits and easily overlooked as it prefers to keep to dense undergrowth. When in the open, it scurries like a mouse along the tops of fences and the edges of walls and borders. Wrens generally feed on and near the ground, and in severe winters, when the ground is covered with a thick layer of snow and ice, many do not survive. Numbers recover quickly, however, if the following years are mild.

Appearance and nesting

A small, compact bird with a thin bill and a short, cocked tail, the Wren is reddish-brown above and paler below, with barred wings and flanks, and a white stripe over the eye.

The Wren's diet *consists mainly of small insects, especially beetles and spiders, which it picks up with its forceps-like bill.*

Male Wrens hold large territories in which they build several nests in holes in walls or trees, or in old nests of other birds. The male sings near a nest to entice a female. If she accepts, she adds a lining of feathers to the nest and lays the eggs. When food is abundant, a male may persuade two or more females to lay in his territory. The unused, unlined nests, known as "cock nests", may be used for roosting.

The female feeds the young with little help from the male. Her scolding *chit* calls of alarm are a common sound in the garden when a human or cat comes too close to the nest. When the young leave the nest, the male takes over their care and even leads them to roost in one of his cock nests or the abandoned nest of another bird.

Basic nutrition

Wrens search among leaves and bark, in crevices in walls, and under leaf litter for a variety of small insects; compost heaps that have been dug over provide a rich source of food. They occasionally eat seeds and berries. When the ground is snow-covered, much of the Wren's food sources can be out of reach, but they still find some food under bushes. In gardens with no shrubs or hedges, "umbrellas" of cut conifer branches can provide snow-free patches in which they can hunt for insects. Amazingly, Wrens have also been known to catch tadpoles, goldfish, and trout fry.

IN THE GARDEN

- Wrens sometimes take breadcrumbs, mealworms, and grated cheese from the ground. They use open and, occasionally, enclosed nest-boxes, and may use either of these for winter roosting (sometimes several birds together to conserve heat).

The globe-shaped nest *is made from dead leaves, grass, moss, and other plant material, and is built with a side entrance.*

With a blur *of whirring wings, the restless Wren in flight resembles an outsize bumblebee as it whizzes around the garden searching for food.*

With its tail held upright *in characteristic pose, the Wren is the shortest European bird. It is often also believed to be the smallest, but is larger than a few other species, such as the tiny Goldcrest. Wrens are shy birds, most likely to visit the garden in winter, especially when food is in short supply.*

Troglodytes troglodytes

Troglodytidae

LENGTH 9–10cm (3½–4in)
WINGSPAN 13–17cm (5–6½in)
VOICE Surprisingly loud, shrill, trilling song; calls include a hard, dry, rattling *tick-tick-tick* and a rolling *churr*.
EGGS Two clutches of 5–6, usually whitish, eggs in April–July.

REARING Female incubates eggs for 16–17 days; fledging is 16–17 days after hatching.

J F M A M J J A S O N D

Robin

VOTED BRITAIN'S NATIONAL BIRD by a public poll in the 1960s, the Robin has spread into British gardens in a way that has not happened over much of the rest of Europe. Its natural habitat of forest with a layer of undergrowth is mimicked by the hedges, shrubs, and trees of British gardens, parks, and roadsides. In other parts of Europe, the Robin is a shy woodland bird.

IN THE GARDEN

Robins love mealworms and will take scraps of bread, meat, potatoes, and fat. Some have learnt to take peanuts and sunflower seeds from hanging feeders. They sometimes nest in open nest-boxes.

Erithacus rubecula

Turdidae

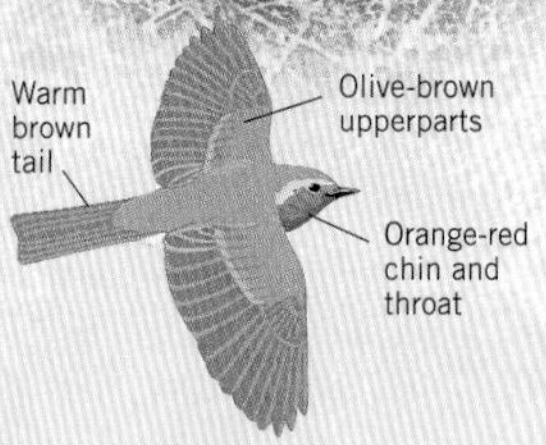

LENGTH 14cm (5½in)
WINGSPAN 20–22cm (8–9in)

VOICE Bursts of liquid warbling; alarm calls are a thin *tseeee* and a repeated *tic.*
EGGS 2–3 broods of 5–6 red-speckled, white, or bluish eggs from April–June.
REARING Female incubates eggs for 14 days; fledging is 13–14 days after hatching.

An unmistakable *garden visitor, the Robin has a large head and round body, appearing even rounder in winter when it fluffs out its feathers to retain body heat.*

Familiar colours

The Robin is easily identified by its round body and distinctive red face and breast above a pale belly. It flies with short, flitting movements, often darting into cover. On the ground, it moves with characteristic hops, pausing often to flick its wings and tail.

The Robin defends *its territory fiercely, singing and fluffing out its red breast feathers to warn off any intruders.*

Private property

Robins maintain and defend territories all year round except for during the summer moult period and in the severest winter weather. A territory is necessary not only for breeding, but also to ensure a private food supply; any Robin without its own sources of food will die within a few weeks. Defence of the territory is therefore extremely aggressive, and if an intruder does not retreat, rivals may come to blows, sometimes with serious and even fatal results.

Male and female Robins defend separate territories in winter, and sing in their defence; they form pairs from December, with the female usually joining the male in his territory. With a good supply of food, Robins will nest earlier in the year. A hair-lined nest of moss and leaves, based on a pad of dead leaves, is built in a crevice in a tree or between rocks, or in a man-made object; sheds, tins, and letter-boxes are favourites.

Both parents feed the young, sometimes splitting the family between them. When the female lays another clutch of eggs, the male feeds the first family alone.

The juvenile has *a heavily spotted, brown body and lacks the characteristic red breast of the adult Robin.*

Highly vocal *all year round, Robins have a rich song in spring, but mellow, sad tones in autumn.*

A natural hunter

Robins mainly eat ground-living invertebrates – insects (especially beetles), snails, worms, and spiders – but occasionally they may also take fish and tadpoles. When hunting, the Robin watches for insects from a low perch, then drops down, seizes its prey, and flies up again. It also hops across the ground, pausing at intervals to watch for moving prey. From autumn to early spring, fruit and berries are also an important part of its diet.

A familiar sight *in British gardens, the Robin follows the gardener's fork, feasting on the invertebrates that emerge as the soil is turned.*

Blackbird

ORIGINALLY A WOODLAND BIRD, the Blackbird has become a familiar figure in the garden. As woodland and farmland habitats have disappeared, so the trees and lawns of mature gardens and parks have become a haven for Blackbirds. Numbers rise in winter when residents are joined by immigrants. After nesting, many leave gardens to take advantage of fruit crops in the hedgerows.

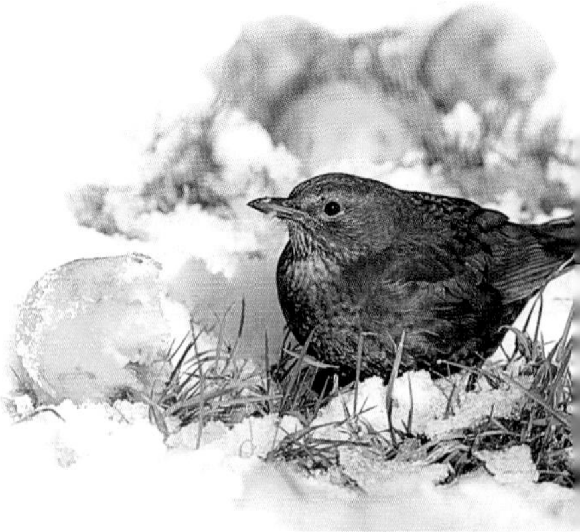

In winter, *the Blackbird's diet switches from earthworms to fruit and berries, including cotoneaster, honeysuckle, and barberry.*

Colour differences

Slightly larger than a Starling, the adult male Blackbird, with its stark, black plumage, offset by bright yellow eye-rings and bill, is an unmistakable garden bird. Female and juvenile Blackbirds are more difficult to identify: the female is dark brown rather than black, with mottling on the throat and chest; the juvenile is similar, but with more spots on the throat and chest, and a dark bill.

The female Blackbird *can sometimes be confused with the Song Thrush, but is generally much darker in colour.*

Raising a family

The Blackbird's rich, warbling song – often delivered from a prominent perch, such as the corner of a rooftop – can be heard from late winter to early spring, when young males set up their territories. It reaches a peak when established males join in. If the weather is mild, breeding starts early. The female builds a solid nest, usually in a shrub or hedge. Dry vegetation, which the male may help her collect, is reinforced with mud. The male sometimes stands guard over the eggs when the female is away feeding. After fledging, the family is divided and each parent feeds particular youngsters, but the male may look after the whole family if the female has a new clutch to incubate. The pair may raise two or more broods in a single season.

Seasonal fare

Blackbirds feed mainly on worms, insects, and other small invertebrates. Fruit and berries are eaten from late summer to early winter. Caterpillars are an important food in the nesting season but, as these are often rare in gardens, young are fed more on worms and adult insects. They forage

Garden ponds *not only provide water for bathing and drinking, but Blackbirds sometimes also catch tadpoles and even small fish to eat.*

IN THE GARDEN

■ Blackbirds visit gardens to take kitchen scraps, bread, fat, seeds, and old fruit, such as apples and pears. They sometimes nest in large, open nest-boxes.

on the ground, using their bills to pick through and turn over leaf litter, and also feed in trees and bushes. They steal food from other birds, such as large snails that have already been broken open by a Song Thrush.

When hunting on a lawn, a Blackbird cocks its head to one side before hopping forward to pull an earthworm from the ground. This head posture may help the bird listen for movements underground, or may help it spot earthworms that are protruding from the soil.

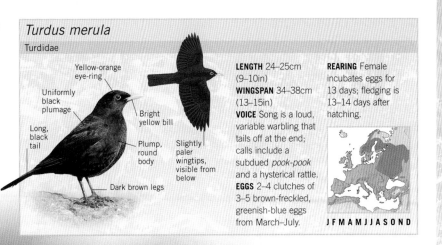

Turdus merula

Turdidae

LENGTH 24–25cm (9–10in)
WINGSPAN 34–38cm (13–15in)
VOICE Song is a loud, variable warbling that tails off at the end; calls include a subdued *pook-pook* and a hysterical rattle.
EGGS 2–4 clutches of 3–5 brown-freckled, greenish-blue eggs from March–July.

REARING Female incubates eggs for 13 days; fledging is 13–14 days after hatching.

J F M A M J J A S O N D

A Blackbird twists *its head to reach the preen gland at the base of its tail, picking up preen oil on its beak. It rubs the oil over its feathers, to maintain their condition and waterproofing.*

In strong sunshine, *Blackbirds may sometimes be seen "sunbathing" with wings and tail spread. This is an important part of feather care and is followed by vigorous preening.*

Song Thrush

A RATHER SHY GARDEN VISITOR throughout the year, the Song Thrush is more often seen feeding on the lawn and in flowerbeds than at the bird-table. In cold weather, or if food is otherwise in short supply, Song Thrushes living in the countryside may join those already in gardens. Recently, the rapid decline in Song Thrush numbers in some parts of Europe has become a cause for great concern.

IN THE GARDEN

Song Thrushes visit gardens to take fat, sultanas, and kitchen scraps from underneath bird-tables. They also enjoy apples left in quiet corners, near to the cover offered by hedges and shrubs.

Turdus philomelos

Turdidae

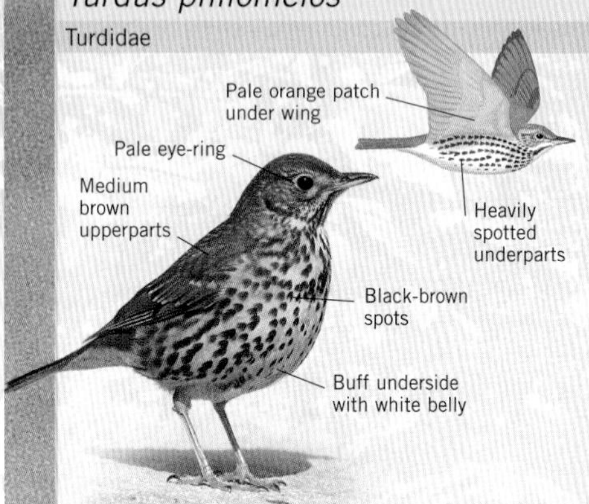

LENGTH 23cm (9in)
WINGSPAN 33–36cm (13–14in)
VOICE Clear, fluting, musical song with a series of short phrases repeated three or four times; calls include a short *tick* and a rattle of alarm.
EGGS 2–3 clutches of 4–6 blue eggs from March–August.

REARING Female incubates eggs for 13–14 days; fledging is 13 days after hatching.

J F M A M J J A S O N D

In dry weather, *when it becomes increasingly difficult to extract earthworms from parched garden lawns, a Song Thrush turns to an alternative food source – snails. With expert twists of the head, it smashes the shells on a rock or "anvil", to reach the soft inner parts.*

The nest of twigs *and grass has a unique, smooth, inner lining made from mud mixed with saliva. The same nest may be re-used for further broods.*

Easy to recognize *even when splashing about in a bird-bath, the Song Thrush has warm brown upperparts and a distinctive spotted breast.*

Distinctive spots

The Song Thrush is a familiar sight on garden lawns. It can be distinguished from the similar Mistle Thrush because the spots on its breast are arranged in lines and shaped like upside-down hearts, while those of the Mistle Thrush are scattered and circular. Song Thrushes are also smaller and browner than Mistle Thrushes, and their flight pattern is direct, compared with the undulating flight of the Mistle Thrush.

Diminishing numbers

In some northern European countries, there has been a worrying decline in Song Thrush numbers in recent years, both in gardens and the countryside. Fears that this was caused by predators, especially Magpies and Sparrowhawks, or by pesticide-poisoning have not been confirmed and research has shown that nesting birds rear as many young as they used to. More young Song Thrushes are dying in their first winter, however, perhaps due to a shortage of food at this time caused by the disappearance of vital habitat on farmland.

Nesting starts earlier than with most birds, and in mild weather the first clutch may be laid as early as February or March. A well-shaded site is usually chosen for the nest, often low in a bush or tree, or amongst the thick foliage of creepers, such as ivy. As summer advances, you may hear fledged young calling to their parents from hideouts in the undergrowth with sharp *chick* sounds.

Song Thrushes are *partial migrants; a few males hold their territories, singing throughout winter, but others migrate, even as far as Africa.*

Snail specialist

The Song Thrush feeds mainly on insects and other invertebrate animals. Worms are an important food, especially in the earlier part of the year, as is fruit (including fallen apples, and berries such as elder, holly, and rowan) in autumn. Snails are mainly an emergency ration, taken in winter frosts or summer droughts when hard ground makes worms and insects difficult to catch. Breaking the snail's shell and sorting through the untidy remains is a laborious and time-consuming task that is not worthwhile when other food is readily available. Only Song Thrushes smash open snails, but watch for Blackbirds waiting to snatch the snail flesh from them.

Earthworms and *other invertebrates make up the bulk of the Song Thrush's diet. Windfall fruit is taken when available.*

Mistle Thrush

NAMED AFTER one of its favourite foods – the berries of mistletoe – the Mistle Thrush is one of the largest European thrushes. Although it breeds widely across Europe, it is never abundant. This aggressive bird vigorously defends a large breeding territory, and often occupies larger gardens with tall trees that provide high song-posts, from which the male delivers its far-carrying, ringing song.

IN THE GARDEN

- Mistle Thrushes sometimes visit gardens to take kitchen scraps, bread, and apples, often defending their food supply from other visitors. They also feed on the berries of some shrubs and trees.

Bold spots

The Mistle Thrush is larger than the similar Song Thrush, and has larger spots on its underside. There is a pale patch around the eye and the white corners of the tail and white underwings are visible in flight. The juvenile is similar, but with a paler head and with whitish spots on the back.

The Mistle Thrush *feeds on the berries of a number of plants and trees, including rowan, holly, hawthorn, and mistletoe.*

Protective parents

The female takes one to two weeks to build a grass-lined nest of earth and plants, often well-hidden in tree foliage but sometimes exposed. The first nest is likely to be concealed in the dense foliage of a conifer. The Mistle Thrush is more wary of people than the Song Thrush. Cats, Magpies, and birds of prey that come too close to the nest are vigorously attacked with swoops and a harsh, rattling call of alarm. Both adults feed the nestlings initially, but the male then continues to feed the first brood alone once the female lays her second clutch. One nest may be used for all the year's clutches. Once fledged, the juveniles form small flocks; larger flocks gather when nesting has finished at the end of summer.

Seasonal changes

After winter flocks break up, some individuals and pairs defend territories around crops of berries (and well-stocked bird-tables) from other birds. Good berry crops can serve as individual food stores until spring, allowing the owners to start nesting earlier and to produce larger clutches. They can be overwhelmed, however, when flocks of Redwings and Fieldfares arrive and strip the bushes clear.

Singing is at its height *in the breeding season, but starts in midwinter, when Mistle Thrushes can be heard even when their exposed perches are lashed by wind and rain.*

The female *Mistle Thrush is similar in appearance to the male; she builds the cup-shaped nest and incubates the eggs for 12–15 days.*

Mistle Thrush young *leave the nest after about two weeks, but are not fully independent for a further 14 days.*

In spring and summer, *animal food starts to become important in the Mistle Thrush's diet, as it turns to insects, spiders, worms, and snails. It mainly feeds on the ground, but also forages in trees and bushes and sometimes catches flying insects.*

Turdus viscivorus

Turdidae

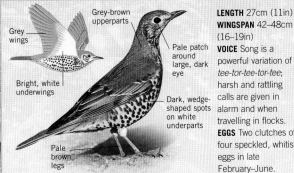

LENGTH 27cm (11in)
WINGSPAN 42–48cm (16–19in)
VOICE Song is a powerful variation of *tee-tor-tee-tor-tee*; harsh and rattling calls are given in alarm and when travelling in flocks.
EGGS Two clutches of four speckled, whitish eggs in late February–June.
REARING Female incubates eggs for 12–15 days; fledging is 12–15 days after hatching.

J F M A M J J A S O N D

Redwing

REDWINGS ARE WINTER VISITORS to much of southern and western Europe. The numbers and timing of their arrival depend on conditions in their summer homes in northern Europe. They are seen mainly on farmland, but visit gardens in cold weather to search for crops of berries – a flock will sometimes land on a tree and strip it of berries in a few hours.

The Redwing's song *is a variable, repeated sequence of short fluting phrases, concluding with a throaty chuckle.*

Turdus iliacus

Turdidae

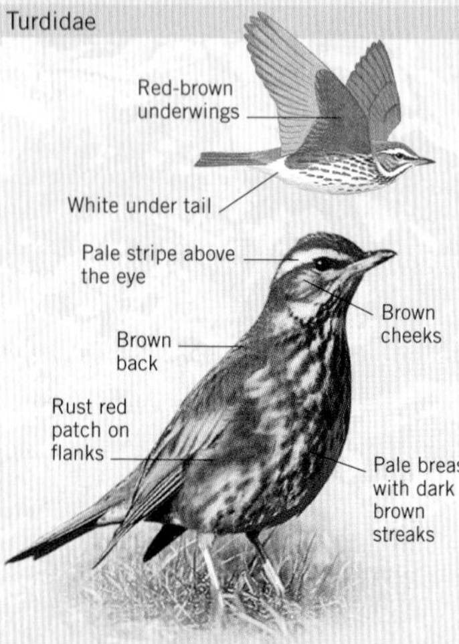

LENGTH 21cm (8in)
WINGSPAN 33–35cm (13–14in)

J F M A M J J A S O N D

VOICE The call, often given in flight, is a soft, lisping *see-ip*.
EGGS Two clutches of 4–6 red-brown speckled, pale blue eggs in May–June.
REARING Female incubates eggs for 12–13 days; fledging is 10 days after hatching.

A distinctive thrush

The Redwing, named after its red underwing and flanks, is the smallest member of the thrush family. It is more easily recognized by the facial pattern of bold, cream stripes above the eye and below the cheek. The sexes and ages are alike.

Redwings are common nesting birds in the sparse woods, scrubs, and suburban gardens of northern Europe, including Iceland, where their twittering song is a familiar sound. They started to breed in northern Scotland 70 years ago and around 50 pairs nest there every year. The cup-shaped nest is usually built in a tree or bush, but may be on the ground, especially in the treeless far north of Europe. It is made of twigs and grass, the inside plastered with mud and lined with fine grass and leaves.

Hunting for insects

The Redwing's diet consists mainly of small animals, especially insects, but also small snails, slugs, and earthworms. In autumn and winter, when animal food becomes scarce, it turns increasingly to berries. Redwings forage for food on the ground, often picking through leaf litter in search of insects.

In freezing conditions, *food shortages in the countryside force Redwing flocks into gardens and parks.*

IN THE GARDEN

Redwings enjoy the berries of holly, cotoneaster, and hawthorn bushes. They feed on apples left on the ground and, rarely, kitchen scraps.

Fieldfare

THE FIELDFARE IS A NORTHERN SPECIES, like the Redwing, but has colonized central Europe over the last 50 years. It is a winter visitor to western and southern parts, forming large feeding flocks, often mixed with Redwings. These flocks are nomadic in their search for food, and a shortage of berries drives them into gardens.

Aggressive defences

A large, long-tailed thrush, the Fieldfare is distinguished from other thrushes by its grey head and rump and chestnut brown back. When in flight, the white underwing patches are a useful feature for identification.

Fieldfares nest in sparse woods and scrub, including city parks, in northern and central Europe. They breed both in solitary pairs, and in colonies of up to 50 pairs. The nest is often built in a tree or bush, although sometimes a site near the ground is chosen. Although the nest site is often exposed, neighbouring pairs of Fieldfares help to defend the colony's nests, and can be extremely aggressive towards intruders. People, cats, and Magpies coming too close are "dive-bombed" with angry cries, and are sometimes spattered with droppings. The birds continue their attacks until the predator retreats.

The diet of the Fieldfare mainly consists of earthworms, snails, and many types of small insect. It eats fruit in winter, especially when animal food is unavailable. Crops of berries are particularly attractive, and a single Fieldfare will try to defend a tree against all comers.

Turdus pilaris

Turdidae

LENGTH 27cm (11in)
WINGSPAN 39–42cm (15–16in)
VOICE Song is a medley of chuckles and whistles interspersed with *chack* notes; calls include a harsh *chack-chack-chack*.
EGGS 1–2 clutches of 4–6 red-speckled, pale blue eggs from May–July.
REARING Female incubates eggs for 13–14 days; fledging is 14 days after hatching.

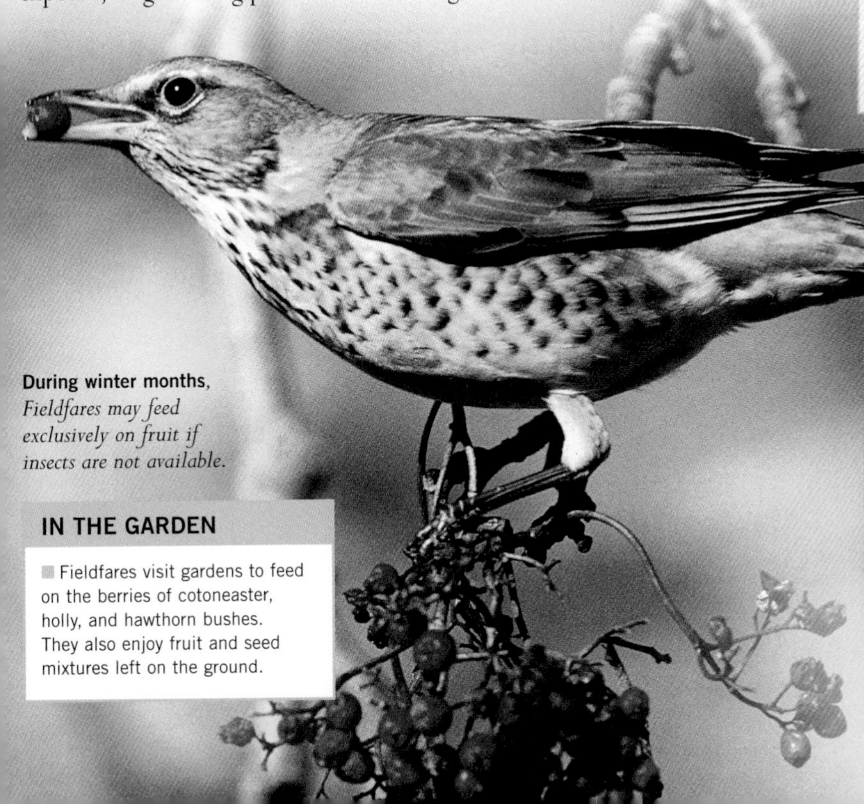

During winter months, *Fieldfares may feed exclusively on fruit if insects are not available.*

IN THE GARDEN

Fieldfares visit gardens to feed on the berries of cotoneaster, holly, and hawthorn bushes. They also enjoy fruit and seed mixtures left on the ground.

Fieldfares construct *a cup-shaped nest of grasses, twigs, and mud, lined with fine grasses.*

Black Redstart

ORIGINALLY A BIRD OF ROCKY HILLSIDES, the Black Redstart has become an urban bird in western Europe. It is found in villages and suburbs in continental Europe, but in Britain it prefers city life, and is found in sites such as railway yards, power stations, churchyards, and derelict areas. Similar in build to a Robin, the Black Redstart is easily identified by its rust-brown, quivering tail.

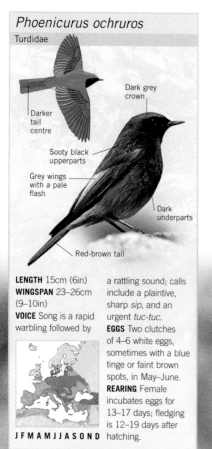

Phoenicurus ochruros

Turdidae

LENGTH 15cm (6in)
WINGSPAN 23–26cm (9–10in)
VOICE Song is a rapid warbling followed by a rattling sound; calls include a plaintive, sharp *sip*, and an urgent *tuc-tuc*.
EGGS Two clutches of 4–6 white eggs, sometimes with a blue tinge or faint brown spots, in May–June.
REARING Female incubates eggs for 13–17 days; fledging is 12–19 days after hatching.

J F M A M J J A S O N D

Urban habitats

The male Black Redstart has a grey crown, while the rest of the head and the upper half of the body are black. The rump and tail are chestnut brown. In the female and juvenile, dusky-brown replaces the black and chestnut except on the tail.

A few British Black Redstarts nest on sea-cliffs, but most nests are found on ledges or in holes in buildings. The female constructs the cup-shaped nest from grass and moss, lining it with wool, hair, and feathers. She is also responsible for incubating the eggs.

Juvenile birds *have a plumage similar to that of the adult female, but with darker brown streaks and flecks on the body.*

Both parents feed the young, continuing to do so for almost two weeks after fledging.

Black Redstarts mainly eat a variety of insects, including small flies, but also other small animals, such as spiders and earthworms. Prey is chased on the ground, plucked from foliage and walls, or caught in the air. Plant food is also eaten, including a variety of different berries and seeds.

Female Black Redstarts *have duller, browner plumage than males, but still have the distinctive red-brown tail.*

IN THE GARDEN

■ Black Redstarts are rare visitors to gardens. They nest on old buildings in towns and cities – even in industrial areas.

Whitethroat

BEST KNOWN FOR ITS SONG, often delivered from cover or as it flies up, the Whitethroat was once a very common farmland bird, but its numbers crashed in the late 1960s and have only partly recovered. It is believed that the sudden decline was caused by severe drought in the region where it over-winters in Africa.

A bold warbler

The Whitethroat is a medium-sized warbler with a long tail and large head. Its upperparts are brown with rusty-brown on the wings, the throat and chin are conspicuously white, and it has white outer tail feathers. The male has a grey head, while the female and juvenile have brown heads.

Like other warblers, Whitethroats are most likely to be seen in gardens after nesting, when young birds are on the move. They occasionally settle in overgrown gardens which provide the cover they require. The nest is usually built low in a bush or among brambles, nettles, or other low growth. The male may build several rudimentary nests before one is selected by a female; she then completes the construction, adding a lining of grasses and hair. Both sexes incubate the eggs and feed the young, which remain with their parents for up to three weeks after fledging.

The Whitethroat's diet changes with the seasons. In autumn and winter, it feeds on wild fruits and berries, but it switches to a variety of small insects in summer.

Sylvia communis

Sylviidae

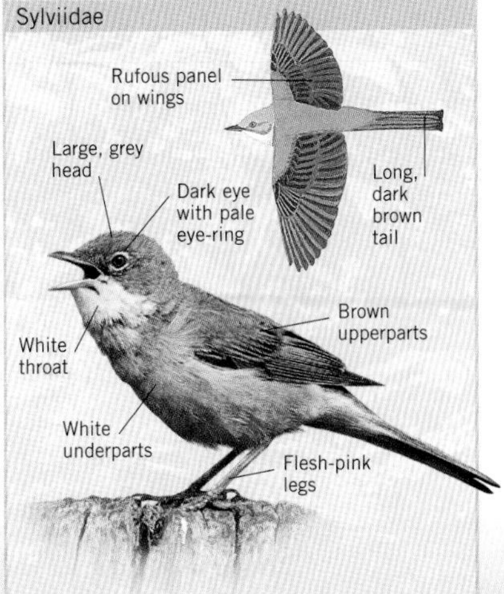

LENGTH 14cm (5½in)
WINGSPAN 19–23cm (7½–9in)
VOICE The song is a quick, chattering warble; calls include a musical *wheet-a-wheet-a-whit* and a scolding *tchurrr.*
EGGS 1–2 clutches of 4–5 pale blue or green eggs with sparse olive and grey marks in May–July.
REARING Eggs are incubated for 9–14 days by both sexes; fledging is 10–12 days after hatching.

In the breeding season, *Whitethroats search foliage and stems for insects, including caterpillars, beetles, and flies.*

The Whitethroat *delivers its lively, warbling song from a song-post or in a fluttering song-flight.*

IN THE GARDEN

■ Whitethroats sometimes visit gardens, feeding on berries, such as blackberries, in late summer and autumn.

Blackcap

THE MUSICAL WARBLE of the Blackcap is thought by some to be the best of all bird songs. It starts as a jumble of harsh notes, followed by a series of rich, fluting tones, often incorporating snatches of other birds' songs, such as Nightingale, Blackbird, and Song Thrush. This can make identification tricky, especially as the song is delivered from deep within the foliage of bushes and trees, but a glimpse of the singer's black cap leaves no doubt.

Blackcaps establish *regular song-posts from which to deliver their rich, warbling song. Although similar in size to Marsh and Willow Tits, the male Blackcap is easily distinguished from these black-capped birds because it has no black on its chin.*

Sylvia atricapilla

Sylviidae

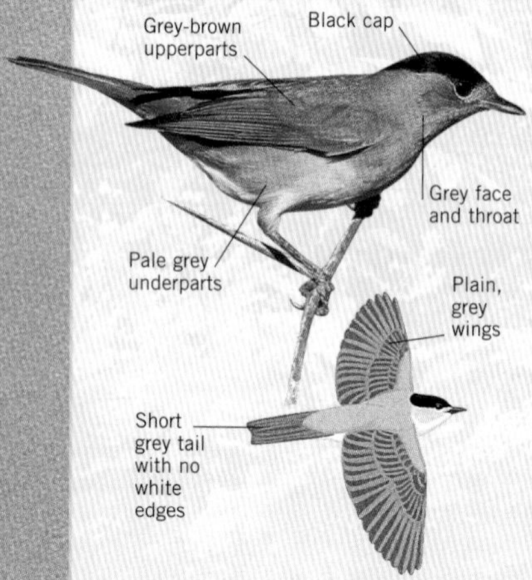

LENGTH 13cm (5in)
WINGSPAN 20–23cm (8–9in)
VOICE Song is series of bright, pure notes with a "rippling" quality, often delivered with a sudden increase in volume.
EGGS One or two clutches of 4–6 buff-coloured eggs with brown marks in April–June.
REARING Eggs are incubated for 10–16 days by both sexes; fledging is 10–14 days after hatching.

J F M A M J J A S O N D

The nest is built *near the ground, often in brambles, shrubs (including hedges), or sometimes in clumps of nettles.*

Bold headgear

A stocky, grey-bodied warbler, the Blackcap is distinguished from the similar Garden Warbler by its characteristic cap, which is black in the male and brown in the female.

Blackcaps are migrants in some parts of Europe, but resident in others, and different populations employ different migratory strategies. In Britain, for example, Blackcaps are not resident but may be seen all year round because the breeding population that migrates south to France, Spain, and beyond, is replaced in late autumn by Blackcaps that have nested in Germany and Austria.

Territory and nesting

Blackcaps choose territories with shrubby undergrowth for nesting and tall trees for feeding and to provide concealed perches to use as song-posts. They may nest in large, mature gardens but are more likely to wander into gardens in late summer, after the breeding season. Most of these birds are probably youngsters that are looking for food and perhaps for breeding places for the next year. They are not very social birds, and are more likely to be seen individually than in groups.

The male starts building several nests but leaves them unfinished; the female chooses one and completes the construction. The neat, cup-shaped structure is made from grass, roots, small twigs, and moss, and is lined with fine grass and hair. When built around human habitation, the Blackcap's low-level nests are vulnerable to predators, especially cats.

IN THE GARDEN

In winter, Blackcaps take kitchen scraps from bird-tables and peanuts from hanging feeders. They also enjoy the fruits of redcurrant, elder, blackberry, and ivy. They occasionally nest in large gardens with tall trees and shrubberies.

The female Blackcap *has a reddish-brown, rather than a black, cap and generally has browner plumage than the male.*

A varied diet

Blackcaps glean insects from the leaves of trees, and occasionally from the ground or in the air. The bulk of the diet is small beetles, bugs, flies, and caterpillars, but worms and snails are also taken. As summer crops ripen, Blackcaps turn increasingly to eating fruit and berries, and these become the mainstay through the winter. The nestlings are fed mainly on animal food, especially caterpillars, flies, and beetles, but they may also be fed some fruit. Nectar and pollen is taken from the flowers of willow, winter jasmine, mahonia, and other plants.

In autumn and winter, *Blackcaps rely on a wide range of fruit, but will also visit garden bird-tables to supplement their diet.*

Flicking its wings *to splash water over itself, a vigorous bath helps a Blackcap keep its plumage clean and free from parasites.*

Garden Warbler

THE GARDEN WARBLER is a woodland bird and its presence in open woods with a layer of shrubs suggests that it ought to be found in mature gardens, but it is shy and does not tolerate disturbance. Garden visits are confined to passing migrants in spring and wandering juveniles in late summer. The Garden Warbler is distinguished mainly by the lack of prominent features.

Both parents *incubate the eggs and help to provide for the young, continuing to feed them for two weeks after they have left the nest.*

Sylvia borin

Sylviidae

LENGTH 14cm (5½in)
WINGSPAN 20–24cm (8–9in)
VOICE Song is a varied, even warbling similar to a Blackcap's; calls include a soft *tchak* and a low *churrr*.
EGGS 1–2 clutches of 4–5 white, pink, or green eggs with brown, purple, or olive markings in May–July.
REARING Eggs are incubated for 11–12 days by both sexes; fledging is usually 10 days after hatching.

A medium-sized, brown warbler, *the Garden Warbler is a summer visitor to most of Europe, after spending the winter in Africa.*

A plain warbler

The Garden Warbler shows itself only in brief glimpses, and has virtually no identifying features, making it difficult to identify by sight. A rather plump-bodied bird, its plumage is dull brown above and buff below, with a faint grey patch on the side of the neck. Male, female, and juvenile are all similar in appearance. Its sweet, warbling song can easily be mistaken for the Blackcap's, but is more even and lacks the final fluting notes.

Breeding and diet

The male Garden Warbler builds several unfinished nests low in bushes and herbaceous plants; the female selects one in which to lay her eggs and completes the construction. The cup-shaped nest is made from twigs, grass, leaves, and plant stems, and is lined with fine grasses and roots.

The diet of the Garden Warbler varies depending on the time of year. In the breeding season, it mainly consists of insects, such as aphids, weevils, and caterpillars, which are picked off leaves and twigs. At other times, fruit and seeds are most important, especially berries, which are eaten before migration in the autumn.

IN THE GARDEN

■ The Garden Warbler is a scarce visitor to country gardens, especially those with "wild" areas and lots of shrubs.

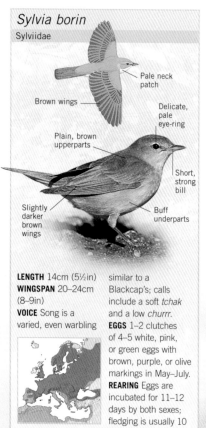

Chiffchaff

THE CHIFFCHAFF and Willow Warbler are so similar in appearance that they can be very difficult to distinguish, except by their songs; even experienced birdwatchers often talk of seeing a "willowchiff". Many are migrants, spending the winter in Africa or southern Europe. They return to their breeding grounds in much of the rest of Europe in early spring.

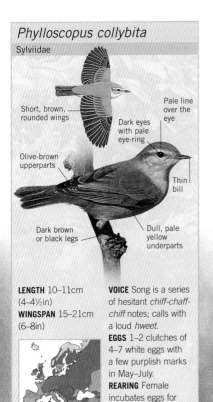

The Chiffchaff *is smaller, generally duller, with a more rounded head than the Willow Warbler and its legs are usually black, not brown.*

Phylloscopus collybita

Sylviidae

LENGTH 10–11cm (4–4½in)
WINGSPAN 15–21cm (6–8in)

J F M A M J J A S O N D

VOICE Song is a series of hesitant *chiff-chaff-chiff* notes; calls with a loud *hweet.*
EGGS 1–2 clutches of 4–7 white eggs with a few purplish marks in May–July.
REARING Female incubates eggs for 13–15 days; fledging is 14–16 days after hatching.

Muted colours

The Chiffchaff is an inconspicuous and featureless warbler roughly the size of a Blue Tit, with olive-green upperparts, yellowish underparts, and an indistinct pale line above the eye. The sexes and the juvenile are similar in appearance.

When male Chiffchaffs in migrant populations return from their winter habitats in spring, they deliver their song, a series of hesitant *"chiff-chaff-chiff"* notes, from the bare tree branches. They may spend a short time in gardens before they settle in woodland, or sometimes in mature gardens with trees and shrubs. Females arrive ten or more days later, and join the males on their territories, where they build a nest of a hollow ball of grass and leaves, usually on or near the ground. From the end of August, Chiffchaffs are seen and heard again in gardens as young birds start to wander around. Shortly afterwards, most of the population heads south for the winter.

Chiffchaffs feed almost exclusively on insects, but they sometimes also eat fruit and berries in autumn and winter.

An active bird, *the Chiffchaff can often be seen launching itself from a twig to catch flying insects. When perched, it continually bobs its tail and flicks its wings.*

IN THE GARDEN

Gardens with large shrubs and a "wild" area are the most likely to attract the Chiffchaff, especially in late summer.

Goldcrest

THE GOLDCREST IS THE SMALLEST European bird and there are even records of it becoming trapped in spiders' webs. It is a member of the warbler family that lives almost entirely in conifer trees or nearby deciduous trees. Often difficult to see in dense foliage, its presence is given away by its distinctive song, which can be heard throughout the year.

A tiny warbler

This tiny bird behaves rather like a tit, searching amongst foliage for insects and spiders. It has olive-green upperparts and pale buff underparts. The whitish ring around the eye and the black-edged orange-yellow crown are distinctive. The male's crown has a small patch of red in the yellow.

Regulus regulus

Sylviidae

LENGTH 9cm (3½in)
WINGSPAN 13–16cm (5–6in)
VOICE Song is a thin, twittering *tweedly-tweedly-tweedly-twiddledidee*; call is a thin *see-see*, used in pairs and flocks to keep in contact.
EGGS Two clutches of 7–10 brown-spotted, white or buff eggs in May–July.
REARING Female incubates eggs for 14–17 days; fledging is 16–21 days after hatching.

J F M A M J J A S O N D

Juvenile birds lack the colourful crown markings. The Goldcrest can be confused with the similar Firecrest, but is slightly smaller, its plumage less brightly coloured, and it lacks the white stripe over the eye.

Goldcrests form monogamous pairs and nest-building is undertaken by both male and female birds. The nest is slung underneath foliage near the end of a branch. Made of moss and lichen, it is held together and suspended with spiders' webs, and lined with feathers and hair. Unusually, the female may lay the second clutch before the nestlings from the first clutch have fledged, leaving their care to the male. Having two large clutches each year allows the Goldcrest to maintain its population despite huge losses in cold winters.

The Goldcrest eats many kinds of spiders and insects, especially flies, aphids, and beetles and their larvae, but it occasionally also takes larger types of insects, such as adult moths.

Conifer branches *are a Goldcrest's preferred nest site. Growing spruce and fir trees in the garden may encourage them to nest, once the trees reach 2m (7ft).*

IN THE GARDEN

- Goldcrests rarely visit garden feeding stations, but in extremely cold weather they may take bird cake, grated cheese, and fat. They nest in cypress, larch, and other conifers, and also in ivy and gorse.

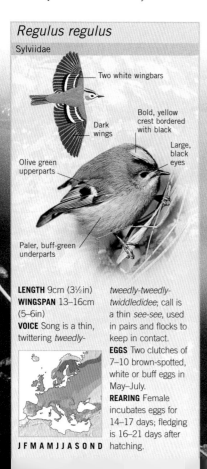

Goldcrests forage *for food in trees and hedges, rarely on the ground, and they are remarkably tolerant of human spectators.*

Pied Flycatcher

PIED FLYCATCHERS NEST IN HOLES in trees and readily take to nest-boxes; in some places, their breeding range has been extended by the provision of suitable boxes. Their habitat is mainly broad-leaved woodland, especially oak or birch, or conifer woods with some broad-leaved trees, but parks and large gardens are also suitable.

Summer visitor

In the breeding season, the male Pied Flycatcher has unmistakable bold black-and-white plumage; the upperparts are black with a conspicuous pattern of white on the wings when in flight, while the underparts are white. Females, juveniles, and non-breeding males are brown in place of black, but are still easy to identify by the white markings on wings and tail, distinguishing them from the Spotted Flycatcher.

Pied Flycatchers spend the winter in tropical Africa, returning to breed in much of Europe. The males return first and choose nest sites before the females arrive. A male entices a female to the nest site by singing and displaying, and the quality of the site is an important factor for females in the selection of a mate. The female Pied Flycatcher builds a cup-shaped nest with leaves, grass, and moss, and both the female and the male assist in feeding the young.

The Pied Flycatcher spends less time chasing flying insects than does the Spotted Flycatcher, relying more on insects – such as caterpillars, beetles and flies – picked from leaves or the ground. Outside the breeding season, it eats a wide variety of small fruits, berries, and seeds.

Some male Pied Flycatchers *mate with two or even three females, but they usually only help to feed their first brood.*

In its winter plumage, *the male Pied Flycatcher resembles the female, with dull brown rather than black upperparts.*

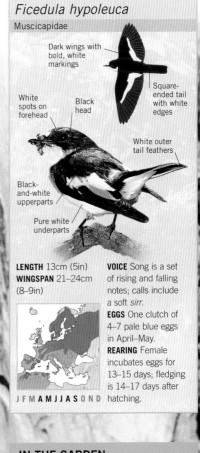

Ficedula hypoleuca

Muscicapidae

LENGTH 13cm (5in)
WINGSPAN 21–24cm (8–9in)

J F M **A M J J A S** O N D

VOICE Song is a set of rising and falling notes; calls include a soft *sirr*.
EGGS One clutch of 4–7 pale blue eggs in April–May.
REARING Female incubates eggs for 13–15 days; fledging is 14–17 days after hatching.

IN THE GARDEN

Pied Flycatchers nest in orchards, parks, and large gardens, and use enclosed nest-boxes with entrance holes 32mm ($1\frac{1}{4}$in) in diameter, positioned 2–4m ($6\frac{1}{2}$–13ft) above the ground.

Spotted Flycatcher

THOUGH DULL IN APPEARANCE, the feeding behaviour of the Spotted Flycatcher makes it fascinating to watch. It lives almost exclusively on flying insects, which it catches by flying out from a conspicuous perch, seizing them in its bill while briefly hovering, and returning to the perch. A summer visitor from southern Africa to most of Europe, it is most easily recognized by this characteristic method of hunting.

Plain colours

The Spotted Flycatcher is easily recognized by its large head and upright posture when perched, as well as by its characteristic fly-catching habits, although Chaffinches and other birds sometimes also employ the same technique. Its greyish-brown plumage, streaked on the head and breast, can appear almost grey. Male and female birds are alike. The Spotted Flycatcher's song – a collection of quiet, squeaky notes – is not often heard.

The Spotted Flycatcher *chooses a sheltered site with a suitable ledge on which to build its nest; this spot inside a garden shed is perfect.*

Late arrival

The Spotted Flycatcher is one of the latest migrants to return from its winter habitat, and consequently, its nesting season starts later than other insect-eaters, such as warblers and tits. This is precisely timed to allow the young to fledge at the height of summer, when hot days mean large numbers of insects are on the wing.

The nest of moss, grass, and twigs, bound by cobwebs and lined with hair and feathers, is built mainly by the female, usually in a crevice of a tree trunk or wall, in a creeper, or in an old nest. Creepers, hanging baskets, and open-fronted nest-boxes attract Spotted Flycatchers to nest in gardens but they are more likely to be seen when passing through on migration.

Juvenile birds *are similar to adult Spotted Flycatchers but with a more heavily spotted plumage, especially on the head and back.*

Mid-air specialist

The Spotted Flycatcher usually feeds on flies, but also on aphids, bees, wasps, and butterflies. Once it has collected the insects in one area, a flycatcher has to move to a new perch, but it returns later for more forays from the original spot. Spotted Flycatchers prefer to catch insects that give the best return for their effort; the most economical are large flies, such as bluebottles. Bumblebees make even larger meals, but they must have their stings removed, which takes time that could be spent on catching another insect, so they are usually only caught in the early morning before flies are active.

IN THE GARDEN

- Spotted Flycatchers feed on flying insects and never visit garden birdfeeders. They sometimes nest in gardens in open nest-boxes with low fronts.

Birds of woodland edges, *Spotted Flycatchers inhabit gardens with perches for hunting, cover for nesting, and water for drinking and bathing.*

Spotted Flycatchers *feed almost exclusively on flying insects, except during unseasonably cold or wet weather when they may have to rely on insects plucked from leaves on the ground, or even turn to berries.*

Muscicapa striata

Muscicapidae

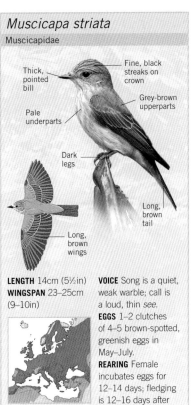

LENGTH 14cm (5½in)
WINGSPAN 23–25cm (9–10in)

J F M A **M J J A S** O N D

VOICE Song is a quiet, weak warble; call is a loud, thin *see.*
EGGS 1–2 clutches of 4–5 brown-spotted, greenish eggs in May–July.
REARING Female incubates eggs for 12–14 days; fledging is 12–16 days after hatching.

Dependent on flying insects *to survive, the Spotted Flycatcher is a brief visitor to Europe, leaving for the warmer climes of its winter home in Africa in late summer, when insect populations start to dwindle.*

Long-tailed Tit

A CHORUS OF REPEATED *zee-zee-zee*, *zirrup*, and *pit* notes heralds the arrival of a flock of Long-tailed Tits working their way acrobatically through the trees and streaming across the spaces between. These delightful little birds are distant cousins of the true tits, and are most often seen in groups. In summer, these are family parties, while outside the breeding season, they form larger feeding flocks.

IN THE GARDEN

Long-tailed Tits take small fragments of meat, fat, and peanuts, and are tempted by fat and uncooked pastry smeared on tree trunks. They are increasingly learning to feed from birdfeeders.

Aegithalos caudatus

Aegithalidae

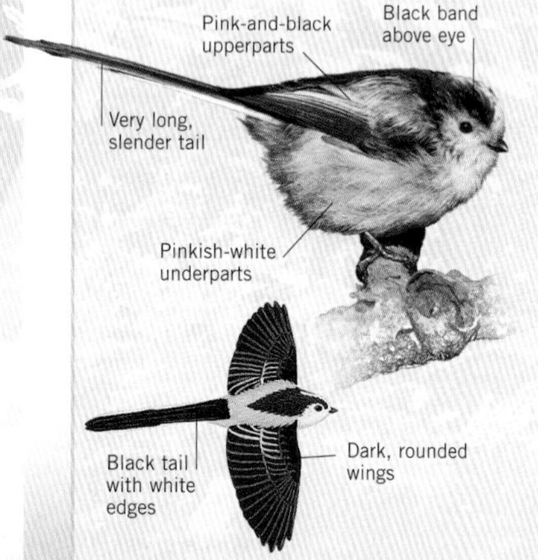

LENGTH 14cm (5½in)
WINGSPAN 16–19cm (6–7½in)
VOICE Song is a twittering trill; calls include a sharp *tsirrup*, a high-pitched, thin, repeated *zee* given in flight, and a short *pit*.
EGGS One clutch of 8–12 reddish-freckled, white eggs in April–June.
REARING Female incubates eggs for 14–18 days; fledging is 14–18 days after hatching.

J F M A M J J A S O N D

Long-tailed Tits *can look quite slender in summer, but in winter, when their fluffed feathers make their bodies look rounder, they have a distinctive "ball-and-stick" appearance.*

Juvenile birds *are similar to adults, but lack the pink markings and have shorter tails, brown backs, and more grey on the head.*

Long-tailed Tits *are relatively new visitors to the garden. They can increasingly be seen on peanut feeders, especially in winter when other food supplies are scarce.*

Distinctive shape

With its long tail and tiny, round body, the Long-tailed Tit is an unmistakable garden bird. Its plumage is mainly black-and-white, but with a pinkish-grey tinge. Male and female Long-tailed Tits are similar in appearance, while juvenile birds have shorter tails and no pink in the plumage. In flight, the long tail is the most obvious aid to identification.

Extended families

Long-tailed Tits do not nest in holes (or use nest-boxes) and their families, including parents, their offspring, and other individuals related to the male, stay together throughout winter. On cold nights, they huddle together to keep their tiny bodies warm. Family groups often join together to make large flocks which, in recent years, have started to visit gardens to feed on peanuts.

At the end of winter, flocks break up and male Long-tailed Tits set up territories. Nest-building starts in early spring and takes both male and female about three weeks to complete because the nest is so elaborate. The nest is placed low down in a bush, bramble thicket, or hedge, or high in the fork of a tree. The structure of the nest (see below) is fairly elastic, which allows it to expand as the young grow. Both male and female feed the young, and continue to do so for two weeks after they have flown the nest. Long-tailed Tits' nests are extremely vulnerable to predators, such as Magpies and Jays, and as many as 50 per cent of nests are robbed. The bereaved parents split up and join a male relative and his mate to help rear their offspring, and there can sometimes be four or five adults at one nest.

Acrobatic dining

Long-tailed Tits eat far fewer seeds than other tits, and mainly take small insects picked from twigs, leaves, and buds. Their diet consists of a variety of insects, including caterpillars and flies, and spiders. They are agile in their search but, unlike other tits, do not hold food under the foot while pecking at it. Instead, they hang upside down by one foot while clutching the food in the other.

Thousands of feathers *are collected to line the nest, making it so snug inside that the incubating female has to fold her tail over her back to fit inside.*

The nest is a *wonderfully constructed ball of moss held together with spiders' webs and hair. The tits decorate it with lichens, which provide camouflage.*

Coal Tit

COAL TITS NEST AND FEED in the branches of conifers, and their presence in gardens has been increased by the fashion for planting conifer trees and hedges. Easily missed as it darts among a crowd of Blue and Great Tits, the Coal Tit lands on a feeder, grabbing a seed and flying off with it, returning a minute later for another. It takes the seeds to eat at leisure in the shelter of a nearby tree or bush, or stores them for later consumption.

A tiny tit

The agile Coal Tit is less colourful than a Blue Tit, but can be confused with Marsh and Willow Tits. It can be identified by the white patch on its nape which stands out against its bold, black head. As it flies away, two white wingbars are visible in contrast to the dark grey wings. Male and female Coal Tits are similar in appearance, but juvenile birds have yellowish rather than white cheeks.

The tiny Coal Tit *uses its diminutive size to great effect, foraging for food on the most slender twigs at the tips of tree branches.*

Pairs and nesting

Outside the breeding season, Coal Tits often join mixed flocks of tits that scour woodlands and gardens in the hunt for food. In spring, pairs return to their territories, their *pee-choo, pee-choo* song betraying their presence. They nest in gardens and parks in towns and cities where there are at least a few conifers. Nest-boxes will occasionally attract Coal Tits, and it helps if the entrance hole of a box is restricted to 24mm (1in) to keep out the other, larger tits.

The nest is built of moss, and is usually lined with hair, distinguishing it from the feather-lined nest of a Blue Tit. When the young Coal Tits first leave the nest, they remain under cover for a few days rather than following their parents, and even return to the nest to roost.

Acrobatic visitors *to garden feeders, Coal Tits often hang upside down to reach the best food.*

Natural hoarder

With its long toes, the Coal Tit can easily grip bunches of conifer needles and cones as it searches for insects with its slender bill. It also feeds on caterpillars and spiders. In autumn and winter, seeds, especially those extracted from cones, make up a large part of the diet. Storing behaviour is common in autumn, when Coal Tits are often seen at feeders, although numbers depend on the availability of natural food in the countryside.

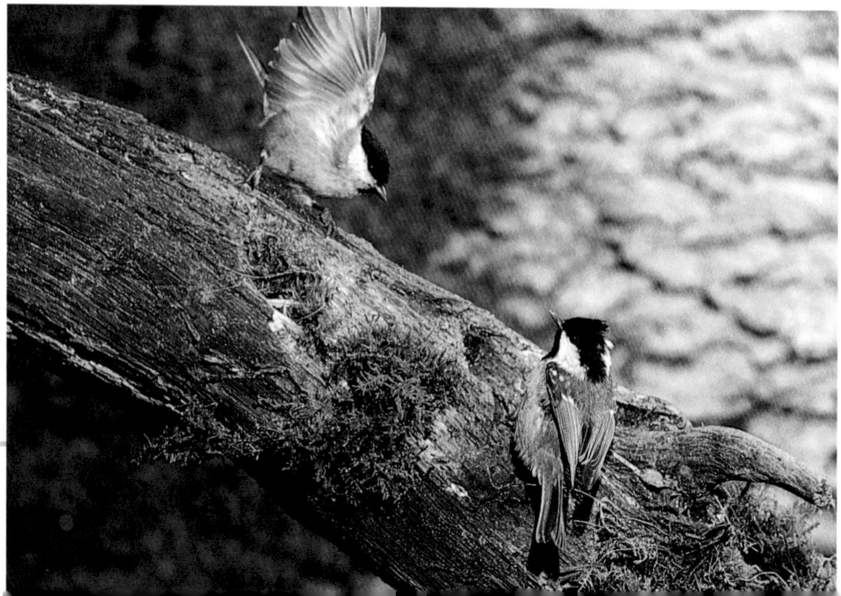

With wings raised, *a Coal Tit warns another with a threatening display. As the smallest member of the tit family, the Coal Tit will defer to all other species of tit.*

At first glance, *a Coal Tit can easily be mistaken for another small tit; look for its large, black bib and diagnostic white nape patch.*

IN THE GARDEN

■ Coal Tits visit garden feeding stations to take peanuts, seeds, and fat. They will occasionally nest in enclosed nest-boxes if placed within a conifer tree or hedge.

A hollow *in a conifer trunk is a Coal Tit's ideal choice of nest site. Suitable holes are hard to find, however, and so these versatile tits also make use of hollows among tree roots, crevices in walls, or even mouse holes.*

Parus ater

Paridae

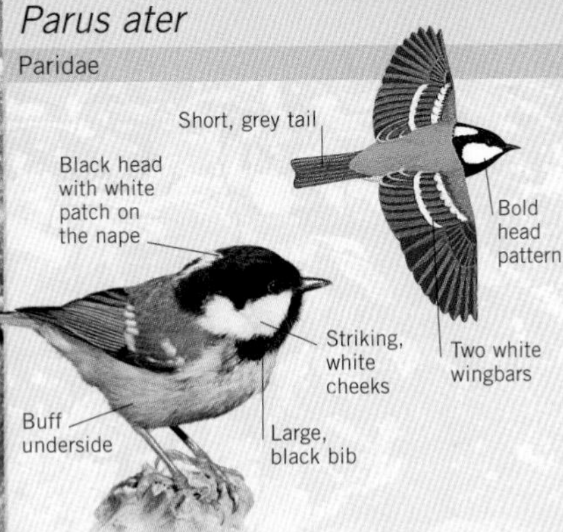

LENGTH 11–12cm (4½in)
WINGSPAN 17–21cm (6½–8in)
VOICE Song is a bright, high-pitched *pee-choo pee-choo*; calls include a *tsee-tsee*, similar to the call of a Goldcrest.
EGGS 1–2 clutches of 7–12 reddish-spotted, white eggs in April–June.
REARING Female incubates eggs for 14–16 days; fledging is 18–20 days after hatching.

J F M A M J J A S O N D

Blue Tit

THE LIVELY BLUE TIT is one of the most delightful birds to be seen in the garden, with its bold, perky behaviour and the acrobatics it performs on feeders and tit bells. A regular visitor to feeding stations, this colourful bird is credited with great intelligence, partly because of its ability to find new sources of food and the dexterity of foot and bill when feeding, but also because of its ability to learn from other birds by imitation.

The inquisitive *Blue Tit's daily search for food and water involves exploring all possibilities. When food or nest sites are in short supply, this bold tit will aggressively defend its precious resources.*

Parus caeruleus

Paridae

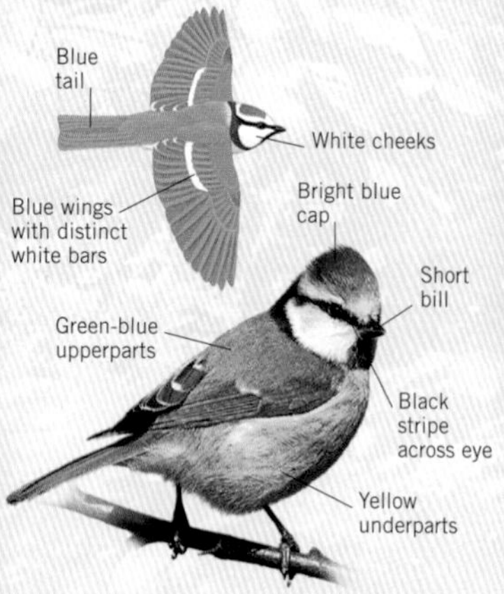

LENGTH 11cm (4½in)
WINGSPAN 17–20cm (6½–8in)
VOICE Song is a trilled *tsee-tsee-tsu-hu-hu-hu-hu*; calls include a thin, quick *tsee*, a harsh *tsee-see-sit*, and a scolding *churr* of alarm.
EGGS Usually one clutch of 7–12 reddish flecked, white eggs in April–May.
REARING Female incubates eggs for 12–15 days; fledging is 16–22 days after hatching.

J F M A M J J A S O N D

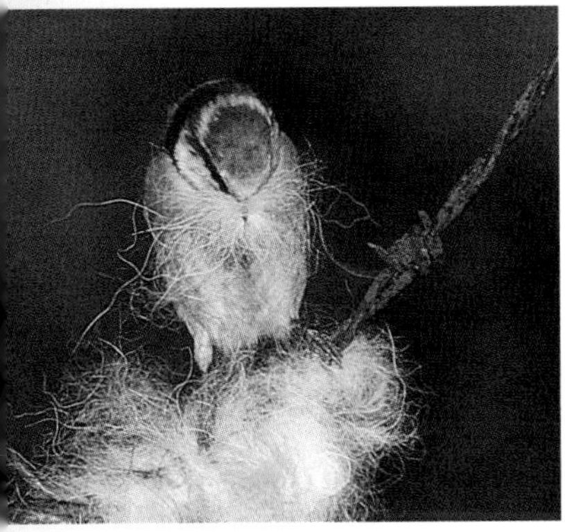

Nesting material *is collected by the female Blue Tit, and includes wool, hair, feathers, and fine dry grass to line the nest.*

Lightweight and agile, *the Blue Tit can feed from practically any angle – including upside down.*

A familiar tit

The Blue Tit is easily recognized, with its distinctive colouring, hopping movement, and bursts of rapid, whirring flight. Smaller than the similar Great Tit, it has blue-green upperparts and yellow underparts, with a faint black stripe on the belly. Its white head has a bold, blue cap and black markings. Males generally have brighter colouring than females.

Raising a family

Blue Tits form pairs when the winter flocks break up in January. Nest-building starts with the female chipping at the entrance of a hole or crevice (even if it is an already suitably sized hole in a nest-box). The time taken to collect material and build the nest varies from a few days to several weeks if work is held up by bad weather. The nest is made of moss, dried grasses, and small twigs.

Blue Tits are the most frequent users of garden nest-boxes, but they do not breed as well here as in woodland. This is because there are fewer native trees in gardens, so the supply of caterpillars needed for feeding the nestlings may be poorer. At the same time, however, garden Blue Tits tend to live longer than their woodland cousins because they feed on the dietary supplements provided at garden feeding stations.

Garden favourite

The Blue Tit's diet includes insects and spiders in summer and a mixture of insects and seeds, especially beech mast, in winter. Blue Tits sometimes visit willow catkins and the flowers of gooseberries, currants, and other garden plants for nectar. A natural resourcefulness enables this species to take advantage of changing food sources, while their tameness allows them to exploit garden feeding stations to great effect. Once a new way to find food is discovered – like piercing the foil tops on milk bottles to steal the cream from the top – Blue Tits quickly learn from one another.

Studies of ringed birds have shown that over 100 Blue Tits may visit a garden in succession, although only a few can be seen at a time. Not many travel more than 10km (6 miles) on their daily round, although some migrate over 100km (60 miles) from their summer breeding grounds.

Juvenile birds *are duller than adult Blue Tits, with yellower cheeks and greenish rather than bright blue caps.*

IN THE GARDEN

■ Blue Tits take fruit, fat, meat, and assorted kitchen scraps from bird-tables and will feed on seeds and peanuts, especially in hanging feeders. They also enjoy suet sticks and blocks and halved coconuts. They nest in the garden in enclosed nest-boxes.

Blue Tits build their nests *in holes in trees and buildings and will readily use nest-boxes, often returning year after year.*

Great Tit

NATURAL NEST HOLES are in shorter supply in gardens than in woods, so garden nest-boxes have a good chance of being used by the Great Tits that regularly visit birdfeeders through the winter. These vocal birds have a wide "vocabulary" and can even recognize each other's songs. They will not react to the familiar song of a neighbour, while a stranger's song brings an immediate response.

Juvenile Great Tits *are generally duller than adult birds, with yellowish rather than white cheeks and a less distinct belly stripe.*

Familiar visitor

The largest member of the tit family, the Great Tit is blue-green above and yellow below with a black head and white cheeks. The black tail has white edges. Females are similar to males, but with a narrower stripe on the underside, while juveniles are duller.

Tits nesting *in urban and suburban gardens lay their eggs one or two weeks earlier than those nesting in nearby woodland, perhaps due to stimulation by artificial lighting.*

A garden resident

The start of nesting depends on spring temperatures, and can vary by as much as four weeks between years. Great Tits readily use nest-boxes, but gardens do not support the diversity of insect life found in woodland; fewer eggs are laid in garden nests, and a greater number of nestlings do not survive. The female builds the nest in a nest-box, a hollow or cleft in a tree, or in a hole in a wall. It is constructed with moss and dry grass, and lined with hair, wool, and feathers. Both male and female Great Tits feed the young while in the nest, and continue to do so for some time after they have flown. The length of time before the young become independent is shortened if the female lays a second clutch of eggs (but a second brood is rare for birds nesting in gardens).

Seed specialist

In winter, Great Tits are common visitors to bird-tables and hanging birdfeeders, while in their woodland habitats, they turn over leaves and stones in search of food. The winter diet consists largely of tree seeds, such as beech mast, acorns, and even hazelnuts, hammered open while held securely against a perch by the feet, or wedged in a crevice that acts as a vice. The flesh of fruit is also sometimes eaten, but the tits are more interested in picking out the seeds. In summer, Great Tits mainly eat insects, such as weevils, bugs, and caterpillars, but also spiders and small snails.

Larger than the other tits, *the Great Tit is not as agile, and spends more of its time feeding on or near the ground.*

The Great Tit *has one of the largest vocal repertoires of any small bird. With practice, it is even possible to recognize the songs of individual birds.*

Parus major

Paridae

LENGTH 14cm (5½in)
WINGSPAN 22–25cm (9–10in)

J F M A M J J A S O N D

VOICE Song is varied; calls include a familiar *tea-cher, tea-cher*.
EGGS 1–2 clutches of 5–12 reddish-spotted, white eggs in April–June.
REARING Female incubates eggs for 12–15 days; fledging is 16–22 days after hatching.

The Great Tit *is easily told apart from other tits, such as the smaller Coal Tit, by the distinctive black stripe on its underside, slightly narrower in the female, and the striking white cheeks that contrast with its all-black head markings.*

IN THE GARDEN

Great Tits are regular visitors to feeding stations, including hanging peanut and seed feeders, scrap baskets, and half-coconuts. They enjoy peanuts, seeds, meat bones, and fat. They are common users of enclosed nest-boxes.

Marsh/Willow Tit

THE MARSH TIT (*Parus palustris*) looks so similar to the Willow Tit (*Parus montanus*) that birdwatchers sometimes call them "brown tits" unless they have had a close look or heard their calls. Despite their names, the Marsh Tit is a woodland bird that favours woods, hedges, and mature gardens, while the Willow Tit prefers willows and birch on marshy ground.

The Willow Tit *has a slightly duller black cap and larger bib than the Marsh Tit, but they are best told apart by their calls and song.*

A matching pair

Marsh and Willow Tits are similar in size to Blue Tits, but are greyish-brown above and dirty white below, and both have black caps and bibs. From a distance, it is very difficult to tell these two species apart unless you hear their distinctive calls and songs.

There are no differences between male and female for either species. Juvenile Willow Tits are similar to their adults, while juvenile Marsh Tits have slightly duller black caps than adult Marsh Tits, making them extremely difficult to tell apart from juvenile Willow Tits.

Marsh Tits build their nests in existing holes in trees or walls, usually at head height or lower. Willow Tits either excavate their own holes in rotten wood or enlarge existing ones. Marsh Tits build a nest of moss, lined with hair, while the Willow Tit's nest is made of grass and plant fibres. Male and female of both species feed their young until they leave the nest, and Marsh Tit parents continue for a further week.

Marsh and Willow Tits eat insects in the breeding season, and more seeds, berries, and nuts than other tits during the rest of the year. Both species regularly hoard food, usually eating it within a few days.

Parus palustris

Paridae

LENGTH 11–12cm (4½in)
WINGSPAN 18–19cm (7–7½in)
VOICE The Marsh Tit's calls include a loud, sneezing *pitchou-pitchou*, distinct from the buzzing, deep, nasal *chay-chay-chay* and thin *zi-zi* of the Willow Tit.
EGGS 1–2 clutches of 6–9 white eggs with a few red-brown spots in April–June.
REARING Female incubates eggs for 13–15 days; fledging is 17–20 days after hatching.

J F M A M J J A S O N D

IN THE GARDEN

- Marsh Tits visit garden feeding stations to take seeds and kitchen scraps and they sometimes nest in enclosed nest-boxes. Willow Tits prefer boxes filled with soft material for them to dig out.

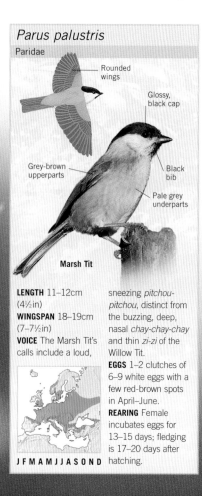

Marsh Tits *are not common garden visitors, but are more likely to be seen in gardens with mature, deciduous trees or near woodland.*

Nuthatch

NUTHATCHES DO NOT TRAVEL FAR and only come into gardens near mature woodland, although they may nest in gardens with large trees. Their presence is given away at any time of the year by the loud, ringing *chit-chit* calls. Frequent visitors to garden bird-tables, Nuthatches often feed with flocks of tits in autumn and winter.

Natural hoarders

Unmistakable when seen clearly, the Nuthatch has a pointed shape due to its long head and long bill, and jerky movements. The body is blue-grey above, buff below, with a prominent black eyestripe. Male, female, and juvenile birds look alike.

Nuthatches spend the winter in pairs on their territories. They nest in holes, plastering mud around the entrances; this probably serves to prevent larger birds, such as Starlings, taking over. The hole is shaped to the right size by the Nuthatch repeatedly passing through while the mud is wet. The female is responsible for constructing the simple nest and incubating the eggs, but the male helps with feeding the young.

When hunting for food, the Nuthatch probes crevices for spiders and insects. From autumn onwards, it collects hazelnuts, acorns, and beechnuts. It wedges them into holes and hammers them open with its powerful beak, making a tapping noise that can be mistaken for a woodpecker. Some nuts are stored in crevices for later use.

Nuthatches build *their nests in natural holes in trees, and also use old woodpecker holes. The nest is a loose pile of wood chips.*

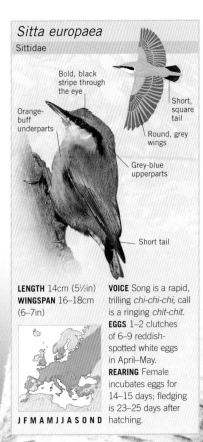

Sitta europaea

Sittidae

LENGTH 14cm (5½in)
WINGSPAN 16–18cm (6–7in)

VOICE Song is a rapid, trilling *chi-chi-chi*; call is a ringing *chit-chit*.
EGGS 1–2 clutches of 6–9 reddish-spotted white eggs in April–May.
REARING Female incubates eggs for 14–15 days; fledging is 23–25 days after hatching.

Uniquely among *European birds, Nuthatches climb headfirst down the trunks of trees as well as up, without using their tails for support.*

IN THE GARDEN

Nuthatches are colourful visitors to garden feeding stations, taking peanuts, sunflower seeds, and bird cake. They also enjoy fat smeared on tree trunks. They nest in enclosed nest-boxes with entrance holes 32mm (1¼in) in diameter.

Treecreeper

THE TREECREEPER is a small, long-tailed bird that runs up tree trunks and out along branches, almost like a mouse. It then flies down to the base of the next tree and works its way up again. Unlike Nuthatches and tits, Treecreepers do not hang head-down and only hop upwards, using their strong tails as props like miniature woodpeckers.

The Treecreeper, *seen here in flight, can be difficult to tell apart from the Short-toed Treecreeper; look for the Treecreeper's clean, white, not duller buff, underparts.*

Certhia familiaris

Certhiidae

LENGTH 13cm (5in)
WINGSPAN 18–21cm (7–8in)

VOICE Song is a high, thin *see-see-see-sissi-sooee.*
EGGS 1–2 clutches of 5–7 brown-spotted, white eggs in April–June.
REARING Female incubates eggs for 12–20 days; fledging is 13–17 days after hatching.

IN THE GARDEN

Treecreepers may visit bird-tables to take peanut and sunflower hearts, and are also attracted by porridge and fat smeared over bark or into holes. If natural nest sites are scarce, they may use specially designed wedge-shaped nest-boxes.

Tree dweller

The Treecreeper is a long-tailed, brown-streaked bird with bright, white underparts and a thin, curved bill. The sexes and juveniles are alike. Treecreepers depend on large trees, both for nesting and for the wealth of insect life they support, and so are only seen in mature gardens, especially in winter.

Treecreepers are likely to remain in or near their territories all year. Their song is rather like a high-pitched version of a Chaffinch's song, but it is thin and not easily heard. The usual site for the nest is behind a flap of loose bark or the cladding of a building, or in a crevice or hollow. Occasionally, a Treecreeper will nest in the gap behind a nest-box. Both sexes build the nest from twigs, grasses, and moss, and line it with feathers, hair, and other soft material. Once fledged, juveniles often join mixed flocks with tits and Goldcrests, where they benefit from the many eyes on the lookout for predators.

The Treecreeper's diet consists almost entirely of small insects, but in winter, it supplements its diet with small seeds, especially those of spruce and pine.

An insect specialist, *the Treecreeper's diet includes crickets, earwigs, and spiders plucked from crevices in bark with its slender, curved, tweezer-like bill.*

Carrion Crow

LIKE OTHER MEMBERS of the crow family, the Carrion Crow is shy of people after centuries of persecution, but when left alone, it becomes tame enough to visit gardens. In parts of Europe, the all-black Carrion Crow (*Corvus corone corone*) is replaced by the Hooded Crow (*Corvus corone cornix*), a subspecies with a grey body.

The Hooded Crow, *widespread in northern and eastern Europe, is now considered by some to be a separate species to the Carrion Crow.*

Plumage variations

When seen in good light, the all-black plumage of the Carrion Crow has a glossy sheen of green and blue. Its curved "Roman" bill and flat crown help distinguish it from the similar Rook. The Hooded Crow also has a black head and wings, but the body is grey. Where their ranges overlap, Carrion and Hooded Crows interbreed, resulting in hybrids with intermediate plumage.

Crows mate for life, and a pair defends its territory for much of the year, chasing out intruders with vigorous calling. The substantial nest, built by both sexes high in a tree or on a pylon or building, is made of four layers: an outer cup of thick twigs snapped from trees cemented with a layer of soil, a layer of fine twigs, roots, earth, and grass, and a lining of hair and bark fibres. While the female incubates the eggs, the male stands guard, warning her of danger as well as bringing food to her.

As its name suggests, the Carrion Crow feeds on roadkill and other dead animals, but it also eats a broad range of other foods, including grain, acorns, potatoes, scraps, insects and their larvae, snails, and worms. It also raids the nests of small birds for the eggs and nestlings.

Corvus corone

Corvidae

LENGTH 44–51cm (17–20in)
WINGSPAN 93–104cm (36–41in)

VOICE Calls include a variety of harsh, grating caws and a hard *konk*.
EGGS One clutch of 3–6 brown-speckled, greenish eggs in April–May.
REARING Female incubates eggs for 18–19 days; fledging is 30–36 days after hatching.

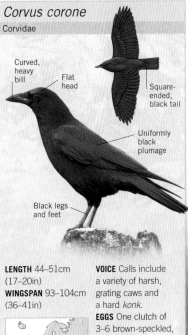

The Carrion Crow *is smaller in size than a Raven, and can be distinguished from a Rook by its all-black, not grey, face.*

IN THE GARDEN

- Carrion Crows are attracted to gardens to take bread, meat, potatoes, and a variety of other kitchen scraps.

Rook

SIMILAR IN APPEARANCE to the Carrion Crow, the Rook differs considerably in its social habits; rather than being a solitary bird, it nests in rookeries, flies in large, ragged flocks, and feeds communally in fields. Too wary to be a common garden bird, the Rook sometimes visits quiet country gardens near a rookery.

Rooks build their nests *in the tops of trees using twigs and sticks, lining them with softer materials like moss, leaves, and grass. Both parents feed the young, and continue to do so for six weeks after they have left the nest.*

Social living

Unmistakable from close range, the Rook is an all-black bird with a slender bill, steep forehead, and a grey, bare-skinned face. The feathers at the tops of the legs are loose in appearance, giving a "baggy trousers" look. When not seen clearly, the Rook can be confused with the Carrion Crow. Male and female look alike, but the juvenile has a black, feathered face and is less glossy, making it much more difficult to distinguish from the similar Carrion Crow.

Rooks nest in rookeries – colonies ranging in size from a few nests to a few thousand. The rookery is usually at the top of a clump of tall trees and the nests are often built close together, although one or two may be on their own. The male Rook selects the nest site and begins construction of the nest, with the female joining in later.

Rooks eat earthworms and insects, such as leatherjackets, beetles, and caterpillars, small mammals, birds' eggs and nestlings, and carrion, as well as newly-planted grain, acorns, and fruit. They feed mainly on farmland, but sometimes come into gardens in summer when they cannot find enough food in the dry fields. In winter, they may scavenge on rubbish tips and in litter bins.

Corvus frugilegus

Corvidae

LENGTH 44–46cm (17–18in)
WINGSPAN 81–99cm (32–39in)

VOICE Calls with a raucous *kaah*; song is a mixture of soft caws, rattles, and cackles.
EGGS One clutch of 2–6 speckled, greenish eggs in March–April.
REARING Female incubates eggs for 16–18 days; fledging is 30–36 days after hatching.

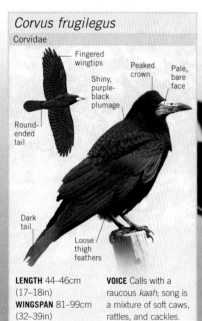

The Rook's song *is a tuneless medley of calls. The male delivers it from a perch in the hope of attracting a mate.*

IN THE GARDEN

■ Rooks visit gardens to feed on hanging bones, fat, cooked meat, and kitchen scraps left on a lawn.

Jackdaw

A SOCIABLE AND ENTERTAINING BIRD, the Jackdaw can be seen in many towns and villages, where it nests in buildings and old trees. It is the smallest of the black crows and often mixes with other species. Apart from its size, it is easily identified by its sharp *tchak* call, from which it gets its name, and a *chaair* note given in flight.

Jackdaws are attracted *to populated areas, nesting in buildings and scavenging from rubbish bins.*

A small crow

The Jackdaw is a black-and-grey bird, smaller in size than a Rook or Carrion Crow. It has a distinctive grey "hood" on the back of its head and its black plumage has a slight bluish-purple sheen. The juvenile is a duller colour than the adult, showing less contrast between the hood and the body, and lacking the pale grey "button" eye.

Lifelong bonds

Jackdaws nest in colonies, usually choosing holes in tree trunks or buildings, or crevices in cliffs. They mate for life, and a flock is clearly made up of pairs of birds. The nest is built from sticks, often in huge quantities, lined with hair, bark, rags, and other materials mixed together with earth. The pair share nesting duties except that the female is responsible for incubating the eggs. Food can be in short supply in summer, which often makes it difficult to raise a full family, and it is at this time that Jackdaws most often venture into gardens.

The Jackdaw's diet consists of all sorts of vegetable and animal foods; they mainly eat cereals, fruit, and insects, but also carrion and scraps, and they steal eggs and nestlings from the nests of other birds.

IN THE GARDEN

■ Jackdaws visit gardens to feed on hanging bones, fat, and cooked meat. They nest in large, enclosed nest-boxes with entrance holes 15cm (6in) in diameter, placed in high, secluded positions.

Corvus monedula

Corvidae

LENGTH 33–34cm (13in)
WINGSPAN 67–74cm (26–29in)

J F M A M J J A S O N D

VOICE Song is a variable medley that includes *tchak* calls and other notes.
EGGS One clutch of 4–6 spotted, pale blue eggs in April–May.
REARING Female incubates eggs for 17–18 days; fledging is 28–36 days after hatching.

Jackdaws mainly *forage for food on the ground, but also hunt for caterpillars and beetles in trees.*

Jay

AN UNMISTAKABLE MEMBER of the crow family, the Jay is a regular visitor to some rural and suburban gardens and urban parks, preferring places where there are plenty of mature trees, especially oak and beech. In its natural woodland home, it usually gives away its presence in the trees by its harsh, screeching cries, or is briefly seen as it flaps jerkily and heavily across clearings on broad wings.

IN THE GARDEN

Jays visit garden feeding stations to take peanuts and kitchen scraps. They often leave their woodland homes in autumn in search of acorns and other seeds and berries.

Garrulus glandarius

Corvidae

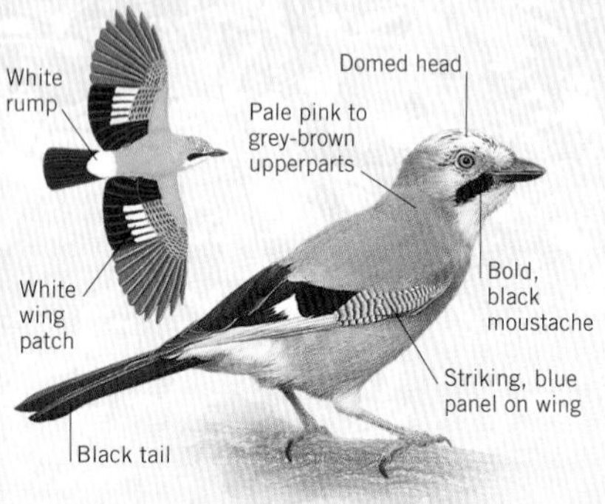

LENGTH 34–35cm (13–14in)
WINGSPAN 52–58cm (20–23in)
VOICE Social and alarm calls are a rasping *krar*; mimics the calls of other crows, Tawny Owls, and even birdsong.
EGGS One clutch of 3–6 brown-flecked, greenish eggs in April–June.
REARING Female incubates eggs for 16–17 days; fledging is 21–22 days after hatching.

J F M A M J J A S O N D

A shy, woodland bird, *the Jay is most likely to venture into the garden early in the morning, before people are about. On the ground or on a tree branch, it moves confidently with a series of bouncing hops and twitches of its long, black tail.*

Young are fed *by both parents while in the nest, and then for a further three to four weeks after fledging.*

A colourful crow

On fleeting glance, a Jay may be mistaken for a Hoopoe, but when seen clearly, it is easily recognized by the pinkish to grey-brown body, distinctive black moustache, and bright flash of blue on the wing. The black-and-white striped crown feathers can be raised into a domed crest. Male and female are similar in appearance. The Jay looks jerky and slow in flight. In autumn, it may be seen flying high over the treetops when collecting acorns.

Nesting and feeding

Unlike other crows, Jays are not social birds, and individuals and pairs live in territories for much of the year. In spring, flocks of up to 30 birds form, probably to bring "single" birds together. At these courtship gatherings, there is much displaying and calling. After they pair, both female and male Jays are monogamous, and form a lifelong pair-bond.

Nesting begins in April, and both male and female share in the construction of the untidy nest. It is mainly composed of twigs broken from trees, and is lined with thinner twigs, roots, hair, and fibres collected from the ground. The male feeds the female while she is incubating the eggs. The nest is quickly deserted if the female is disturbed and many nests are lost to predators.

Acorns are a major part of their diet for most of the winter, but Jays also eat other seeds and fruit, as well as insects (in particular, beetles and caterpillars), snails, carrion, and occasionally mice and voles. They also steal from the nests of small birds but, like other crows, do so mainly when they have young to feed.

In autumn, Jays collect huge numbers of acorns, and also hazel, beech mast, and conifer seeds. They carry their harvest back to their territory – sometimes over distances of many kilometres – where they bury it, hammering the nuts and seeds into the soil with their beaks. They transport food by holding it in the beak, and also in a special pouch under the mouth and in the gullet.

In winter, when other sources of food are scarce, a Jay will return to retrieve its hidden food store. It can remember exactly where each item has been buried, and is able to find its store even through a 30cm (12in) thickness of snow.

Catching a glimpse *of a Jay bathing in your garden is fortunate – more often, these easily frightened birds are seen flying away.*

The nest is built *in the fork of a tree, in a tall shrub, or sometimes on a building, usually some height above the ground.*

"Anting" may help Jays *keep their plumage free from parasites. Here a Jay sits on a wood ants' nest with its wings and tail spread. The ants do not sting, but squirt formic acid, which may kill parasitic feather lice.*

Magpie

MAGPIE NUMBERS HAVE INCREASED dramatically in the countryside in the last few decades – a result of reduced persecution by gamekeepers. They are also highly successful in urban areas, where refuse, bird-tables, and roadkill provide them with plentiful food. Many more of these opportunistic birds survive the winter than if they relied on natural food, and they enter the breeding season in good condition.

Pica pica

Corvidae

LENGTH 44–46cm (17–18in)
WINGSPAN 52–60cm (20–23in)

J F M A M J J A S O N D

VOICE Calls include a harsh *kyack* and a repeated *shak-shak-shak*.
EGGS One clutch of 3–9 speckled, greenish eggs in March–April.
REARING Female incubates eggs for 18 days; fledging is 24–30 days after hatching.

Magpies are rarely confused *with other species. They remain in gardens year round; indeed few individuals stray more than a few kilometres from where they hatched.*

Bold in its feeding habits, *the Magpie will take almost any food – including the velvet from the antlers of a stag. Velvet is very nutritious, made up of blood vessels enclosed in skin and covered with fine hair.*

Nest-building may *start in winter, with both adults of the pair contributing to the work. The ideal nest sites are thorny trees, but some birds may even build nests on the ground.*

A distinctive resident

The long tail, striking plumage, and large size make the Magpie an unmistakable garden bird. The black feathers on the body are iridescent with green, blue, and purple, while the belly and outer wings are white. The sexes are similar in appearance. In level flight, Magpies can appear a little laboured, but they are surprisingly agile when swooping for food or manoeuvring through trees.

Juvenile birds *closely resemble the adults, although they have shorter tails and their plumage is less glossy.*

Pairs and families

Magpie pairs often remain in their territories through the winter, but non-breeding individuals live in flocks. Young Magpies establish a territory either by sneaking into the corner of an existing territory or through "magpie weddings". The young pair attempt to settle in an established territory, and the noisy attacks of the resident birds attract other Magpies, which gather to watch the spectacle. The Magpie's nest is a substantial, domed structure of sticks and twigs, lined with mud and plant material, and usually built in a tree or tall shrub, although in some parts of Europe, Magpies nest on buildings or electricity pylons. The nest has a single side-opening and is roofed over with sticks as protection against attack by other crows, which destroy the nest as well as killing the nestlings. Some nests are re-used from year to year, and the large structures become very obvious in winter, after trees have shed their leaves. The family stays near the nest for several days after fledging, and young birds often form loose flocks; 100 or more may gather in late afternoon before flying to the roost at sunset.

Agile when feeding *on the ground, the Magpie moves with a distinctive high-stepping walk interspersed with brisk jumps. Its general-purpose bill is powerful enough to strip meat from carcasses.*

Opportunist feeders

Magpies are not fussy eaters; they take anything from beetles, spiders, and slugs, to seeds and fruit, as well as carrion and animal droppings. They store food in times of plenty for later retrieval and consumption. They are known to hunt and kill other birds and small mammals, and there is no doubt that Magpies keep watch for nesting birds and destroy clutches and broods. For this reason they have traditionally been persecuted by gamekeepers. However, recent research has shown that Magpies do not have a significant effect on populations of garden birds, except perhaps on a very local scale.

IN THE GARDEN

■ Magpies are regular visitors to feeding stations, taking scraps of bread and meat. They are attracted to gardens with hedges, trees, and shrubs, and nest in tall trees or on buildings.

Starling

THEIR BOLD NATURES and voracious appetites have not made Starlings popular in the garden – often they will clear the bird-table before other birds can claim their share. They can also be noisy when they nest under the eaves of houses. Yet their lively behaviour makes Starlings attractive birds to watch as they perform a repertoire of fascinating activities, and at close range, their plumage is surprisingly beautiful.

In autumn, *as fruit crops ripen, they become an important part of the Starling's diet.*

Appearance and nesting

Starlings are unmistakable when seen at close quarters, the glossy, blackish feathers revealing an iridescent sheen of metallic blues, purples, and greens. After the summer moult, the new feathers are tipped buff and white, creating a spangled appearance; this is most marked in young birds. The spangling is lost by spring because the feather tips wear away. In the breeding season, the male's bill has a blue-grey base, while the female's is pink-white. Female birds are more spotted than males but less glossy. Starlings move across the ground with bold, striding steps. While in flight, they have an arrowhead outline.

The juvenile Starling *is much plainer than the adult, and has mouse-brown plumage and a dark bill.*

The male Starling defends a small territory around a hole in a tree or building, where he builds a rough nest. Where resident, the male will often remain in this territory throughout winter, using the nest for roosting. The female Starling lines the nest with fine grasses, feathers, moss, and other materials. The female is also responsible for incubation, but the male sits on the nest when she leaves it for brief periods. Both the male and the female provide food for the nestlings. Later, the young can be seen on garden lawns, begging for food from one of their parents.

Versatile omnivore

Starlings have a varied diet of both animal and plant material, but they mainly eat earthworms, leatherjackets, and other small creatures. Nestlings are fed completely on an animal diet. When feeding on a lawn, a Starling inspects the ground with frequent, rapid thrusts of its bill. The bill is equipped with strong muscles that force it open at each probe into the soil. Swivelling its eyes forwards to peer down the hole, the Starling focuses on the end of its bill to identify anything worth eating, while at the same time, watching for any lurking predators, such as cats.

Outside the breeding season, *Starlings swarm each evening to join large communal roosts. The flocks gather and circle in the air with great precision, each bird watching its neighbours very carefully to avoid collisions.*

Sturnus vulgaris

Sturnidae

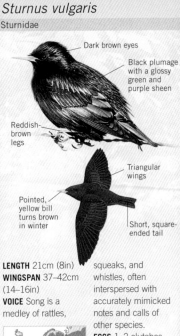

LENGTH 21cm (8in)
WINGSPAN 37–42cm (14–16in)
VOICE Song is a medley of rattles, squeaks, and whistles, often interspersed with accurately mimicked notes and calls of other species.
EGGS 1–2 clutches of 4–6 pale blue eggs in March–April.
REARING Female incubates eggs for 11–15 days; fledging is 21 days after hatching.

J F M A M J J A S O N D

Nest material *is largely collected by the male Starling, and he also builds the rough nest of grass and stems. He may also decorate it with green leaves and flower petals collected from plants that have insecticidal properties – this probably protects the nest by killing nest parasites.*

IN THE GARDEN

■ Starlings are regular garden visitors, taking bread, scraps, hanging bones, and peanuts. They sometimes use large, enclosed nest-boxes, but are more likely to nest in a hole in a tree or under the eaves of a house or barn.

In the breeding season, *the male Starling sings from a prominent perch, like the edge of a gutter; this is usually close to the nest-site.*

House Sparrow

THE HOUSE SPARROW is aptly named. Through its successful exploitation of human settlements for shelter and food, it has been able to colonize many parts of the world which would otherwise have been too hot, cold, wet, or dry. In recent years, however, many European House Sparrow populations have been declining at an alarming rate.

IN THE GARDEN

House Sparrows visit garden feeders, taking scraps, seeds, and peanuts. They sometimes nest under the eaves of buildings or in enclosed nest-boxes, from which they occasionally displace tits.

Passer domesticus

Passeridae

LENGTH 14cm (5½in)
WINGSPAN 20–22cm (8–9in)
VOICE A variety of *cheep* and *chirp* calls, used to maintain contact and as social calls within flocks; the song is a simple medley of these calls.
EGGS 2–3 clutches of 3–5 brown-blotched, white eggs in April–August.
REARING Eggs are incubated for 11–14 days by both sexes; fledging is 11–19 days after hatching.

J F M A M J J A S O N D

Dust-bathing helps *the House Sparrow maintain the condition of its plumage. This usually follows water bathing, and involves making the same motions as in normal bathing, but using dry, loose soil or dust on a garden path or in a flowerbed.*

Once pairs form *they remain together for life, although infidelity is commonplace and accounts for many young.*

Distinctive visitor

The male House Sparrow is easily identified by its distinctive plumage: its brown upperparts are streaked with black, and it has grey cheeks, crown, and rump, and a black bib. Female and juvenile birds are not as boldly patterned as the male and lack the grey on the rump and crown and the black on the head and throat. Sparrows fly with rapid bursts of whirring wingbeats.

The female House Sparrow *is plainer and more uniformly brown than the male, and at fleeting glance could be mistaken for a female Chaffinch.*

Once familiar in city parks, House Sparrows were often seen hopping around among customers at open-air café tables, pilfering scraps of food. In gardens, they were often not appreciated because flocks of these bold little birds would take food before shyer species arrived. Recently, however, numbers have declined seriously across Europe. This may be due to a lack of the food sources vital for sparrow nestling survival in the first few days of life.

Human connections

House Sparrows rarely nest away from buildings, although they occasionally use holes in trees, or usurp the nests of other birds, such as martins and Swallows. Less often, they make their own domed nests of grasses in a tree or hedge. Males advertise the nest site by chirruping with their chests pushed out to show off the black bib. After the young have fledged, the adults continue to use the nest as a snug roost throughout the winter, while the young roost together in evergreens and amongst ivy.

House Sparrows are basically seed-eaters but nestlings are fed on insects. They have a varied diet, increased by their bold nature and ingenuity. They shake leaves to dislodge insects, pick them from spiders' webs and car radiators, and even steal food from the beaks of other birds. By copying tits, they have learnt to steal milk from bottles and hang from feeders.

A nest of grass *lined with feathers and plant fibres is built by both parents, and both sexes incubate the eggs and feed the nestlings.*

House Sparrows *gather in large flocks for feeding and roosting. The flocks often contain birds from several neighbouring colonies.*

Tree Sparrow

TREE SPARROWS have recently suffered greater declines in the British countryside than any other birds. Although often overlooked because of their similarity to House Sparrows, Tree Sparrows were once common birds in open country. Within the last 30 years, their numbers have dropped by over 90 per cent, perhaps due to changes in farming practices.

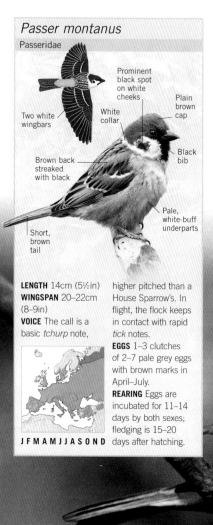

Tree Sparrows *build their nests in holes in trees, buildings, and cliffs, and in nest-boxes, sometimes forcing out other, smaller species.*

Passer montanus

Passeridae

LENGTH 14cm (5½in)
WINGSPAN 20–22cm (8–9in)
VOICE The call is a basic *tchurp* note, higher pitched than a House Sparrow's. In flight, the flock keeps in contact with rapid *tick* notes.
EGGS 1–3 clutches of 2–7 pale grey eggs with brown marks in April–July.
REARING Eggs are incubated for 11–14 days by both sexes; fledging is 15–20 days after hatching.

J F M A M J J A S O N D

Bold markings

The Tree Sparrow is very like the distinctly larger House Sparrow, but can be distinguished by the markings on its head and face; the chestnut crown lacks the grey centre of the House Sparrow, and there is a black spot on the white cheek. Juveniles also have these diagnostic markings, but their plumage colours are duller.

Tree Sparrows form loose colonies in farmland, parks, and the edges of suburbs where there are large gardens. A male advertises his small territory with a *tchurp* note. The pair construct the nest from leaves, stems, and rootlets, lining it with moss, hair, and feathers. The same nest site may be used for several years, but these wary birds are very sensitive to disturbance, and nests should not be approached.

Tree Sparrows mainly forage on the ground, or in low bushes. They eat a range of plant and animal food, especially seeds, while insects are important for rearing young.

IN THE GARDEN

In places where they are common, Tree Sparrows sometimes visit feeders to take kitchen scraps, bread, and seeds. They readily use enclosed nest-boxes.

Male and female *Tree Sparrows are alike in appearance, unlike House Sparrows, which have distinct sex differences.*

Brambling

BRAMBLINGS ARE WINTER VISITORS to southern and western Europe, but they very rarely nest there, migrating to northern Europe and Asia for the breeding season. In years when supplies of beech mast fail in the north, Bramblings may arrive in their winter habitats in much larger numbers.

Seasonal changes

Similar in appearance to the Chaffinch, the Brambling can be identified by its conspicuous white rump and black tail. In spring, the male develops a striking plumage with black head and back, and orange breast and sides. The female and juvenile retain the dull winter plumage of brown and grey with faint orange on the breast and sides.

Nesting and diet

Bramblings nest in colonies in birch or mixed birch and conifer forests. The female builds the nest from bark, heather, moss, and grass, and lines it with feathers, hair, and moss. She also incubates the eggs, but the male assists in providing food for the nestlings.

The Brambling's main food is tree seeds – such as those of beech, birch, ash, and spruce – but it also eats weed seeds and takes seeds from fallen apples that other birds have opened. In winter, Bramblings mainly eat beech mast, even digging through layers of snow up to 40cm (16in) thick to find it. They supplement their diet with insects in summer, foraging in trees and bushes for caterpillars and beetles, and catching flying insects in the air.

The female Brambling *constructs the rather untidy nest high in a tree, either against the trunk or in a fork.*

In their winter homes, *if the beech mast crop is poor, Bramblings are more likely to come into gardens, where they mix with Chaffinches.*

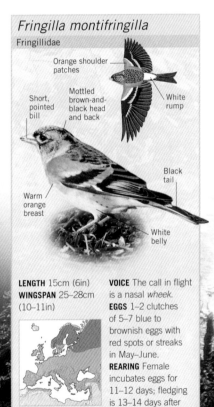

Fringilla montifringilla

Fringillidae

LENGTH 15cm (6in)
WINGSPAN 25–28cm (10–11in)

J F M A M J J A S O N D

VOICE The call in flight is a nasal *wheek.*
EGGS 1–2 clutches of 5–7 blue to brownish eggs with red spots or streaks in May–June.
REARING Female incubates eggs for 11–12 days; fledging is 13–14 days after hatching.

IN THE GARDEN

- Bramblings take sunflower seeds and peanuts from the ground, but some have also learned to use feeders.

Chaffinch

PRIMARILY A WOODLAND BIRD, the Chaffinch is also common in gardens and parks that have tall trees and prominent perches from which it can deliver its song. Chaffinches are especially likely to visit gardens if natural food is in short supply, and their willingness to feed in gardens may be one reason why their numbers have not dropped like those of some other familiar species.

IN THE GARDEN

Chaffinches eat a variety of seeds and scraps, including peanut granules and sunflower hearts. They usually forage under bird-tables, picking up the spillage, but they sometimes take food from a table.

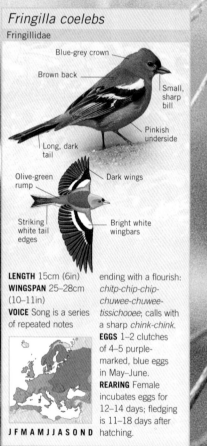

Fringilla coelebs

Fringillidae

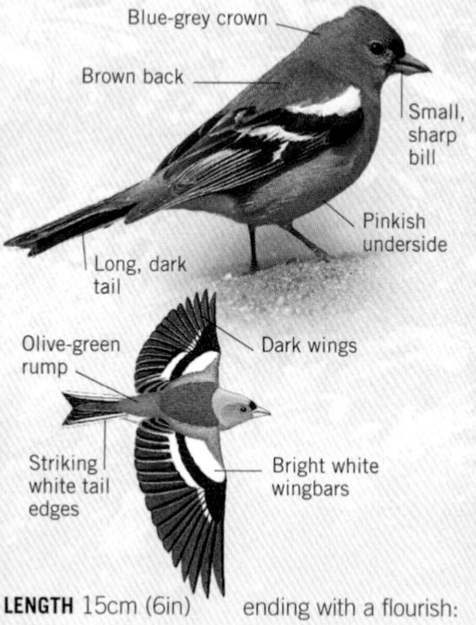

LENGTH 15cm (6in)
WINGSPAN 25–28cm (10–11in)
VOICE Song is a series of repeated notes ending with a flourish: *chitp-chip-chip-chuwee-chuwee-tissichooee*; calls with a sharp *chink-chink*.
EGGS 1–2 clutches of 4–5 purple-marked, blue eggs in May–June.
REARING Female incubates eggs for 12–14 days; fledging is 11–18 days after hatching.

J F M A M J J A S O N D

A rather plump finch, *the Chaffinch is similar in shape, plumage, and even in behaviour to the Brambling, and the two can often be seen feeding together in the winter. To tell them apart, look for the Chaffinch's pink, not white, belly and its greenish rump.*

The delicate nest *is built entirely by the female Chaffinch, and she makes over a thousand trips to gather the nest material.*

Distinctive plumage

The Chaffinch is a colourful member of the finch family, easily identified by the conspicuous white bars on its wings and tail. Adults moult in early autumn, and are paler in colour throughout the winter. In early spring, the male's buff feather tips wear away, revealing the characteristic pink face and body and slate-blue crown of the male Chaffinch's breeding plumage.

Unlike many other small birds, Chaffinches walk as well as hop when on the ground, often with a slight nodding of the head. They are not as agile when in trees. Their flight is light and undulating.

Territorial notes

The Chaffinch's cheerful song is a familiar sound in the spring and summer, while its calls can be heard all year round. Its vocal repertoire varies, with many local dialects (in the same way that human languages have regional accents). At the start of the breeding season, when the winter flocks break up, male Chaffinches start to sing in their territories on fine days. They visit selected song-posts – prominent perches often at the tops of trees – where they sing loudly to mark out the boundaries of their territory, and also to attract females. Once a pair forms, the territory will become their feeding ground as well as the nesting place.

Nest-building begins in spring, and is earlier if the weather is warmer. The female builds the nest, which is made mostly of grass and moss, in a fork in a tree or bush. She lines it with feathers and rootlets and decorates the outer surface with lichens and spiders' webs. The male accompanies her as she works but does not help; his priority is to prevent rival males entering the territory. The female is responsible for incubation and she also provides most of the food for the nestlings.

In characteristic pose, *the male perches upright with tail drooped and head raised, advertising his presence with a burst of song.*

The olive-brown female *Chaffinch is less colourful than the male, but has similar striking, white wingbars and tail edges.*

Ground feeding

In autumn and winter, Chaffinches mainly eat seeds that have fallen to the ground, including beech mast, grasses, chickweed, and charlock. They forage in trees and bushes in the nesting season, hunting for spiders, caterpillars, flies, and other invertebrates. They also feed on flying insects, catching them by flying out from a perch to pluck them from the air, like a Spotted Flycatcher.

A seed specialist, *the Chaffinch has a deep, broad bill with sharp cutting edges, perfect for removing the husks from seeds.*

Linnet

THIS SMALL FINCH used to avoid gardens, but is now being seen more often as the countryside becomes less attractive to seed-eaters and it learns to feed on millet and sunflower hearts. Linnets are usually found in open country of hedged farmland and scrub, where they feed on the seeds of arable crops and weeds.

A female Linnet *forages for food in a cabbage patch. Linnets are ground feeders, unlike Redpolls which feed mainly in trees.*

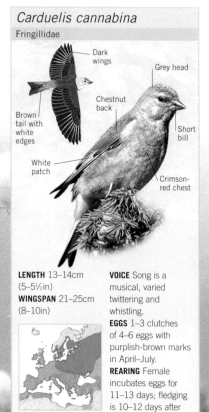

Carduelis cannabina

Fringillidae

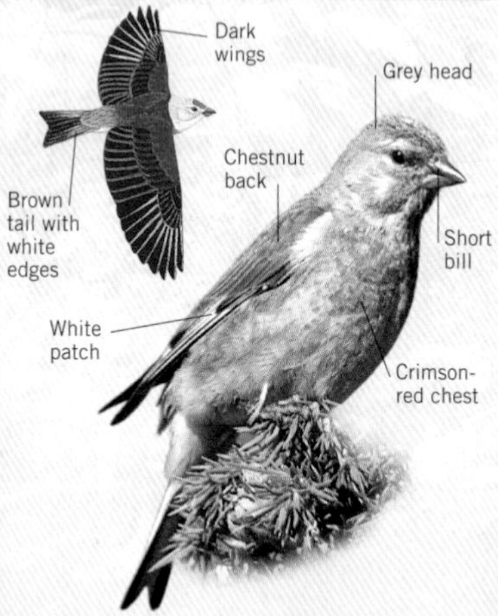

LENGTH 13–14cm (5–5½in)

WINGSPAN 21–25cm (8–10in)

J F M A M J J A S O N D

VOICE Song is a musical, varied twittering and whistling.

EGGS 1–3 clutches of 4–6 eggs with purplish-brown marks in April–July.

REARING Female incubates eggs for 11–13 days; fledging is 10–12 days after hatching.

A small finch

Linnets have undistinguished, streaked brown plumage with white edges to the flight feathers and on their tails. During the breeding season, the male has crimson on the crown, chest, and flanks, and chestnut on the back. The female has streaked brown plumage, rather like the male in winter, while the juvenile looks like a female but is less streaked.

Linnets nest in small groups of up to a dozen pairs, each pair building its nest within a few metres of others. The nest is a cup of twigs, stalks, roots, and moss lined with hair and wool. It is placed about 1m (3½ft) above the ground in dense cover, such as in a gorse bush or a young conifer.

Linnets eat a wide variety of small seeds, and also, occasionally, small invertebrates. Unlike most other finches, they also feed their young on seeds. Two favourite foods of the Linnet are flax, also known as linseed, hence the common name "Linnet", and hemp or cannabis, hence the scientific name "*cannabina*".

The Linnet's diet *consists almost entirely of seeds, including weed seeds such as thistle, charlock, knotgrass, dandelion, and dock.*

IN THE GARDEN

- Linnets are not common garden visitors, but occasionally venture in to take millet and sunflower hearts.

Redpoll

AN ACROBATIC LITTLE FINCH, the Redpoll is named after the crimson patch on its head. A relative newcomer to mature gardens, it lives in open woodland, heaths, hedgerows, and young conifer plantations. It can often be found in mixed flocks with Siskins, feeding at the tops of trees.

Female Redpolls *lack the pink breast of males in their breeding plumage, but have the distinctive red forehead.*

Appearance and nesting

The Redpoll exists in two closely related races in Europe, which have recently been designated as separate species. Northern Redpolls (*Carduelis flammea flammea*, or "Common") are slightly larger and paler than the western race (*C. f. cabaret*, or "Lesser"). The Redpoll can be told apart from the similar Linnet by its red forehead, black chin, pale rump, and two whitish wingbars. Males have a pink breast and rump in the breeding season, absent in the female. Both sexes are less colourful in winter.

Redpolls are gregarious outside the breeding season, forming flocks for feeding and roosting. In the breeding season, they often build their nests close together in small groups, usually fairly low down in trees or bushes. The nest is constructed from twigs, stalks, and stems, and lined with roots, grass, and flowerheads.

Seed specialist

The diet of the Redpoll mainly consists of small seeds, especially those of birch and alder, together with various grasses, willowherb, meadowsweet, and many weeds. They feed in trees but also come to the ground, especially in winter. In the nesting season, they eat insects and their larvae.

Carduelis flammea

Fringillidae

LENGTH 11–15cm (4½–6in)
WINGSPAN 20–25cm (8–10in)

VOICE Song is a staccato twittering with a rattling *cha-cha-cha-charr.*
EGGS Two clutches of 4–6 bluish eggs with reddish-brown specks in May–June.
REARING Female incubates eggs for 10–12 days; fledging is 9–14 days after hatching.

Redpolls *are more likely to come to feed in gardens if they have silver birch trees or a wild area with lots of seeding weeds.*

IN THE GARDEN

■ Redpolls are attracted by sunflower hearts and nyjer seed, and may visit ponds and bird-baths to drink.

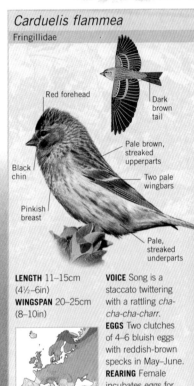

Goldfinch

THIS JEWEL OF A BIRD is unlikely to visit a tidy garden unless there are offerings in feeders. More gardeners, however, now leave seedheads on herbaceous plants after flowering has finished. These, and patches of weeds, are the best initial attraction for Goldfinches, but they then soon learn to visit garden feeding stations.

The slender, tweezer-like bill *of the Goldfinch is the perfect tool for extracting thistle seeds from their seedheads.*

Eye-catching plumage

With bold, colourful markings on its head and wings, the Goldfinch is an unmistakable and attractive garden visitor. It has red, black, and white markings on the head, and the black wings have a golden yellow bar. The sexes are alike, but the female has less red on the face. Juvenile birds lack the colourful head markings.

Carduelis carduelis

Fringillidae

LENGTH 13cm (5in)
WINGSPAN 21–25cm (8–10in)

J F M A M J J A S O N D

VOICE Call is a liquid *switt-witt-witt*; song is a musical twittering.
EGGS 1–3 clutches of 5–6 red-freckled, white eggs in May–August.
REARING Female incubates eggs for 11–12 days; fledging is 13–18 days after hatching.

Nesting and diet

Goldfinch territories are small, and several pairs may nest close to each other. Courtship involves both sexes spreading their wings and tails to show off their colourful plumage. The female builds a cup-nest of moss, roots, and lichens, lined with wool and thistle-down, often near the end of a branch.

Apart from insects, such as aphids and caterpillars, eaten in the nesting season, the diet of Goldfinches is mainly small seeds. Garden favourites include teazel, lavender, and lemon balm, and they are attracted to weedy patches of burdock, thistles, dandelions, and groundsel. They also eat the seeds of some trees, like elm, birch, and pine. A small flock of Goldfinches is a delightful sight, most likely to be seen in gardens during April and May when wild seed crops are exhausted.

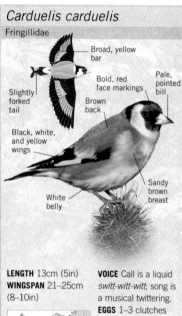

IN THE GARDEN

Goldfinches visit gardens to feed on the seeds of a variety of shrubs and trees. They occasionally visit garden feeders to take sunflower hearts and nyjer seeds.

Widespread in Europe, *Goldfinches are partial migrants; part of the population winters in its breeding range, while part travels to southern Europe to spend the winter.*

Greenfinch

NOW VERY COMMON IN GARDENS, the Greenfinch gradually colonized towns and cities over the course of the 20th century. Originally rather a shy bird of scrub and hedgerows, it has adapted so well to garden life that the population has thrived despite the changes to the countryside that have harmed other seed-eaters.

Greenfinches *are easily distinguished from sparrows by the yellow wing patches, forked tail, and stout bill.*

Garden regular

Few gardens with birdfeeders are without gangs of Greenfinches making the most of the ready supply of seeds. The male Greenfinch is distinctive, with its bright green and yellow plumage, while the female is a duller olive brown. Juvenile birds resemble the female but have less green and yellow and are more streaked.

Greenfinches nest in small colonies of about half a dozen pairs, usually in dense shrubs and creepers. Conifers and other evergreens are often used, especially for early nests before deciduous leaves are out. The female builds the nest of twigs, grass, and moss and lines it with hair and rootlets. She also incubates the eggs, but the male helps feed the young and may become entirely responsible when the female starts to build a new nest before the first family has started to fly.

Greenfinches are almost entirely dependent on a wide assortment of seeds, especially weed seeds, such as thistle, charlock, dandelion, and burdock, but also tree seeds including elm, yew, and cypress. Only a few invertebrate animals are eaten in the nesting season.

IN THE GARDEN

- Greenfinches are common visitors to garden feeding stations, taking peanuts and sunflower seeds and hearts from hanging feeders, and foraging on the ground under feeders and tables to collect seed fragments dropped by other birds.

In winter, *Greenfinches enjoy fleshy fruits, such as blackberries. They selectively eat the seeds, discarding the flesh.*

Carduelis chloris

Fringillidae

LENGTH 15cm (6in)
WINGSPAN 25–27cm (10–11in)
VOICE Song is a medley of notes ending in a loud wheeze; calls include a repeated *chi-chi-chi-chi* and the male's rasping *sweee.*
EGGS 1–3 clutches of 4–6 red-spotted, white eggs in April–June.
REARING Female incubates eggs for 12–14 days; fledging is 14–15 days after hatching.

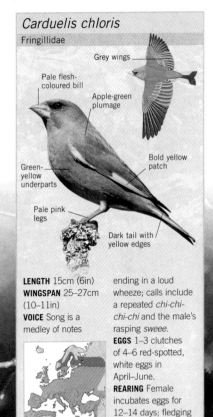

Siskin

SISKINS HAVE ONLY started to visit gardens in the last 50 years. They first came occasionally to hanging bags of peanuts, but now feed regularly in some gardens. The spread of conifer planting has increased their breeding range throughout Europe, making it increasingly likely that Siskins coming into a garden are nesting not far away.

Siskins are most *likely to be seen at the end of winter, when natural seed supplies are exhausted and many are preparing to migrate.*

Carduelis spinus

Fringillidae

LENGTH 12cm (4½in)
WINGSPAN 20–23cm (8–9in)
VOICE Calls include a *tsooee* and a twitter given on the wing; the song is a sweet twittering that culminates in a wheeze.
EGGS 1–2 clutches of 4–5 red-streaked, pale blue eggs in April–July.
REARING Female incubates eggs for 12–13 days; fledging is 13–15 days after hatching.

Garden newcomer

The Siskin is a small finch with a markedly forked tail and the acrobatic habits of a tit. In flight, the yellow bars on its wings and on the sides of its tail are obvious. The male is bright yellow and green with a conspicuous black cap and black on the wings. The female is streaked and lacks the black and bright colours, while juveniles are even more streaked and less yellow. The thin, twittering song, with "*doolee*" and wheezy notes, is delivered from a perch or on a switchback song-flight.

The female Siskin builds the compact nest with small, lichen-covered twigs and lines it with rootlets, hair, and feathers. It is usually sited near the end of a conifer branch, high off the ground. The female also incubates the eggs, but both parents feed the young.

The natural foods of the Siskin are the seeds of conifers, alder, birch, elm, thistles, and dock, while insects are fed to growing nestlings. It searches for food at the tips of slender twigs, where it hangs upside down as it pecks at cones and bunches of seeds. It uses the same acrobatic technique to reach peanuts and seeds in hanging garden feeders.

Similar in colour *to the Greenfinch, the Siskin is easily identified by its smaller size and streaked underparts.*

IN THE GARDEN

Siskins visit garden feeding stations, especially to take peanuts from hanging feeders, but also for fat and small seeds.

Bullfinch

THE BULLFINCH can easily pass unnoticed, despite its colourful plumage, because it keeps to thick foliage where only the flash of its white rump is easily seen. The best clues to its presence are often the soft, whistled calls, which carry surprisingly well through dense undergrowth. It uses these to maintain contact with other Bullfinches.

Duller in colour *than the male, the female Bullfinch is still easily recognizable with its characteristic black cap and white rump.*

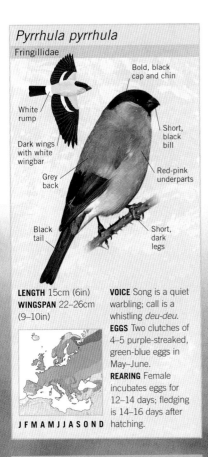

Pyrrhula pyrrhula

Fringillidae

LENGTH 15cm (6in)
WINGSPAN 22–26cm (9–10in)

VOICE Song is a quiet warbling; call is a whistling *deu-deu.*
EGGS Two clutches of 4–5 purple-streaked, green-blue eggs in May–June.
REARING Female incubates eggs for 12–14 days; fledging is 14–16 days after hatching.

IN THE GARDEN

■ Bullfinches very occasionally visit garden feeding stations, taking peanuts and sunflower hearts from bird-tables.

A secretive finch

With its large head and unmistakable plumage, the Bullfinch is an easily recognizable finch. Its head, wings, and tail are black, and it has a bright white wingbar and rump. The sides of the head and underparts are warm pink in the male, duller pink-buff in the female. Juvenile birds lack the black cap and pink coloration.

Unlike many other garden birds, Bullfinch pairs often stay together through the year. In spring, the male takes the initiative in choosing the nest site. He leads the female to suitable locations in a thick hedge or conifer, but she builds the delicate nest of fine twigs and rootlets. The young are fed by both parents while in the nest and for up to three weeks after fledging.

The Bullfinch's preferred diet is seeds, but when stocks run out at the end of winter it turns to eating buds. It particularly enjoys the developing buds of fruit trees and, before recent population declines, it sometimes caused problems for fruit growers. Its usual diet, however, is the seeds of ash, birch, dock, nettle, and bramble. Insects, as well as seeds, are fed to the nestlings. In gardens, Bullfinches feed on clover and dandelions in the lawn.

Adult Bullfinches *are almost entirely vegetarian, eating a variety of plant material, from berries and seeds to shoots and buds.*

Reed Bunting

AS THEIR TRADITIONAL HABITATS – reed beds, wet pastures, and marshes – have disappeared, so Reed Buntings have started to nest in drier places, such as in fields of cereal and rape crops and conifer plantations, or by reed-filled ditches and ponds. In winter, they sometimes look for food in gardens when snow and ice deprive them of their natural resources.

After moulting, *the male Reed Bunting's black head markings are obscured by buff feather tips, but these wear away before the breeding season.*

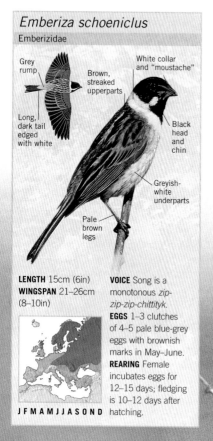

Emberiza schoeniclus

Emberizidae

LENGTH 15cm (6in)
WINGSPAN 21–26cm (8–10in)

J F M A M J J A S O N D

VOICE Song is a monotonous *zip-zip-zip-chittityk.*
EGGS 1–3 clutches of 4–5 pale blue-grey eggs with brownish marks in May–June.
REARING Female incubates eggs for 12–15 days; fledging is 10–12 days after hatching.

Seasonal differences

In the breeding season, the male Reed Bunting has a striking black head and chin and a white collar; at other times of year, these markings are less obvious. The back is brown streaked with black and the underparts and rump are grey. The winter male, female, and juvenile are more sparrow-like, but have traces of the white "moustache".

The nest is usually found close to marshy areas or in fields, sited in a tussock or among bushes. It is built by the female from stems and leaves and lined with hair, moss, fine grass, and reed flowers. She incubates the eggs alone, but the male helps her feed the young. The young leave the nest before they can fly and call to their parents from nearby vegetation. The parents lead predators from the nest by "injury-feigning" – running with their wings spread to attract attention.

The seeds of marsh plants, grasses, and grain are the Reed Bunting's main food, but they also eat insects in summer. Young are fed entirely on insects, such as beetles, bugs, and caterpillars.

The plumage *of the female Reed Bunting is similar to the male's, except for the distinctive head markings. The female's head is brown not black and has white-and-black stripes.*

IN THE GARDEN

■ Reed Buntings visit gardens to feed on the ground on sunflower seeds and hearts, and may also, rarely, visit peanut feeders.

Yellowhammer

THE YELLOWHAMMER is a farm bird that used to feed in large flocks on stubble fields in winter and nest along hedgerows and the edges of woods. It has never traditionally been a garden bird, except for visits when the countryside is snow-covered. Recent changes in farming, however, are now forcing the Yellowhammer into gardens more often.

The female *Yellowhammer is very similar to the winter male. Both have duller yellow plumage than the summer male.*

Emberiza citrinella

Emberizidae

LENGTH 16cm (6in)
WINGSPAN 23–29cm (9–11in)
VOICE Best known for its metallic, trilling *"little-bit-of-bread-and-no-cheese"* song; calls include a sharp *tzit*.
EGGS 2–3 clutches of 3–5 white to purplish eggs with brown-red marks in April–September.
REARING Female incubates eggs for 12–14 days; fledging is 11–13 days after hatching.

J F M A M J J A S O N D

A colourful bunting

The Yellowhammer derives its name from "*Ammer*", an Old English word for bunting. The male's bright yellow body is very distinctive; the head and underparts are yellow with few streaks, the back is brown with a rufous rump, and the tail has conspicuous white outer feathers. Females are duller with more streaks, while the juvenile is even more streaked than the female.

The male sings his well-known and far-carrying refrain from a perch above the nest, which is built on or near the ground in hedge-bottoms, in brambles, under bushes, and in young plantations. It is constructed from grasses, stems, and leaves and lined with hair and fine grass and rootlets. Rearing the family is left largely to the female, but the male helps feed the young and takes over completely when his mate starts another clutch.

The diet of an adult Yellowhammer consists of a wide range of seeds. The young are fed insects and other invertebrates. The birds often form flocks to feed on the ground, especially near weedy fields that have been taken out of production.

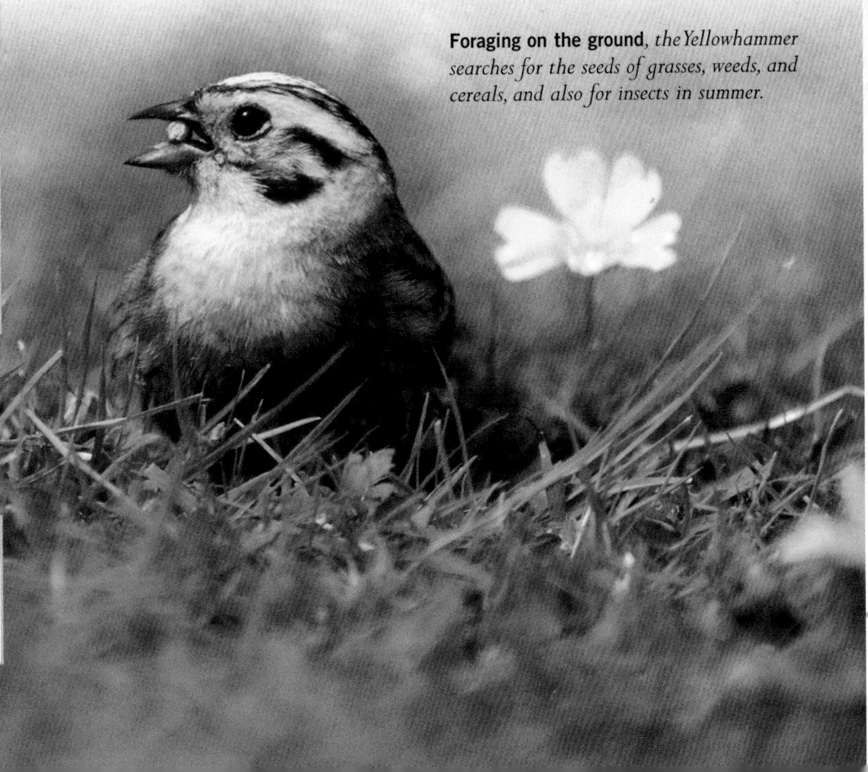

Foraging on the ground, *the Yellowhammer searches for the seeds of grasses, weeds, and cereals, and also for insects in summer.*

IN THE GARDEN

- Yellowhammers feed on the ground, near cover, on grain and sunflower hearts. They occasionally come to bird-tables.

Bird classification

THE SCIENTIFIC SYSTEM for naming plants and animals was devised in the 18th century by the Swedish naturalist Carolus Linnaeus. The names given to birds reflect their evolutionary lineage and degree of relatedness, so a knowledge of bird classification and naming is more than just an academic pursuit – it allows us all to understand and predict similarities and differences between species.

The Hooded Crow *is a subspecies of the Carrion Crow. They can interbreed but mostly live in different places.*

Birds, and all other living things, have a two-word Latin name – always printed in italics. The first word gives the genus (a grouping of species); the addition of the second word identifies a particular species. For example, *Passer* is the Latin for sparrow. The House Sparrow is *Passer domesticus,* and the very similar Tree Sparrow is *Passer montanus*. Sharing the same genus name indicates that the two species are closely related. The scientific name of the Dunnock is *Prunella modularis*, so the name tells us that it is not closely related to the sparrows. Based on similarity, genera (the plural of genus) are grouped into families, and the families into orders. Swallows, House, and Sand Martins all belong to the family Hirundinidae in the largest order, Passeriformes (perching birds), but the superficially similar Swifts are in the order Apodiformes, indicating fundamental differences in their biology and their lineage.

ORDERS AND FAMILIES

This table sets out the relationships between, and classification of, the birds described in this book. The information is more than just a dry list, and close examination reveals some unexpected facts. For example, the Long-tailed Tit is not closely related to other tits and the Barn Owl is rather different from all the other owls.

ORDER	FAMILY	COMMON AND SCIENTIFIC NAMES
Ciconiiformes	Ardeidae	Grey Heron (*Ardea cinerea)*
Anseriformes	Anatidae	Mallard (*Anas platyrhynchos)*
Accipitriformes	Accipitridae	Sparrowhawk (*Accipiter nisus)*
Falconiformes	Falconidae	Kestrel (*Falco tinnunculus)*
Galliformes	Phasianidae	Pheasant (*Phasianus colchicus)*
Gruiformes	Rallidae	Coot (*Fulica atra)*
		Moorhen (*Gallinula chloropus)*
Charadriiformes	Laridae	Herring Gull (*Larus argentatus)*
		Black-headed Gull (*Larus ridibundus)*
Columbiformes	Columbidae	Collared Dove (*Streptopelia decaocto)*
		Feral Pigeon (*Columba livia)*
		Woodpigeon (*Columba palumbus)*
Cuculiformes	Cuculidae	Cuckoo (*Cuculus canorus)*
Strigiformes	Tytonidae	Barn Owl (*Tyto alba)*
	Strigidae	Long-eared Owl (*Asio otus)*
		Tawny Owl (*Strix aluco)*
		Little Owl (*Athene noctua)*
Apodiformes	Apodidae	Swift (*Apus apus)*
Piciformes	Picidae	Green Woodpecker (*Picus viridis)*
		Great Spotted Woodpecker (*Dendrocopos major)*

Herring Gull

Little Owl

ORDER	FAMILY	COMMON AND SCIENTIFIC NAMES
Passeriformes	Hirundinidae	House Martin (*Delichon urbica*)
		Swallow (*Hirundo rustica*)
	Motacillidae	Pied/White Wagtail (*Motacilla alba*)
	Bombycillidae	Waxwing (*Bombycilla garrulus*)
	Prunellidae	Dunnock (*Prunella modularis*)
	Troglodytidae	Wren (*Troglodytes troglodytes*)
	Turdidae	Robin (*Erithacus rubecula*)
		Blackbird (*Turdus merula*)
		Song Thrush (*Turdus philomelos*)
		Mistle Thrush (*Turdus viscivorus*)
		Redwing (*Turdus iliacus*)
		Fieldfare (*Turdus pilaris*)
		Black Redstart (*Phoenicurus ochruros*)
	Sylviidae	Whitethroat (*Sylvia communis*)
		Blackcap (*Sylvia atricapilla*)
		Garden Warbler (*Sylvia borin*)
		Chiffchaff (*Phylloscopus collybita*)
		Goldcrest (*Regulus regulus*)
	Muscicapidae	Pied Flycatcher (*Ficedula hypoleuca*)
		Spotted Flycatcher (*Muscicapa striata*)
	Aegithalidae	Long-tailed Tit (*Aegithalos caudatus*)
	Paridae	Coal Tit (*Parus ater*)
		Blue Tit (*Parus caeruleus*)
		Great Tit (*Parus major*)
		Marsh Tit (*Parus palustris*)
		Willow Tit (*Parus montanus*)
	Sittidae	Nuthatch (*Sitta europaea*)
	Certhiidae	Treecreeper (*Certhia familiaris*)
	Corvidae	Carrion/Hooded Crow (*Corvus corone*)
		Rook (*Corvus frugilegus*)
		Jackdaw (*Corvus monedula*)
		Jay (*Garrulus glandarius*)
		Magpie (*Pica pica*)
	Sturnidae	Starling (*Sturnus vulgaris*)
	Passeridae	House Sparrow (*Passer domesticus*)
		Tree Sparrow (*Passer montanus*)
	Fringillidae	Brambling (*Fringilla montifringilla*)
		Chaffinch (*Fringilla coelebs*)
		Linnet (*Carduelis cannabina*)
		Redpoll (*Carduelis flammea*)
		Goldfinch (*Carduelis carduelis*)
		Greenfinch (*Carduelis chloris*)
		Siskin (*Carduelis spinus*)
		Bullfinch (*Pyrrhula pyrrhula*)
	Emberizidae	Reed Bunting (*Emberiza schoeniclus*)
		Yellowhammer (*Emberiza citrinella*)

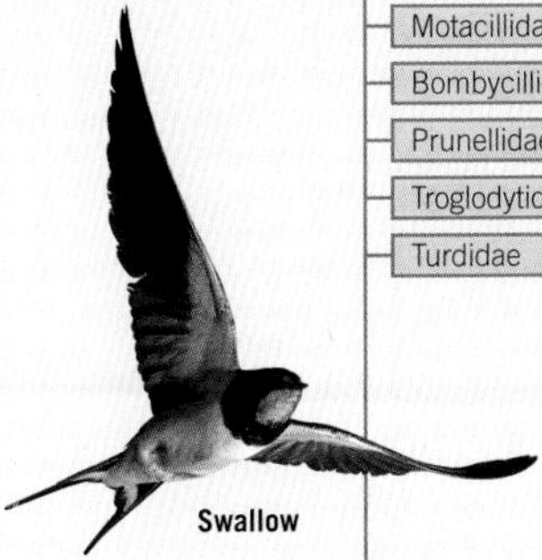
Swallow

Wren

Black Redstart

Pied Flycatcher

Jackdaw

Marsh Tit

Magpie

Linnet

Reed Bunting

Glossary

Adult A fully mature bird, which is able to breed and is in its final plumage that no longer changes pattern with age

Barred With marks that cross the body, wings, or tail

Behaviour How a bird moves, calls, sings, nests, and carries out all aspects of its life, in a manner that is more or less characteristic of its species

Breeding plumage An imprecise but useful general term; usually refers to the plumage worn when birds display and pair

Brood Young produced from a single clutch of eggs, and incubated together

Call Vocal sound, often characteristic of a single species, communicating a variety of messages

Clutch A group of eggs in a single nest, usually laid by one female, and incubated together

Colony A group of nests of a social species that has some social function

Covert A small feather in a well-defined tract on the wing or at the base of the tail, covering the base of the larger flight feathers

Dabble To feed in shallow water by sieving water and food through comb-like filters in the bill, hence "dabbling duck"

Declining Of a population undergoing a steady reduction over a period of years

Display Ritualized, showy behaviour that is used in courtship and/or by a bird claiming a territory; other forms of display include distraction display, in which a bird attempts to lure a predator from its nest

Drumming An instrumental sound often made by vibrating the bill against a branch

Eruption A large-scale movement of birds from their breeding area, when numbers are high but food is short

Eye-ring A ring of colour around the eye

Eyestripe A stripe of colour running as a line through the eye

Family A category in classification, grouping genera that are closely related; also the family group of a pair (or single adult) with young

Feral Living wild, in a sustainable population, but derived from captive stock or from domestic stock that has escaped, or that has been introduced into an area where the species either does not naturally occur or, as in the case of the Feral Pigeon, from which it has disappeared as a truly wild bird

Genus A grouping of species (or, sometimes, a single species if the genus is "monotypic") that are closely related, recognized by the same first word in the scientific name; plural "genera"

Immature Not yet fully adult or able to breed; some species, such as larger gulls, have a sequence of changing immature plumages for three or four years, while others are unable to breed for several years but show no sign of such immaturity in their plumage pattern

Juvenile The plumage of a bird in its first flight, before its first moult

Moult The shedding of old feathers and growth of new replacements, in a systematic fashion that is characteristic of the species

Migrant A species that spends part of the year in one geographical area and part in another, "migrating" between the two

Order A category in classification, grouping families according to their presumed relationship

Pigeon's milk A cheesy secretion from the crop of pigeons, rich in protein and fat, which is fed to developing nestlings

Race A more or less distinct group within a species, defined by geographical area; also "subspecies"

Rare Found in very small numbers or low densities, or an individual bird found outside its normal range (a "rarity" or "vagrant")

Roost A place where birds sleep, or the act of sleeping. "A roost" infers a communal nature

Secure Of a population that is not currently or foreseeably threatened

Song A vocal performance with a pattern characteristic of the species; may attract a mate, or repel intruders from a territory

Song-flight A special and usually distinctive flight in which the song is performed

Species A group of living organisms, individuals of which can breed and produce fertile offspring, but which do not or cannot usually breed with individuals of other species

Streaked Marked with lines of colour aligned lengthwise along the body

Subspecies A more or less distinct group within a species, defined by geographical area; also "race"

Underwing The underside of the wing

Upperwing The upper surface of the wing

Vagrant An individual bird that has accidentally strayed outside its normal range; also a species that is only found in such circumstances in a given area, such as the Northern Parula, a "vagrant" in Europe

Wingpit The base of the underside of the wing, the "axillaries"

Wingbar A line of colour across the coverts on the closed wing or along the extended wing as a bar or stripe

Young An imprecise term to indicate an immature bird, from a nestling to a full grown bird in immature plumage

Index

Page numbers in **bold** refer to entries in the bird and plant profile sections; numbers in *italics* refer to illustrations.

F

G

H

I

J

K

L

M

About the RSPB

A registered charity, founded in 1889 and granted its Royal Charter in 1904, the RSPB (the Royal Society for the Protection of Birds) is Europe's largest voluntary wildlife conservation organisation. The Society has more than one million members, some 150,000 of whom belong to its junior branch, the RSPB Wildlife Explorers.

In addition to its national headquarters in Bedfordshire, the RSPB has six regional offices, a Scottish Headquarters with three Scottish regional offices, and country offices in Wales and Northern Ireland. As well as wardening staff based on the Society's nature reserves, various other personnel are outposted (mainly conservation officers). The Society rents a small office which is maintained in London, close to Parliament. In all, the RSPB employs nearly 1,000 permanent staff, more than 120 field teachers with a further 300 seasonal or part-time contract staff. The conservation effort is supported by an additional 7,000 volunteers who currently donate around 358,000 hours of their valuable time every year. And in 2003, 314,000 people took part in the RSPB's annual Big Garden Birdwatch.

The prime objective of the Society is the conservation of wild birds and their habitats, and increasingly, the flora and other fauna that share those habitats. Habitat and species work is based on sound science – the result of research and survey work which is often carried out in close co-operation with statutory or other voluntary bodies. This in turn produces a nationally agreed system of assessing priorities and leads to the preparation and implementation of detailed Action Plans. The acquisition and management of nature reserves continue to be important parts of the RSPB agenda: the Society currently owns or manages 176 nature reserves covering nearly 300,000 acres. In addition to their more obvious role as protected sites, most reserves cater for visitors (some in very large numbers), and several have a prime educational function. Education in the wider sense is an important ingredient of RSPB work – in recent years there has also been a growing programme of disseminating conservation advice to an increasingly wide audience.

Bird conservation is about much more than nature reserves and special protection schemes for rare or threatened species, important though both these aspects continue to be. An effective conservation programme must embrace the total environment and have regard to everything going on within it. To that end, the RSPB has broadened its scope (and the expertise of its staff) considerably over the last two decades to cover farming, forestry, marine issues and all forms of planning and development, as well as issues such as the rural economy, global warming, energy use and transport. Highly professional staff are always on hand to discuss these and other environmental matters with Government and MPs.

One of the most significant developments on the international scene has been the formation of BirdLife International, an umbrella body for bird conservation organisations worldwide. The RSPB is UK partner for BirdLife and is closely involved with many of its overseas programmes as well as with its own projects in Europe, Africa, and Asia. The emergence of the European Union as a major force in world politics, and therefore in global conservation, has led to the Society being increasingly involved in European matters, even to the extent of opening a small office in Brussels.

Closer to home, there is a growing importance of gardens for our native wildlife as the wider countryside is affected by changes in how it is managed and even bigger issues – such as climate change. Gardens in Britain cover an area twice the size of Luxembourg, a significant potential nature reserve in itself. Feeding the birds in our gardens has become something of a national pastime in recent years – two-thirds of us now regularly feed the birds in our gardens, spending over £80 million per annum and using up some 30,000 tonnes of wild bird seed and 15,000 tonnes of peanuts. It all helps birds to survive, particularly during severe weather. Feeding in spring and summer is now also proving to be advisable. As parent birds struggle to rear their families, a regular supply of birdfood helps the adults to concentrate on finding natural food for the young and stay in good health at their busiest time of year.

How we manage our gardens can have considerable benefits for birds and other wildlife too. Planting native plants, shrubs, and trees, providing a water feature, and creating a variety of habitats will attract a respective increase in the range of wildlife in our gardens. It is important to remember that the way we garden also affects the environment beyond our boundaries. For example, water shortages are serious problems for people and birds. Many marshy places where Moorhens, frogs, and dragonflies live are drying out because of increasing use of water in our homes and gardens. And peat extracted from magnificent lowland peat bogs for the horticultural industry has destroyed all but six per cent of this wonderful habitat.

Gardens can be special places for people, for birds, for ever, so enjoy reading this book, and feeding and watching the wildlife in your back yard.

Acknowledgments

Cobalt id would like to thank the following for their assistance with this book: Peter Holden for additional text and invaluable editorial guidance; Rob Hume for additional text, illustrations, and informed comment; Richard Bird for indexing; Richard Chappell, Ennis Jones, and John Ferguson for their enthusiastic help in the photography of their special gardens; Roger Crabb for illustrations of bird gardens and advice on wildlife gardening; all at FLPA for their help and guidance on image sources; Viking Optical; Trevor Codlin (digiscoping.co.uk); Christine Percy and all at Swarovski UK Ltd; and Rebecca Johns.

Commissioned photography: David Tipling, Peter Anderson
Commissioned illustration: John Plumer

Abbreviations key: t = top; b = bottom; l = left; r = right; c = centre. Pictures in columns are numbered top to bottom; pictures in rows are numbered left to right.

Andrew Lawson: 66.

Ardea: 47c, 77tl2; Bill Coster Pictures Ltd 12tc; Bob Gibbons 44bl, 47br; Brian Bevan 36tr; Chris Knights 46cr1, 80br, 169tl; Dennis Avon 77tl1; John Daniels 31b, 34tr, 124tr; M Watson 21b4; S Roberts 119br; Steve Hopkin 41tr.

Bruce Coleman: Colin Varndell 156b, 160tr; Harald Lange 38tr; Kim Taylor 94tr.

Cobalt id: Marek Walisiewicz 11c; Paul Reid 87rc.

Chris Gomersall: 20cr, 91b1, 91b2, 108tr, 159tr.

CJ Images: 18b4, 19b3, 22b3, 27b1, 28b8, 31tl2, 36bl; CJW 20b4; David White 5r5, 10, 18b1, 18b2, 19b2, 19b4, 19b5, 20b1, 20b5, 21b1, 21b2, 21b5, 22b1, 22b2, 22b4, 26b1, 26b4, 27b2, 27b3, 27b4, 28c, 33t1, 33t2, 33t3, 34bc, 35bc, 35br, 36bc, 37bl, 37bc, 40c, 62l1, 62l2, 62, 66l2, 66l4, 175c, 203br, 209b; M Read 36br; Outhouse 28b1, 28b2, 28b3, 28b4, 28b5, 28b6, 28b7.

FLPA: A Christiansen 132b; AR Hamblin 105b1, 107b2, 109tr2, 136b, 137tr, 154ct, 208tr, 210tr; A Wharton 47tr; Alan Parker 130tr, 149tr; Albert Visage 111tr2; B Borrell 94br, 172b; DA Robinson 143b; DT Grewcock 200tr, 77r5, 145tl; D Warren 37br; David Dalton 46bl; David Hosking 12br, 36l, 40bl, 80tl, 118tr, 134b, 139tr, 140bl, 141tl, 153tr, 153cb, 161tr, 164bl, 180bl, 183br, 185, 185tr, 187br, 187tr, 194tr, 196b, 197c, 203cr, 206, 207tl; Derek A Robinson 199tr; Derek Middleton 170tr; Don Smith 144br; E&D Hosking 32tr, 33cr, 112tr, 112b, 115c, 128b, 155bl, 200bl; E Hosking 77bl, 155ct; F Merlet 109tl; Foto Natura Stock 91b3; Fritz Pölking 98bl; G Nystrand 179b; GT Andrewartha 163bc; H Clark 65r2, 81b2, 101cr, 102c, 103c1, 148tr, 155, 177b, 192tr, 217tl; Hanna Hautala 157tr, 105b4; J Swales 117b1; Jeremy Early 93r1; John Hawkins 35tr, 94bl2, 97r5, 105b3, 109tr1, 113b, 128tr, 137bl, 152, 159tl, 163br, 168ct, 168bl, 169, 180cl, 183bl, 193b; John Watkins 94bl1, 96b, 97r3, 160cl, 184cl; John Zimmermann 154br; Jurgen & Christine Sohns 175br; L Batten 139cl; MB Withers 105tl1; M Walker 176tr; Martin Withers 94bl3; Neil Bowman 157b; P Heard 92tr, 137br, 184tr, 195b, 198b; R Austing 101tr; RP Lawrence 198tr; R Tidman 142b, 171br, 178tr; R Wilmshurst 77r3, 77r4, 111tr1, 125tl1, 170b, 203tl; Ray Bird 13tr, 33t4; Richard Brooks 100cr, 105b5, 161, 204tr, 211b; Robert Canis 32cr; Roger Hosking 126b, 197br; Roger Tidman 40br, 69r1, 81tl, 99r2, 105tl2, 167tl, 176b; Roger Wilmshurst 70l4, 93r2, 114tr, 131b, 133b, 134tr, 138b, 143tr, 144bl, 147c, 164tr, 166, 168br, 173b, 183tl, 199bl, 201, 212tr; S Maslowski 113cl; Silvestris 92br; Tony Hamblin 106tl, 107b3, 120b2, 120b3, 146b, 149b, 184bl, 197tl; Tony Wharton 103c2, 154bl; W Wisniewski 135b.

Garden Picture Library: Juliette Wade 44br; Lynne Brotchie 65; Sunniva Harte 62l3.

Garden World Images: 48bl.

Natural Visions: Brian Rogers 45c; Heather Angel 47bl, 50bl, 50br, 57tl, 61tl, 65r1, 95, 105b2, 151ct.

Jerry Harpur: 69.

John Glover: 97.

Mary Evans Picture Library: 9bl.

Mike Lane: 27cl, 93r3, 102cr, 107t1, 107b1, 110tr, 115cr, 115b3, 202b.

Mike Read: 11br, 18b3, 19b1, 20b2, 30tr, 90b1, 90c, 95r3, 99r3, 99r4, 106br2, 115b2, 120cl, 121br, 125r, 126tr, 135tr, 140br, 146tr, 163tl, 163tr, 174, 191c, 205tr.

NHPA: Alan Williams 189tl, 208b; Ann & Steve Toon 127tr; Dave Watts 190b; EA Janes 215tr; Eric Soder 18cl, 100bl; Joe Blossom 13; John Buckingham 24tr, 158tr, 214b; Laurie Campbell 127b; Manfred Danegger 81b5; Melvin Grey 182b; Paal Hermansen 46cr2; Roger Tidman 178b, 205b; Stephen Dalton 4, 46tr, 81b1, 81b4, 103t, 130t, 147b, 181ct; Susanne Danegger 41.

Oxford Scientific Films: Bob Gibbons 61br; Colin Milkins 187tl; Deni Bown 48tr, 60tl; Dennis Green/SAL 37tr; Lothar Lenz/Okapia 33br; Mark Hamblin 190tr; Michael Leach 48br; Niall Benvie 139br.

Roger Crabb: 49cl1.

RSPB: 32b, 34bl, 77r1, 95r5, 107t2, 108br, 183tr; Alan Barnes 95r1; Bill Paton 116b2, 145; Bob Glover 17c, 34br, 95r2, 107t3, 116b1, 159b, 179tr, 197tr; Carlos Sanchez 144tr, Chris Gomersall 18b5, 21tl, 97r1, 141b; Chris Knights 81b3, 153tl, 156tr; Colin Carver 191b; David Kjaer 195tr; David Tipling 108bl, 117b3; Eric Woods 192b; Ernie Janes 62l4, 97r2, 160bl; Geoff Simpson 49cl2; George McCarthy 16b, 95r4, 117tr; Gerald Downey 212b; Jan Halady 8c; Laurie Campbell 167tr; Malcolm Hunt 12tl, 177tr; Mark Hamblin 26l, 77r2, 91tr, 99r5, 105tr, 109br, 125tl2, 129cl, 151br, 158b, 193tr, 207tr, 210b, 211tr, 213b; Maurice Walker 91tr; Mike Lane 92bl, 140c, 204b; Mike McKavett 108bc; Mike Richards 11tr, 209tr; Peter Perfect 102bl; Phillip Newman 110br, 171b, 173bl; Ray Kennedy 30bl, 207br; Richard Brooks 90b2; Richard Revels 45tl; Robert Smith 87br; Roger Wilmshurst 93r4, 129br, 201br; Steve Austin 215b; Steve Knell 78tl, 106br1, 172tr, 194b; Tony Hamblin 16tr, 73r4, 99r1, 104b, 148bl, 165cr, 167br.

Science Photo Library: Dr Kari Lounatmaa 31tl1.

Windrush Photos: 21r, 70l3, 100t, 113tr; Alan Petty 181, Andy Harmer 120tr, D Mason 93r5, 120b1, 131tr, 175tl; David Tipling 2, 5r3, 5r4, 6, 20b3, 21b3, 27t, 35bl, 74, 79bl, 82tr, 97r4, 99, 111tl, 115b1, 118b, 122, 129tr, 133tr, 150br, 151tr; F Desmette 90b3; G Langsbury 8bl; George McCarthy 80bl1, 114b, 117b2; Gordon Langsbur 35c; HE Lloboy 165b; J Hollis 1b; JL Roberts 117b4; Les Borg 188cl; Maurice Walker 116tr; Pentti Johansson 150; Peter Cairns 142tr; Réne Pop 98br; Richard Brooks 88; Roger Tidman 80bl2; Tom Ennis 22c.